Government and Politics
in Northern Africa

Government and Politics
in Northern Africa

I. WILLIAM ZARTMAN

FREDERICK A. PRAEGER, *Publisher*
New York • London

FREDERICK A. PRAEGER, PUBLISHER
64 UNIVERSITY PLACE, NEW YORK 3, N.Y., U.S.A.
77–79 CHARLOTTE STREET, LONDON, W.1, ENGLAND

Published in the United States of America in 1963
by Frederick A. Praeger, Inc., Publisher

Printed in the United States of America

To my parents

CONTENTS

MAPS

PREFACE

This book came into being because of a need. Northern Africa is one of the world's least studied areas, at least in terms of English language writings. Tunisia, long the West's staunchest friend, at the top of the continent; Libya, an oil-rich country that may soon rival Algeria; and Somalia, a growing trouble spot for Western policy: All are barren areas in American scholarship. Other countries—Morocco, Algeria, Sudan, and Ethiopia—have been accorded more attention, but hardly in a measure comparable to their importance. Only the United Arab Republic (Egypt) has been the subject of a large number of political analyses. The reason, to a great extent, is probably the uncertain position of these countries. They are part of both the Arab and the African worlds, and as a result have been treated as part of neither. All of them, except Somalia and Algeria, attained their independence before the wave of liberation swept the continent in 1960 and, more significant, before some of the modern analytical tools for understanding emerging nations were developed. North Africa (the Maghreb)—Tunisia, Morocco, and Algeria—has always been the domain of France, in scholarship as well as politics; Egypt has been the domain of the Arabists; the rest have been ignored. Yet these countries are profoundly part of Africa. The large number of contemporary treatises on government and politics both in the Middle East and in Africa south of the Sahara therefore need to be supplemented by a study covering the in-between area.

There is also an ideological need. If some of these countries have gained recent attention, it has been primarily on the level of emotion and polemics. Colonialism and dictatorship have been the usual lenses for examinations of Algeria and the United Arab Republic. The result has been to becloud rather than to clarify issues. In fact, the poles of colonialism and independence, of dictatorship and democracy, do not provide adequate perspectives for judging

ix

this area. Its nature and its problems require a more sophisticated way of understanding political systems and governmental structures. It is hoped that this study will promote such an understanding of the government and politics of northern Africa by showing what democracy and independence mean to the emerging nations of the area.

There are a number of debts to be acknowledged in connection with this study, although responsibility for the material lies wholly with the author. The University of South Carolina made the work possible through a research grant. The maps were drafted in the Department of Geography, University of Ghana, by David Hilling and C. L. Amarquaye. Real gratitude is due the readers of individual chapters, who gave their assistance unselfishly, despite personal inconvenience in several cases: Francis de Tarr, G. Henry M. Schuler, P. M. Holt, Douglas Ashford, William Lewis, John E. Moes, and Raymond Moore. Help also came from three of my students: Aurelia Woolsey, Ann Burgdorf, and Crawford Cook. Mrs. Cloris Grogan has been a very efficient and helpful typist. My wife, Marie-Danièle, has, as always, worked with me in innumerable little ways, with faithful interest and attention.

I. William Zartman

University of South Carolina

Government and Politics
in Northern Africa

I

DEMOCRACY AND INDEPENDENCE

The recent history of the emerging nations of northern Africa has been marked by the struggle for self-government. During the post-war period, all the states—Morocco, Algeria, Tunisia, Libya, the United Arab Republic (Egypt), Sudan, Ethiopia, and Somalia—have emerged from foreign domination. In terms of international politics and law, this emergence has taken the form of a struggle for independence. But in terms of domestic politics and law, it has meant the transition from dependence to self-government. There is then posed the problem of how many nationals to include in the concept of "self." In this sense, democracy is the other side of the coin of independence: The existence of the one brings the new country's leaders face to face with the challenge of establishing the other.

If the newly independent society is no longer to be governed by a foreign power, it must be governed by some or all of its own members. The most extreme formulation of this aspiration is government by the people themselves, according to a democratic system. If the problem was so posed—implicitly or explicitly—for the nationalists of northern Africa during their preparations for independence, it was because the same answer was being suggested by important *idées-forces*, mainly the notions of populism and constitutionalism.

Nationalist leaders who grew up under colonial rule found themselves struggling against forces that had a monopoly of power. Legal authority, economic wealth, military force, international support—all were concentrated in the colonial rulers and were often shared with their traditionalist supporters in the colonial society. Only one source was open to the nationalist leaders: the

3

power of the people. The struggle for independence often involved an attempt by the nationalists to counter colonial power with outside support, in terms of legal arguments, money from abroad, military supplies from sympathetic nations, and finally recognition by foreign allies of the right to independence in the absence of such recognition by the metropole. But the struggle was above all devoted to capturing popular support for nationalist aspirations and to using it in resistance or elections. Although certain elite groups sometimes collaborated with colonial rule, in no country was foreign domination supported by the general masses. Nationalist leaders made use of mass support in their appeals, sometimes even before they had acquired it completely, and they worked to build up a mass nationalist movement.

In doing so, they committed themselves to involve the masses in government after independence. Moreover, self-government often meant the displacement of a large segment of the traditional elite. There were two forces left to carry on government after independence—the new nationalist elite and the people whom they said they represented. When independence came, these people were eager to have a hand in government, as they had been promised. The leaders were thus boxed in by their own appeals and their own actions.

Similar pressures were built up in the realm of theory. As the nationalist leaders were victims of their own appeals, so the colonial rulers were committed by their own ideology. Notions of liberty, equality, and fraternity, of parliamentary democracy, and of national self-determination not only were the principles taught to the growing educated elite, but were also the values current in the postwar international atmosphere. In an era when independence was often attained through a number of gradual and confusing steps (interdependence, autonomy, trusteeship, transitional administration), the constitution, documentary proof of independence, became an extremely important goal. It was generally assumed that "constitution" meant "democratic constitution," even if provision for a continuing monarchy was written into its articles. In fact, in the current atmosphere, democracy seemed to be the guardian of independence; unlimited monarchies had shown their inability to stand up against foreign domination, and independence entrenched in the people seemed to be in firmer hands.

This attitude led to curious results. On the one hand, since democratic constitutions could not reflect existing systems of government, they frequently turned out to be simple enumerations of goals; they could be of the most idealistic type, with no one being concerned about their distance from reality. The ultimate in this respect is found in the constitutions of Egypt, which are conceived not as permanent documents but as steps to be attained now and replaced later. Most of the other countries still have difficulty in attaining the ideals of their first constitutions.

On the other hand, republican forces in the monarchies of Morocco, Ethiopia, and Libya learned with chagrin that constitutions are not necessarily democratic. When, with the advent of independence, some of the traditional elements not only remained in power but proceeded to write their power into perpetuity through the use of constitutions, republican forces found themselves opposed to the documents they thought they favored. This situation, too, only increased the pressure for democratic involvement of the people in government.

The Dilemma of Democracy

But independence is easier to attain than democracy. The fact is that when the northern African nations achieved their independence, none of them was ready for democracy. And none of them is today. In all countries, there are elites of different sizes that are capable of governing national affairs. But in no country is the populace in a position to rule itself—despite the commitments made by the leaders, the values of the outside world, and the hopes of the people themselves. This, then, is the dilemma of democracy and independence in newly self-governing states.

The obstacles to democracy in the emerging nations of northern Africa lie essentially in the nature of the people, the nature of the leadership, and the relation between the two. The majority of the population is still an unintegrated mass. In component terms, it is deficient in experiences, expectations, aspirations, and channels. Let us discuss the first three now, the fourth later.

It is trite to note that the inhabitants of northern African countries are still living in a backward and even primitive condition; this has been expressed too often as a sort of condemnation. In fact, the very lack of modern experiences keeps the mass from being able to participate in government. Although the people are frequently quite knowledgeable in the processes of local politics— a condition that makes the lowest level the logical place to start participation in elections—they have no concept of the demands of national government and often no contact with its operations. Characteristic illiteracy keeps their world small and the communication of experiences limited. Experiences that matter have to do with subsistence, natural calamities (often accounted for in magico-religious terms), and a peaceful, secure continuance of life along traditional lines. For example, Libyans in the Fezzan are called on to elect deputies who will pass legislation on oil prospecting and the use of oil revenues; but many of the Fezzanis have never seen oil, let alone oil wells, and can scarcely be expected to examine the candidates' competence with understanding. Local authorities in Ethiopia find it difficult to understand why a tourist should want to photograph the national monuments that he has been invited to Addis Ababa to see; free exchange of information within Ethiopia operates under the same sort of restrictions.

The expectations of the unintegrated masses are similarly limited, to a large extent, by their narrow horizons of experience. The "revolution of rising expectations" is often pictured today as if it were sweeping the underdeveloped countries toward modernization in record time. But this phenomenon is a social revolution, not a political one, and the speed of its effects is comparable to that of the Industrial Revolution—of which it is, in a sense, a part —rather than to that of the French Revolution. A large portion of the northern African population has not yet developed new and greater expectations about its own personal status, nor has it come to learn what can be expected of its government. Indeed, the prestage of this revolution often takes the form of wildly exaggerated dreams: Tunisians told Frenchmen that their refrigerators and automobiles would be taken over as a natural consequence of independence. Populations that have seen their most cherished goal, independence, attained by direct political action can often little understand why all their problems—economic and social, as well as political—cannot be solved rapidly by their new governments. Thus, Moroccan bank employees (including doorkeepers) struck in late 1961 for wage raises and vacations comparable to those of the bank management; at the same time, the union protested against the rising cost of living. An army revolt took place in southern Sudan in 1955 as the result of resentment against interference by Arab administrators from the north; but there was no alternative expectation—except to be left alone.

The aspirations of the populace of these nations are of the

vaguest sort. In most areas, there seems to be a growing national consciousness. In the desert of Somalia or the mountains of Morocco, people will still identify themselves as members of a tribe rather than of a nation, but for the most part there is an awareness that the nation exists. However, there is little awareness of national goals, national interest, or a common good. One reason why politics is played with general themes and slogans in developing nations is that the populace is unable to conceive of and discuss programs in national terms; and of course populism perpetuates this weakness. Between the broad slogans and the narrow parochial world of personal experiences lies a vast territory of which the people have no experience. An Egyptian *fellah* (farmer) might conceivably demonstrate against British troops or against Israel, but what he really cares about is the rise and fall of the Nile, and of his material fortunes with it; and even the ordinary citizen of Cairo is in a very similar position. Somali leaders talk of pan-Somalia, but the Somalo-Ethiopian border war of late 1960 was essentially a tribal vendetta between the Esas and the Danakils, not a popular demonstration of irredentism.

The second series of obstacles to democracy lies in the nature of the leadership. It can certainly be said, without exaggeration, that the leaders of all the emerging nations of northern Africa have accomplished an impressive task in guiding their nations across the threshold of independence to administration of their own affairs, and many have also achieved a drastic transformation of their own thinking from concentration on the single goal of independence to attention to diverse national problems. Deleterious as it may be to real solutions of national problems, the "colonial hangover," in which nationalist leaders continue to emphasize anticolonialism even after independence, is only a natural result of their former fixation on independence.

But the leadership has weaknesses that also mirror the problems of the masses. One is a reluctance to submit to the periodic judgment of the people the offices that the leaders have divided among themselves. Elections in 1960 defeated the Moroccan Minister of Economy's bid for a seat on the Rabat city council and the Libyan Speaker of the House in his campaign for re-election; Egyptian leaders in 1953 and Algerian leaders in 1962 faced hostile demonstrations by the public who had helped put them in power. Leaders of underdeveloped, as well as developed, nations quickly find that the public is a shaky peg on which to hang political longevity.

There are other, deeper obstacles to democracy in the nature of the leadership—principally, the absence of institutions and of a national interest. The underdeveloped countries of northern Africa have underdeveloped governments. This does not only imply an *ad-hoc* approach to governing; it also means a search for patterns of decision-making, a fluid use of many instruments—in sum, an evolution (sometimes unconscious) toward institutionalization of government. During the developing period, leaders look about to find and create comfortable systems of decision-making. As institutions develop and public pressure and readiness to take part in government grow, there is an increasing tendency to work public participation into these patterns. But the institutional systems have not yet been perfected. Two extremes are found in neighboring states. The government in Libya seeks to fill out the constitutional framework already established for it, and in the process public involvement is forced to increase, but not without some clashes of power. President Nasser of Egypt has tried again and again to find suitable ways of governing, and each time moves closer to confirming—even if not sharing—his power through public participation. Morocco and Ethiopia, two monarchies in the throes of evolution, temporarily balked in mid-term, and only Morocco has developed the political institutions that make public participation meaningful.

Emerging nations are not yet keenly aware of their national interest. At present, the states of northern Africa still bear the scars of their anticolonial beginnings. Political forces face the embarrassing dilemma of successful revolutionary movements whose leaders find, in all good conscience, that what they wanted was freedom for themselves but not for others. They see division in opposition when the nation needs unity, colonialism in criticism when the country needs patriotism, and treason, therefore, in anything that challenges the nationalist movement. Party interests thus tend to take precedence over considerations of state. In this situation, democratic opposition and the interplay of opposing forces are seen as a dangerous luxury, and there is no context of national interest within which political debates can take place. In Algeria, opposition is regarded as superfluous, and in Sudan, it is banned; in the U.A.R. and Tunisia, it is viewed as seditious; and in Ethiopia and Libya, opposition forces are disorganized. Even where legal opposition parties exist—in Morocco and Somalia— their appeals are frequently divisive rather than constructive. Lack of basic agreement on a national interest breeds an atmosphere that makes democracy difficult.

The third series of obstacles to democracy lies in the relationship of the mass to the elite. The most significant aspect of this relationship is the "gap." Between the Lazarus of the masses and the Dives of the traditional elite there is a great gulf fixed, with little social mobility, economic graduation, or political interpenetration. In some cases, such as Egypt, Algeria, and Tunisia, the new elite bridges the gap by maintaining its contact with the mass from which it sprang. But this bridge is not totally effective. Until it is made universal, education only accentuates the gap by creating a new modern elite that is worlds apart from the uneducated people. "The overcoming of the gap requires the dispersion of initiative and interest more widely throughout society."[1] The presence of the gap precludes the effective operation of democracy.

There are two special political aspects of the gap that point up its significance as an obstacle to democracy. One is the absence of national unity. In a sense, the gap itself breaks national unity along a horizontal fissure. As long as experiences, expectations, and aspirations remain dual, so far apart in two distinct segments of society, it is hard to conceive of a unified nation. However, most of the countries of northern Africa are split along vertical lines into sharp regional divisions. This may be reflected in the provincial structure of the state, as in Libya; but it usually has its roots in the area's geography, as in Morocco, Algeria, and Sudan. Its extremes are clearly seen in one pair of neighbors: Ethiopia suffers basic ethnic divisions perpetuated by its deeply chasmed topography, while the Somali people, a single ethnic unit, are still divided by ancient tribal animosities. In a region where mountains and deserts are such important features, and where, for the most part, the inhabited regions are either coastal plains or oases (including the Nile valley, the world's longest oasis), regional particularism is bound to be felt in the political structure.

The other aspect of the gap is its lack of bridges. Even if popular aspirations were highly developed in northern Africa, there would still be few channels for conveying them from the mass to the elite. Preparation of a society for democracy, then, depends on the development of intermediaries, spokesmen, institutional bridges, and channels. Political parties, labor unions, representative organs of local government, press and radio, even economic-development projects that involve participation and training, and

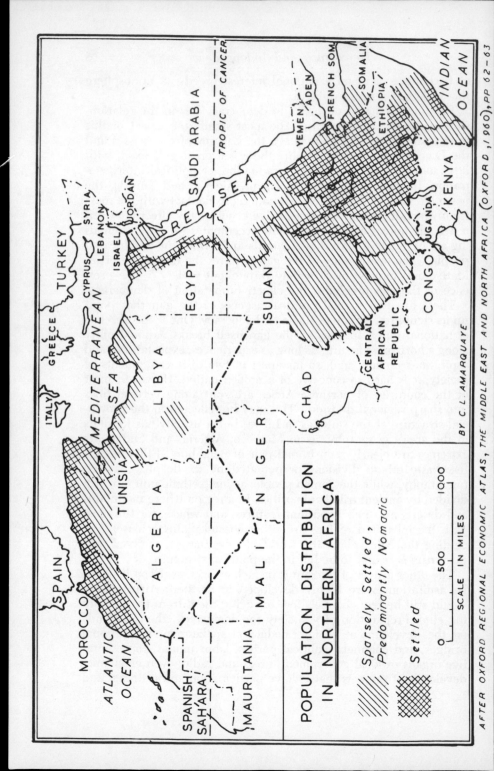

POPULATION DISTRIBUTION
IN NORTHERN AFRICA

Sparsely Settled,
Predominantly Nomadic

Settled

SCALE IN MILES

0   500   1000

BY C. L. AMARQUAYE

AFTER OXFORD REGIONAL ECONOMIC ATLAS, THE MIDDLE EAST AND NORTH AFRICA (OXFORD, 1960), PP 62-63

certainly elections all deserve emphasis. The development of a middle class is the parallel in the social field, and also has its political effects. But emerging nations are, by their own admission, too impatient to follow the classic pattern of social integration as it evolved in the nations of Europe and in the United States. Just as in the field of economic development, they are in a hurry. Political development is thus attendant on the building of bridges, rather than on their natural growth. Until the gap is spanned politically, democracy cannot begin to be effective.

Ways Around the Dilemma

The problem of democracy is posed with insistence in the northern African states, but the nature of the mass and the elite, and the gap between them, keeps democracy from taking shape. No northern African leader can ignore this dilemma. Even if he tries to avoid it, instead of consciously facing it, he must deal with it in some way. The responses in the eight independent states of northern Africa differ widely, but they fall into three general categories: The elite governs, democracy is redefined, political development continues.

Despite the appeals to democracy in northern Africa, government is actually an elite function. The shape of the political system, however, depends on local conditions. The three prevalent systems can be referred to as traditional oligarchies, tutelary systems, and party systems (terms adapted from Shils and from Almond and Coleman[2]). It should be emphasized that these descriptions cover not merely the government but the entire political system of the nation, which may in fact contain the government as only one of several conflicting elements (particularly true of the party systems).

Ethiopia and Libya are considered to have traditional oligarchic political systems. Traditional oligarchies in northern Africa have not known the political catalepsy that the dynastic governments of Yemen and Saudi Arabia have had; the reason is found primarily in the colonial experience of the African countries, which gave rise to disruptive forces within the local populations. However, they do have dynastic monarchies that maintain power to the exclusion of other political formations. Although considered traditional, these systems do not go so far as to refuse the slogans of democracy; in fact, the leaders themselves have led their countries in their first timid steps toward public participation in political life. But this evolution is still firmly in their control and is not subject to pressures from political forces outside the oligarchy. There is no guarantee of permanence to such a system—in fact, the reverse is more likely—but the composition of political forces is such that political development has not yet proceeded to the point where the oligarchy in either country is sitting on a volcano. From this standpoint, these countries differ from another monarchy, Morocco.

The U.A.R., Tunisia, and Algeria are tutelary systems. In many respects, their systems deserve the more descriptive title of "single-party democracies." "Tutelary systems" is preferred, however, as being more inclusive and less contradictory. Egypt's political system is not the product of a single party; rather, the party (such as it may be) is the product of the system. Yet, in Egypt, as in Tunisia and Algeria, a modernistic hierarchical group controls the political life of the country, relying on concentrated executive power and a high degree of two-way contact with lower political echelons, resulting in an often deceptive impression of a democratic system. In contrast to the traditional oligarchies, these systems do contain some organs for bridging the political gap. But these organs are political rather than governmental, consultative rather than decision-making, and do not strongly limit the freedom of action of the elite.

Morocco, Sudan, and Somalia have party systems, although in the first two the parties exist under a nonparty elite. The history of these countries before independence had many similarities with that of countries that now have tutelary systems, but in each case the nationalist movement lost its unity to a number of factions. In Somalia, external party unity masks a tenuous coalition of tribal interests. In Morocco, the dominant nationalist movement broke in half, lost its predominance, and thus made room for other, smaller groups. In Sudan, the parties reflected sectarian and political differences from the beginning, although the political differences were more noticeable in the leadership than in their following. In all cases, the parties provide a certain degree of training and participation in political life. In Sudan and Morocco, however, they do not dominate government. The 1958 generals' junta in Sudan and the personal leadership of Hassan II (now King) since 1960 in Morocco have constituted governing forces that have dominated the parties in both countries (in fact, the Sudanese junta has outlawed the parties). In some ways, popular participation in the parties is greater than party responsibility in the government. The tension thus created is obvious. Although the systems of government vary in all three countries, a factionalized nationalist movement is the predominant characteristic of political life in each.

Democracy, therefore, does not really exist in northern Africa. The fact that "we, the Egyptian people" declared "a democratic republic" in 1956 did not make the Egyptian Government any less of a military regime. King Hassan's first Throne Speech, in 1962, announcing that "the regime chosen and adopted by Morocco is democracy in the political realm, justice in social matters, equilibrium on the economic level, and nonalignment in foreign policy" was not a work of political alchemy that changed the lead of elitist rule into the gold of popular government. But both examples do suggest that leaders are sufficiently aware of their dilemma to try to rationalize their way out of it. This, then, is the second response to the democratic dilemma—the redefining of democracy.

Probably the element common to all the redefinitions is a distinction between procedural democracy, in the Western sense of parliamentarianism, and substantive democracy, in which popular aspirations are known and satisfied despite the absence of formal parliamentary machinery. Parliaments are relegated to the position of consultative, approbatory organs, and elections are frequently replaced by plebiscites, in which the "Jack-in-the-ballot box" always has the same face. But the leaders claim that through familiarity and intuition—and often through mystical popular bonds, in both republican systems (Egypt and Tunisia) and monarchical ones (Morocco and Ethiopia)—they can sense the public will, of which the public itself is often unaware. Whatever new name it may go by, this notion is not new. It is as old as kings and philosophers, and it has been known variously as paternalism and benevolent dictatorship in the past. Its novelty today lies in the adoption of the word "democracy" and in its existence in a rapidly changing world of emerging nations.

Redefinition is at least partially necessary. It has already been seen that there are obstacles to democracy in northern Africa; there are also dangers in it. The mere procedure of voting is not enough to guarantee meaningful public participation in government and effective transfer of public wishes to decision-making organs; moreover, handing over government to an unprepared and unintegrated public is most likely to lead to chronic disunity and instability, and finally to the chaos that tempts potential dictators.

As two experts have pointed out: "Indeed, in societies with little experience of decentralized authority and little consciousness of national goals, too rapid a delegation of power is a sure route back to repressive authoritarianism."[3] Of the two, hastiness is often a greater injustice to democracy than redefinition.

On the other hand, there are also weaknesses in substantive democracy—or in ostensible attempts to attain it. There is no reason to believe that the two generally conceived poles of government—democracy and dictatorship—are the only alternatives; it makes little sense, therefore, to condemn as dictatorial all that is not rigorously democratic. But nondemocratic systems place a tremendous burden on their rulers, not only in the problem-solving sense of government, but in government as the use of power. Obviously, the weakness of governments that call themselves substantive democracies is their propensity to regard their wishes as public wishes, to consider their needs the needs of state, and to see their own well-being as the national welfare.

The third response to the democratic dilemma—continuing political development—is a natural outgrowth of these conclusions; unlike the other two, it concerns the mass above all, rather than leaders. Against a background of economic development and social change, and in an atmosphere of popularistic slogans of democracy, political development continues whether the elite favors it or not. Experiences of colonial rule, the lure and pressures of urbanization, the integrative effects of better transportation and communication, unifying and divisive tendencies brought about by a money economy, the pressures of a sudden population growth, employment and productive possibilities of modernized agriculture and industry, the expansion of concepts and skills through education, the development of national consciousness, inculcation of the ideas of public responsibility, and increased contact with state machinery exercising a welfare function—all these are forces in the social, economic, and political field which, combined together, have started in northern Africa an autonomous process of political development.

Like economic development, political development has its take-off stage, produced in northern Africa by the tension between nationalist drives and colonial regimes. Take-off resulting from only indigenous forces is a much slower and more difficult process, as countries with insufficient colonial contact, such as Libya and Ethiopia, have shown. But once this stage has been passed, evolutionary development in northern African countries has tended to proceed on its own. If government policies and the attention of the elite do not include measures to assist and channel this development toward training citizens for responsible participation in government, tensions develop within the polity, and a clash is bound to ensue. Unfortunately, even if the leaders do prepare themselves and their people for participation in government, there is no guarantee that these measures will be successful or that the pressures generated through political development will not create tension and conflict anyway. New governments can minimize these tensions with measures designed to bridge the gap, but the pressures can hardly be decreased by being ignored or repressed.

Confronted with this inescapable fact, the new national elite is in a situation greatly similar to that of the colonial powers. The metropole had the self-imposed responsibility of preparing its colony for independence; it did its job poorly or well, but it was a prisoner of its own ideology. Its very presence put in motion the forces that would eventually drive it out. The new nation's leaders have the self-imposed task of preparing their country for democracy; they may do their job with varying degrees of success, but their task is cut out for them, too, by their own slogans. It is in the nature of both democracy and the methods of some of the modernizing elite that success in this task may mean the end of their jobs, just as it did for the colonialists.

Given the goals proclaimed, the leaders of emerging nations have a twofold task. They need to develop government as a problem-solving mechanism by establishing adequate institutions and by adopting applicable policy. They must also teach their population to articulate its needs and wishes, and must create integrative mechanisms to "relate the interests and demands of society to political power."[4] In other words, accepting the rationalization of substantive democracy, the governments of northern Africa can be evaluated according to how well they handle the present needs of their countries and how well they prepare for the future expression and satisfaction of their peoples' responsible aspirations.

In the last analysis, these two criteria are actually one. "The success of a development program in a democratic country must depend to a large extent on how far it expresses the wishes and aspirations of ordinary people and on how far they feel themselves identified with it and with the government which is responsible for carrying it out."[5]

It is easier and more realistic to appreciate the progress, tensions, and weaknesses of northern African political systems by applying this criterion than by seeking a simplistic judgment based merely on one's concepts of democracy or dictatorship. It thus becomes possible also to evaluate northern African governments in terms of their own ideals, instead of by holding up as yardsticks irrelevant foreign concepts.

The Stages of Freedom

A country's political evolution generally passes through three stages: traditional, transitional, and modern. However, little attention has been given to the exact nature of this evolution as it progresses. In fact, it is both complex—made up of many separate evolutions—and concomitant, since these separate evolutions take place at varying but interrelated speeds. A few general observations can be made about the three stages. Essentially, the polity appears to be moving from one plateau of stability to another. The first plateau is the political system in which the polity felt "comfortable" as a traditional society, and the second is one that will fit the country's particular conception of modern society. The general characteristic of the first plateau is a static society, economy, and polity, while stability is achieved on the second one through mobile relationships—continued economic growth, social mobility, political processes. In between, the transition stage is devoted to rearranging relationships, accommodating new forces, and searching for a new level of stability.

There are five concomitant evolutions in this three-stage political development:

1. Within the legal system, there is a shift from authority based on custom, through a statutory stage, toward constitutionalism. In a customary society, the ruler operates within broad socioreligious limits, by which every member of society "knows" his place. In the transitional period, laws are passed and promulgated, but are changeable by other laws without any reference to a higher criterion. The constitutional period is characterized not only by a constitution, but also by judicial review of legislation according to the constitutional standard and by the guarantee of rights in reality as well as on paper.

2. Within the mass, there is an evolution from an inert position,

untouched by government, to an instrumental position, where people are manipulated but not effectively consulted, and on to an integrated status, where they participate in public life.

3. On the other side of the social gap, there is a corresponding evolution within the elite from traditional, through mixed, to modern status. In the first stage, power is based on land ownership, descent and respect, relationship with the monarchy, or religious authority; in the final stage, it derives from monetary wealth, education and occupational skills useful in government service, and popular support.

4. Within the political organization, an initial reform group broadens its goals and membership into a nationalist movement and then develops toward becoming a political party. In the absence of elections, the nationalist movement may continue to exist after independence without becoming a full-fledged party. However, there are two distinct types of party organizations: the multiparty system and the single-party system. The former is to be expected where a country, through size or through ethnic or geographical divisions, favors a pluralistic society, where free elections are held, or where the concept of national consciousness has not developed far enough to overcome residual localism. The single-party system will develop where the appeals of anticolonialism are carried over into the post-independence period as the dominant slogans satisfying the movement's members, where the movement's program as government commands the adherence of all members, or where the movement is organized (sometimes about a strong, charismatic leader) to the point that it can manipulate the means of sanction and gratification to the suppression of competing groups.

5. Within governmental ideology, there is an evolution from a narrow goal of personal interest, through a broader but exclusive goal of national power, to a complex of values called national interest. In traditional societies, government has usually been a business rather than a profession, and government employees have been "fortunate participants in the central drama of life"[6] rather than civil servants in the literal sense. In the transitional period, the acquisition of national power is a group goal, and even justice and equality become subservient to or equated with power. Even after the attainment of independence, the ethic of national power continues to be felt in anticolonial foreign policies and in the nationalist movement's continuing struggle to remain the domi-

nant unified political force. Only when this period is outgrown is there a search for a national interest to justify state action.

These are the concepts by which the governments and politics of the independent states of Africa north of the Sahara will be examined and described here. The study of each country will be divided into four sections: An introductory section will show how independence was achieved and what forces were on hand when the country attained its present status. The second will examine the position of the elite in both decision-making and representative functions, and will also present an analysis of the philosophy of government, if one has been expressed by that country's elite. The next section will turn to the position of the mass and, after a general description, focus especially on those organs which serve to prepare for public participation in government and to bridge the gap. The final section will examine the formal rules that govern the polity—including the constitution, legal system, judiciary, and rights of the people—and will conclude with a brief review of the nation's present policies.

II

MOROCCO

Morocco attained its independence on March 2, 1956, after forty-four years as a French and Spanish protectorate. Although Moroccan existence as a political unit stretches back, through numerous interruptions, to Roman times, the awakening of a national consciousness did not come until 1930.* In that year, the French protectorate, through the Berber *dahir* (edict), attempted to divide and conquer the country by making a legal distinction between the Arab and the Berber populations. By 1934, the basic elements of the nationalist movement were formed; the young Sultan was hailed as "king" in popular demonstrations in Fez, and a Moroccan Action Committee was set up to formulate grievances and demand reforms.[1]

The sultanate has always been the office of leadership in Morocco. It derives its power by descent from the Prophet and by consent of the people. This mode of leadership was respected by the protectorate, which was, in fact, established to bolster the weakened sultanate against its enemies through military support and governmental reforms. Although Mulay Mohammed ben Yussef, born in 1911, had been chosen Sultan by the French protectorate in 1927 because he seemed to be the most compliant of the late Sultan's sons, he turned gradually into both the agent and the symbol of nationalist goals. In 1943, he was encouraged by President Franklin D. Roosevelt to seek independence within the prin-

---

* A regional foreshadowing of this modern nationalism was found in the Rif Republic of Abdelkrim Khattabi between 1924 and 1926. Abdelkrim, who died in exile in Cairo in 1963, was a vehement supporter of North African nationalism, especially as expressed by the Algerian Government and the Moroccan left opposition.

ciples of the Atlantic Charter; in 1947, he made his first public demand for Moroccan independence, speaking in the International Zone of Tangier to symbolize the territorial unity of his kingdom. Caught between a growing nationalist movement on the one hand and a get-tough policy of the French Residents-General on the other, the Sultan gave in to first one and then the other until 1953. By then, a compromise on the essential issue of Moroccan sovereignty was no longer possible, and he was summarily exiled to Madagascar by the protectorate. As a result, the Sultan's symbolic leadership of the nationalist resistance was confirmed, and his return from exile in 1955 prepared the way for independence.

While the Sultan stood as a symbol of Morocco's drive for unity and independence, an active political elite, backed by a number of semiclandestine groups, gradually organized to bring about independence by direct action. By 1937, the nationalist movement had split into four geographic and personality factions, each with a similar but competing program. The increasingly aggressive line of resistance, and particularly the unity brought about by the substitution of a single goal of independence for a number of reforms, led to the formation of an independence movement (the Istiqlal) in 1944, which was followed by a Moroccan National Front in 1951. The Front united (although loosely) the four major nationalist factions under the leadership of the original 1934 elite.

Three groups emerged within the nationalist movement. The original leaders, especially after 1952, were deported (for example, Allal al-Fassi) or went into exile (Ahmed Balafrej, Mohammed Laghzawi)* to direct the international aspect of the movement and to provide guidance to the home front from the security of foreign shores. A "second generation" of younger leaders sprang up to lead the active resistance on Moroccan soil (Mehdi ben Barka, Abderrahim Bouabid). Many of these men were later jailed or deported, but they remained in closer contact with resistance activity than the original leaders had. Some of them were connected with terrorist groups (Mahjub ben Seddiq, Mohammed al-Basri) or with the Army of Liberation (Mahjubi Ahardan, Abdelkrim Khatib). The third group, an active faction of the popular masses, listened to the old leaders and worked under the younger generation in guerrilla, terrorist, and propaganda activity, some-

---

* Names cited in parentheses here and similarly throughout this and subsequent chapters are given as important examples rather than as complete lists.

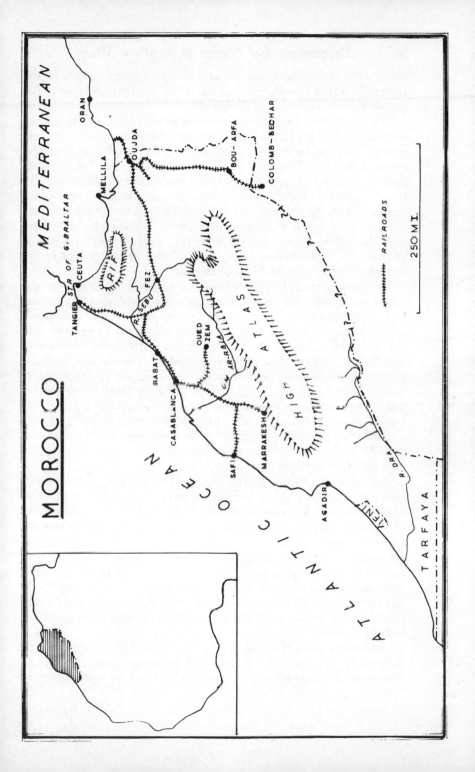

times even taking decisions as well as actions into their own impatient hands. From this group came the popular martyrs (Allal ben Abdullah, Mohammed Zerqtuni).

The resistance became synonymous with the independence movement. The goal, the movement, the party, and even the clandestine newspaper became welded together under a powerful name—Istiqlal. When the goal was attained, the "old guard" leaders returned to reassume political leadership, enabled to do so by the actions of the younger leaders—who took second place again—and of the enthusiastic masses. The Istiqlal Party took advantage of the independence movement to assert its dominant position, but it agreed to join with the other, smaller resistance groups in a "Government of National Unity" presided over by an independent nationalist, Mbarek Bekkai.

The parties provided the cadres for the new government, the urban resistance was for the most part absorbed into the police, and members of the Army of Liberation—the last diehard group to recognize the monarchy's independence—were integrated into the Royal Moroccan Army or given posts in the local administration. Other civil servants were recruited from among former employees of the ministries under the protectorate or from newly trained Moroccan youth, giving Morocco a large civil service (40,000) following independence. Over this ensemble with widely varied political backgrounds, King Mohammed V ruled as an apolitical arbitrator and a symbol of Moroccan unity.[2]

The Structure of the Elite

The Moroccan King is the "trustee of sovereignty" and the "symbol of national unity and protector of the rights and liberties of the citizens." As reigning monarch, he is chief of state, but he also holds a position of religious primacy as Imam and, traditionally, has been considered commander-in-chief of an army that is his personal adjunct. His governmental powers in the legislative, executive, and judicial fields are final, but he shares them with other institutions of government. The evolution of the monarchy in Morocco since 1956 has been toward reassertion of the King's personal role in government, along with consolidation of his position as head of state.

Until May, 1960, King Mohammed V was able to maintain his position as an apolitical arbitrator of Moroccan political life. All important government officials were appointed by him, either in close consultation with leaders of national organizations (parties, unions, resistance groups) or from lists submitted by them; his cabinets, selected after broad and lengthy consultations, were chosen from a slate of political figures and technicians presented by a premier-elect. No important body carried out its work without his participation at some stage, either in actual deliberations, in private working sessions, or in a review of results before their publication as a *dahir*. Although the King remained the sole agent of formal legislation, bills were prepared by the cabinet before their submission to him for final review and approval. The King made known his wishes for legislation by giving out broad policy lines in public speeches or by communicating his desires informally to the appropriate minister. But formal initiative remained with the individual cabinet member.

A broad consensus of public goals and means existing between the King and his ministers, and a royal policy of avoiding interference in particulars, minimized friction over government policy during this period. In a very few instances, direct clashes took place, resulting occasionally in the shelving of legislation or the curtailing of royal programs. Chronic differences were solved by the King through a change in government personnel. The result was a program of moderation carried out by a government that suffered from a lack of ministerial continuity.

In October, 1956, the initial Government of National Unity was reorganized under Prime Minister Bekkai, with the Istiqlal holding a majority of the ministries. When the Prime Minister endorsed a resolution by minority parties criticizing the Istiqlal's demand for full power, however, these ministers resigned in a growing atmosphere of partisan bitterness. The succeeding government, formed in May, 1958, was given to the party causing the crisis—in proper parliamentarian style—and Party Secretary Balafrej headed a nearly all-Istiqlal cabinet. Intraparty rivalries rendered its life short and limited its productivity. In December, 1958, new ministers were chosen "in a personal capacity," although the composition of this fourth government reflected Prime Minister Ibrahim's affiliation with the Istiqlal's dissident activist wing, which had caused the crisis. Except for the personal, rather than the collective, responsibility of ministers in the last cabinet, these four governments were all constituted according to rules similar to those by which party governments in France and England are chosen.

Pressures from several sides changed this situation in May, 1960. The heir apparent, Crown Prince Mulay Hassan, was becoming personally impatient with his own position outside the formal mechanisms of government and politically impatient with the absence of clear policy and stable leadership. The political parties were becoming impatient with the political moderation of the King, as well as with his constraining influence on their use of governmental power for partisan purposes. The King was dissatisfied with the partisanship of the government at a crucial time, when the first nationwide elections were scheduled to take place, but he was also physically tired. An attempt to form a government with the Crown Prince as Premier was refused by the parties. Because of the various conflicting elements in the situation, the King himself assumed leadership of the government, the Prince was appointed Deputy Prime Minister and given effective executive power, and ministerial posts were filled with party representatives and technicians, again acting in a personal capacity. Henceforth, as the King reigned, the Prince ruled.

On February 26, 1961, King Mohammed V died during a minor operation, and Hassan II ascended the throne. The country was plunged into deep mourning and political uncertainty. The thirty-one-year-old Hassan brought an unusual combination of attributes to the throne. His Western ways and dress, his "Prince Hal" youth, and his dynamism were combined with a faithful attempt to reincarnate the religious example and the symbolic unity that his father had embodied, and a belief that "power must be personalized to be popular." The tours he made, following the traditional custom, to receive allegiance in the principal towns throughout the realm were occasions of popular rejoicing similar to those stimulated by his father. But personal acclamation remained the coin of unity more than ever since independence.

The new King's views of government coincide with his idea of personal leadership. The cabinet is to be "a team of responsible men grouped together about a chief, capable of giving the powerful impetus necessary to lead the people in their fight for progress and against poverty." The people "need to follow a man [and] a team. But for this team which I have built up of men in whom I have confidence . . . I must act as standard-bearer, I must open the way." Parties are conceived of rather as a secondary means of organizing support about the King, instead of as popular associations designed to formulate policy and programs. "I will be frank," said the Prince. "I cannot at the present time make the exercise of power less direct. Why? Because our people are not ready to be mobilized about a program or a doctrine." His cousin, Mulay Ahmed al-Alawi, then Information Minister, rephrased the same thought: "Hassan II will be the King of the Moroccan people as well as King of all the political parties." Adroitly, the King uses the parties in such a way that government successes redound to his credit, and failures serve to weaken the parties.

A new government, chosen in June, 1961, reflected this concept. The Prince remained Prime Minister, aided by his close personal collaborator, Ahmed Reda Guedira, Minister of Interior and Agriculture. Balafrej was Foreign Minister, and the spiritual leader of the Istiqlal, al-Fassi, was Minister of State for Islamic Affairs. The rest of the ministries were given to political and technical figures qualified by personal loyalty to the King rather than by party following. However, personal leadership is geared as much to the goal of governmental stability and the achievement of a program as it is to the embodiment of national unity. "We have had too many ministers too early," said the King. "I will not name any more for a long time. It is fitting that those who have begun this difficult apprenticeship be able to finish it."

To Hassan II, a governmental program is dictated as much by the obvious needs of the Moroccan people as by aspirations of which they might be only vaguely or emotionally aware. The King has said, "In this period of uncertainty, of struggle against underdevelopment, of lack of trained cadres, the people need a man in whom they have confidence. . . . Our desire is to promote real social democracy by rapidly guaranteeing the means of achieving dignity: internal peace, employment, housing, increased culture, and decent food." In a number of fields of social policy, such as housing, education, and rural development, real progress has been made.

However, the young King soon realized that direct personal rule was incompatible with the political evolution of the country. Changes in the cabinet were made three times in the latter half of 1962; in January, 1963, the three leading Istiqlal ministers—including al-Fassi—resigned to enter the opposition, and in March the Minister for Mauritanian Affairs returned to Mauritania. A return to the system of Mohammed V, where the King was shielded from direct political participation by the presence of a Prime Minister, again appeared desirable, and was written into the constitution.

The brief evolution of Moroccan government since independence included two attempts by Mohammed V to prepare the country for representative government, followed by the final installation of democratic institutions under Hassan II. Through the creation of representative organs, first on the national level and then on the local level, the late King wished to provide training institutions for the smooth transition into constitutional monarchy. But this move also created forces pushing for republicanism and for more rapid development toward parliamentarianism than the King had wished, without showing corresponding responsibility. These early experiments failed, and their failure provides a partial explanation for Hassan II's concepts of personal leadership.

Mohammed V's first experiment was the creation of a prototype Senate and House, with strictly advisory functions, an appointed membership, and vaguely defined responsibility. A three-man Crown Council, created in October, 1956, to give traditional leaders a voice in government, was regarded by the King as a rudimentary upper house. In addition to giving advice on many matters, its members performed ceremonial functions and acted as the King's representative when a traditionalist figure was needed. However, one member (al-Ahcen al-Yussi) resigned in December, 1958, having been implicated in a traditionalist revolt against the government, and another (Mulay al-Arbi al-Alawi) resigned in January, 1960, in protest against repressive police measures. The eclipse of the third (Mokhtar as-Soussi) on the accession of Hassan II removed the last traditionalist voice from the formal governmental structure.

A seventy-six-member National Consultative Assembly was appointed in August, 1956, for two years, and was later extended to May, 1959. Its membership was chosen on the basis of functional and partisan (and implicit geographical) representation, to provide popular leaders with an occasion to discuss legislation, to comment on the budget, and to interpellate ministers. During its existence, political enmities sharpened among its members, particularly between factions of its Istiqlal majority, and the political neutrality of its president (Ben Barka) was thrown to the winds of partisanship. Yet, at the same time, it demanded with increasing insistence a greater role in government, without fulfilling constructively the preparatory role it had already been given.

The Assembly was allowed to lapse, ostensibly in anticipation of nationwide elections. But when the elections were finally held, they had lost their original significance as the first step in the indirect selection of a national parliamentary or constituent assembly. In May, 1960, 798 rural communes and 27 incorporated municipalities elected local councils. The elections took place in an atmosphere of calm, and they showed the maturity of the population in choosing representatives to decide local affairs. The *dahir* establishing their functions was not prepared until after the elections, and it did not reflect much official confidence in the country's first electoral experience. Local administrative control is still retained by the mayors (*pashas*) and rural administrators (*qaids*), under the effective rule of the appointed governors of the sixteen provinces and two urban prefectures. The local councils fill scarcely more than a consultative role. New local elections were held following the national elections of 1963.

In 1963, a new and more comprehensive attempt to establish democratic institutions was made. A bicameral Parliament was elected and was given an important role in the legislative process. Although the King retained a final veto, he suggested that he would be at least as discriminating in the use of this formal power as his father was of his informal power; "in any constitution, many things are created by custom, and many others are forgotten by non-use," he commented on the new institutions. The 144 members of the House of Representatives were elected in May, 1963, for four years. Sixty-nine of the seats went to the two wings of the former independence movement—twenty-eight to the left-wing National Union of Popular Forces (UNFP) and forty-one to the Istiqlal Party—and sixty-nine seats went to the Front for the Defense of the Constitutional Institutions (FDIC), an electoral association favored by the King. Since the remaining six members were elected as independents, the House contains several possibilities of coalition and political maneuvering in order to obtain the majority necessary to pass laws. The lower house, to which the government is responsible, may be dissolved by the King and sent back to the electorate. The House of Councilors is indirectly elected, two-thirds of its membership from among an electoral college composed of the communal and newly created provincial councils, and one-third from among members of the Chambers of Agriculture, Commerce and Industry, and Artisans, and of the labor unions. The upper house has a part in the legislative process but no right of censure over the government, and its members are elected for staggered six-year terms, a third of the seats being renewed every two years. The parliamentary institutions established in 1963 contain a balance of power and responsibility that was not found in the earlier attempts. On each level of government, the elected councils are obliged to cooperate with a strong nonelected figure—*pasha* or *qaid*, governor, and King. The result in theory is an admirably balanced system. Its effectiveness in practice depends on the willingness of the King and the parties to operate within the constitutional framework.*

The Position of the Mass

Public participation in government is therefore just beginning. There are effective channels for forming and formulating public will, but until 1963 these channels were separated from the organs of government by an institutional gap. This gap clearly reflected the sociological gaps that separate the illiterate, provincial, impoverished, and largely tradition-oriented mass from the governing elite. The creation of political bridges only increases the corollary need for other bridges, for increased opportunity and mobility within the society, and for training in the meaning of public opinion, national issues, and responsible government. "The applause which greets the young King is much more an invitation to act than an expression of sightless confidence."[3] As population continues to grow (at 3.25 per cent annually), and unemployment with it, the gap becomes more dangerous, at least in the urban areas. As popular pressure builds up, dissatisfaction in the cities runs the danger of plunging the nation into revolutionary turmoil. The chronic dissatisfaction that breeds revolution has not yet reached the countryside, however. One of Morocco's greatest problems is how to awaken and ameliorate the agricultural sector—which includes 40 per cent of the national income and 70 per cent of the population—without giving rise to rural unrest.

Quasi-democratic participation in local government is a tradition of Berber society, and this heritage partly accounts for the maturity of the population shown in the elections. The rural tribal council (*jemaa*) governed its tribe or fraction in an oligarchic

* The boycott of the municipal elections of July 28, 1963, by the UNFP, UMT, and Istiqal, and the arrest of a number of opposition leaders shortly before these elections on charges of plotting against the King tend to alter seriously the Moroccan political situation and put the effective operation of the constitution in doubt.

manner, choosing its members and its headman (*sheikh*) through popular consensus expressed in a show of hands. Council membership was flexible enough to include both rival candidates when a choice of one would have a divisive effect on the tribe. The rural population is therefore experienced in local affairs and small-scale politics. When the rural communes were established prior to the 1960 elections, only a third of them reflected tribal divisions, and the rest were created as new, viable social and economic units. When the electoral districts for the House of Representatives were established, 118 of the 144 seats were filled from mixed and rural constituencies.

In the cities, where the problems of government are infinitely more complex and less familiar to the electorate, the choice of many able councilmen and the single-party color of many councils reduce the danger of divisive partisanship and mismanagement.* Probably the greatest contribution of the elections toward integrating the masses lay in their educative value, for the serious campaigns carried on by the government and the parties alike did much to teach the people the meaning of democratic processes. In the House of Representatives, twenty-six members are elected from the nine largest cities. In town and country, elections have been relatively honest and orderly, and abstentions have resulted more from political choice than from apathy. However, the decision to hold at least half-a-dozen elections during 1963, the year that parliamentary institutions were set up, runs the risk of tiring the people of voting and increasing abstention.

Attempts at direct public participation in governmental projects, on the other hand, have tended to substantiate the King's view of the need for dramatic personal leadership. In the summer of 1957, an imaginative project enrolled 10,000 unemployed young Moroccans in the construction of a "Unity Road" across the Rif Mountains, tying together the two zones of the ex-protectorates. Political and civic education for the youths was a part of this project. Despite a search for future programs of this type, partisan opposition and inertia kept it from being repeated, and the road itself fell to the ravages of rain.

In the fall of 1957, the Agricultural Ministry inaugurated "Operation Plow," again with the King's active support; state-owned

* Unlike most Arab countries, Morocco has imposed no restrictions on the participation of women in elections. Ten women even ran—but lost—in the 1960 election, and one fared no better in the Representatives' election in 1963.

tractors were used to plow small private farms, and the *fellahin* (farmers) were subsequently to cooperate in local agricultural councils under the technical direction of agricultural specialists. After reaching its peak the following year, the project has steadily declined, through administrative disfavor as well as rural disinterest in the local councils and unallayed suspicions of modern methods.

Other experiments in direct participation have been more successful. In the early years of independence, party and administrative leaders organized volunteer labor to construct schools in rural areas. Throughout the nation, 700 classrooms were built in 1958, 636 classrooms and 156 dormitories in 1959, and 600 more in 1960–61—all by local volunteers working under administrative direction. The Anti-Illiteracy Campaign, another example of channeled enthusiasm, began with 300,000 "pupils" in April, 1956, under the King's patronage. Although enrollment had fallen to 26,500 by 1959 and instruction was given on a very low level, the program permitted a broad attack on adult illiteracy and at the same time provided an occasion for rudimentary civic education. In early 1962, the radio was put to use to combat illiteracy in one pilot province, with some success.

Following the initiative of individual *qaids,* local volunteers have engaged in campaigns to remove stones from formerly marginal fields, building trails, markets (*souqs*), and irrigation systems; in one district near Marrakech in 1958, 27,000 inhabitants cleared over 15,000 acres and made other public improvements. Another hopeful beginning is a 15,000-member commune in the Rabat area, where a U.N. project in rural development has galvanized local participation and brought rapid results since its inception in August, 1960. This project will be used as a pilot program for communal development, economic betterment, and social integration in three other provinces, involving 450,000 people. In each of these cases, imagination and initiative on the local level were effective in channeling popular enthusiasm and aiding mass integration. The broadest series of local projects is the National Promotion program, involving 35,000 people in 1961 and an average of 80,000 per month in 1962. The program reduced unemployment by creating labor battalions for agricultural and public-works projects; workers were paid small wages and given a daily ration of wheat (supplied by American aid). For the fiscal year 1963, the National Promotion was integrated with related ministries' projects and coordinated with local needs and wishes through the initiative and consultation of the provincial governors and communal councils; under the constitution, the direction of the National Promotion program was combined with the five-year plan under the control of the Superior Council of the National Promotion and the Plan, the highest appointed body in the realm.

Through labor unions, an important segment of the developing population is partially integrated into public life. The Moroccan Labor Union (UMT) was founded with Istiqlal encouragement in March, 1955, as a nationalist workers' organization affiliated with the International Confederation of Free Trade Unions (ICFTU). It has an active membership of about 200,000 (a third of its claims), drawn mostly from the coastal belt of urban industry, but also from the mines and farms of the interior. In national congresses, regional and federation councils, and local meetings, the unions pass resolutions on matters of public policy and on specific labor demands; these resolutions are formulated by the union leadership, but they at least permit rank-and-file exposure to and identification with policy statements. Under Mohammed V, the UMT was consulted on major policy decisions; sat in the National Consultative Assembly, the Superior Council of the Plan, and other advisory bodies; and had access to the Palace. The decreased importance of advisory bodies and the fewer consultations of Hassan II limited the UMT's subsequent role in shaping governmental policy. As a result, the attention of labor was channeled away from substantive policy and turned to procedural demands for increased participation in government and to narrow labor demands. Since the advent of constitutional government, the increased importance of the Superior Council for the National Promotion and the Plan and the creation of an upper house of Parliament—both of which bodies contain labor representatives—may provide labor with the opportunity for a more constructive voice in government.

Although labor unity was upheld by Mohammed V and the Istiqlal during the early years of independence, after the Istiqlal split into two factions during 1959, a new General Union of Moroccan Workers (UGTM) was formed in March, 1960, to carry the party split into labor ranks. The UGTM was only moderately effective in drawing adherents away from the UMT and has not been granted recognition by the ICFTU; it has about 20,000 members. During 1961 and 1962, elections held to choose representatives of civil servants on personnel commissions in several ministries resulted in a clean sweep for the UMT candidates.

Thus Moroccan labor has long been caught in a vicious circle that is both economic and political. With no normal channels of influence open to it, it took advantage of the only remaining weapon, the strike. In 1961, the loss of working days due to strikes rose to a monthly average of 24,325, compared with 11,650 in 1960.[4] The cost of living increased by 6 per cent during 1961 and doubled for some common items, while productivity fell. Labor is both the cause and the captive of this squeeze. Growing external pressure from the Common Market, which takes up more than two-thirds of Morocco's trade, and internal recession following a bad spring drought in 1961 forced an austerity program on the government. The 1962 harvest was the best in several years, but inflation mounted as labor costs continued to rise.

Two other pressure groups have a greater effect on Moroccan government, bringing their members into contact with politics and policy. The Moroccan Agricultural Union (UMA), with a membership of 200,000 large and small landowners, is an organization that has been strong enough to block agrarian reform and to bring about legislation relieving small farmers of direct tax burdens; both these policies were successful, however, because they coincided with the ideas of the King. Chambers of Agriculture were elected throughout the country during 1963. The Moroccan Union of Commerce, Industry, and Artisans (UMCIA), with approximately the same numbers, represents management and handicrafts. Industrial and commercial groups, but not artisans, are also represented in fifteen Chambers of Commerce and Industry, elected in May, 1960, and again in 1963; because of the dominant numbers of small grocers among the 100,000 members of this group, the Chambers are frequently made up of labor and activist sympathizers. Chambers of Artisans were also set up in 1963.

The political parties are the most important of the potential organs of public participation in Moroccan government. Their development and their place in the government of Hassan II provides the key to an understanding of Moroccan government and politics. Following independence, the Istiqlal was the dominant political force in Morocco (after the King). In the first Government of National Unity, it was allotted ten of the twenty-two cabinet posts, the same proportion that was used in choosing party representatives to the National Consultative Assembly (although here the party dominated in fact, since functional representatives were also Istiqlalis). The other ministries were divided between the Democratic Istiqlal Party (PDI), in excess of its real strength, and the independents, including the small, intellectual Liberal Independent Party.

The Istiqlal campaign to turn nationalist sympathizers into party members and to constitute a "homogeneous" (all-Istiqlal) government led to its acquisition of eight of the fourteen ministries of the second Government of National Unity. The PDI was excluded, and its opportunistic opposition and internal factionalism reduced it to a force of only minor importance. The pre-independence division between old-guard Istiqlal leaders and second-generation activists, supported by labor, led to increasing factionalism during the third (ostensibly "homogeneous") government. An open split in the party along these lines came in January, 1959, and by August, 1959, a new political constellation was formed. The National Union of Popular Forces (UNFP) grouped former Istiqlal activists with other splinter elements in the country. Its strength lies in the populous industrial cities of the coast and among the tribes of the south (the Souss River valley), but an array of competing leaders (Bouabid, Seddiq, Ibrahim, Ben Barka) and a lack of support in the *bled* (countryside) keep its power limited.

A civil-liberties law permitting the formation of new political parties brought into the open a fourth group, the Popular Movement, based largely on rural and mountain Berber elements formerly associated with the Army of Liberation. The Istiqlal continues to draw its support from the traditionalist cities and surrounding rural areas of the interior. Thus, each party, although roughly nationwide, has a regional and social base. In the local elections of May, 1960, the Istiqlal won nearly half the 10,350 seats, the UNFP a third, and the Popular Movement less than a tenth. A quarter of the seats went to independents, mainly in the rural areas, who rejected all party control. With the formation of the fifth government, just before the local elections, the UNFP chose to be in the Opposition, and the ministers were drawn from the old-guard Istiqlal, the Popular Movement, and the independents. Hassan II's government of June, 1961, also fell short of national unity by omitting the activists, who refused to participate.

With the coming of national elections in 1963, the Istiqlal regained its political independence by entering into the Opposition, and the King regrouped his supporters into a new electoral association, the FDIC, including Popular Movement (Khatib), Liberal Independent (Guedira), and independent (Laghzawi) leaders. The FDIC is far from having the grass-roots organization necessary for a true political party, and it runs largely on the prestige of the King. But its appearance opened up possibilities of new political constellations in Morocco. Between 1959 and 1963, a rudimentary two-party system had evolved. Differences, however, were much less substantive than procedural, and they reflected the grievances already noted in labor views. The UNFP Opposition rejected symbolic unity centered on the royal figure and demanded instead real participation on the basis of a constitutional system, including increased powers to existing institutions, such as the communal councils, and the direct election of a constituent assembly. The Istiqlal's reasons for entering the Opposition are even more procedural and personal, and its program less clear. While it would seem that all the Opposition groups would now have to do would be to enter into loyal cooperation within the framework of the constitution and under the King, it will take time before the actual role of the King, the working relations of the parties, and the provisions of the constitution have evolved into practice. In the meantime, the three large parties may regroup into a new two-party system, centered on the two forces of the independence struggle, the King and the Istiqlal. A description of government and politics in Morocco, based on the interrelation between the King and the parties, must therefore turn to the constitutional rules as its final element.

Law and Policies

Morocco entered the constitutional stage of legal evolution in 1963. After the breakdown of a constitutional commission appointed by Mohammed V in late 1960, the Palace itself took over the work of writing the constitution. It was published in November, 1962, and accepted by 3.7 million out of 4.6 million registered voters on December 7. While maintaining the position and final power of the monarchy, the constitution provides a liberal and flexible framework for the evolution of Moroccan government. The cabinet is responsible both to the King and to the lower house of the elected bicameral Parliament; legislation is accomplished by Parliament and by referendum, but the King alone may promulgate laws. There is no judicial review, but even before the constitution, Islamic principles of government, French precedent, and major pronouncements of the King were used as criteria for judging broad juridical questions; the Supreme Court has a constitutional chamber that rules on the constitutionality of certain governmental operations. A hierarchical court system is headed by the Supreme Court and four Courts of Appeal, below which is a dual system of Modern Chambers (following European law) and Moroccan Justice (following customary law). Although justice is rendered in the name of the King by judges who are considered his personal representatives, the principle of judicial independence is adhered to strictly, and the King enters the judicial process only through his right of pardon.

Morocco is one of the rare countries in Africa where political opinions and associations are almost completely free and open. Civil liberties are safeguarded by a series of *dahirs* promulgated in 1958 after a long political battle and also by the constitution. Rights of association, assembly, labor unions, press, and expression are thus protected, in laws patterned largely after French legislation. Clauses permitting the exercise of executive judgment, such as those forbidding any attack on the "principles of the monarchy," have been called into operation on a very few occasions to limit freedom of the press, for "principles of the monarchy" are elements of the intense debate of governmental procedure. Political parties—except for the Moroccan Communist Party (PCM)*—have their legal rights to existence and free operation guaranteed, but the fear of government retaliation against the press has sometimes kept the real substance of political debate out of print. The Moroccan National Radio and Television is a government monopoly, but the numerous newspapers in French and Arabic are outspoken and highly partisan.

Minority rights depend more on social custom than on legal guarantees for their protection. Morocco is a mixture of Arab and Berber, and the dominant culture is Arab. Since the Berber *dahir* of 1930 was the immediate cause of Moroccan nationalism, there is no discrimination in any way against the Berber "minority" (in reality, by blood, a majority), and local remnants of friction are

---

* The PCM, banned under the protectorate, was again outlawed in 1959 after the publication of the civil-liberties *dahirs*. Its members are still active, but total support is estimated at 1,500. Despite the ban on the party, the PCM presented three "independent" candidates for the lower house in 1963, all of whom lost.

unimportant. In 1960, there were also 160,000 Jews in Morocco. Although Moroccan Jews were specifically greeted as members of the Moroccan community following independence, and a ministerial post was reserved for a Jew in the first government, the situation worsened after Morocco joined the Arab League in 1958 and the Arab Postal Union in 1959. Mail communications were cut with Israel, and in these years latent and long-standing social animosity hardened against the Jewish community. Moroccan officials make a verbal distinction between Moroccan Jews and Zionists, and prima-facie evidence of "Zionism" is an attempt to emigrate to Israel. In response to rising international criticism in 1960 and 1961, passports were made available to Jews, on the condition that they not be used to go to Israel (although a trip to France and then to Israel is an openly secret way of circumventing this restriction). There is no legal discrimination against Jews in Morocco, and they play an important role in the nation's economy and have been elected to communal councils. But customary Arab dislike of their fellow Semites is evident in social relations, and most Jews, in turn, consider themselves more Jewish than Moroccan.

There is no legal or even organized social discrimination against Europeans, and they, too, retain an important role in the industrial and agricultural sectors of the economy. The continuing exodus of Frenchmen is due more to a feeling that Morocco is no longer "their country," to a slowdown in economic activity, to restrictions on currency exchanges with the franc zone, and to limited confiscation of certain plantations than to legal or social friction with Moroccans. By the beginning of 1963, there were 160,000 Frenchmen in Morocco.

Another aspect of the legal order is the role of the security forces. The police force is the largest group of civil servants and is an effective arm of the central government. Security was rapidly established throughout Morocco after independence, with the exception of a few violent shudders of the body politic at the end of 1956 and in 1958. However, as the labor Opposition has taken more and more to direct action, the police have adopted an increasingly active role; strikers and government critics frequently are given a rough going-over before they reach the courts, and the conflict between the government and the Opposition is thus exacerbated. The Army is more an internal security force, standing behind the police, than an external defense force, and is organized for this role above all. The Royal Armed Forces, a 30,000-man military body including token naval and air units, are personally loyal to the King, who has been their chief of staff since their creation in 1956. The Army's conservative, apolitical nature also reinforces its attachment to the throne.

Foreign policy also has an intimate connection with the pressures of domestic politics. Morocco's policy guideline of "nondependence" was an invention of the activists in 1957 when they were still part of the Istiqlal; under Hassan II, the same policy has been a means of undercutting the activist opposition and of covering the King's conservative domestic philosophy. The founding of the Casablanca Group (with Egypt, Algeria, Guinea, Ghana, and Mali) on Moroccan initiative in January, 1961, also coincided with a period of domestic difficulties for the King's government.

Morocco hopes to regain its historic unity by recovering large territories to the south. The acquisition of Tarfaya province from Spain in April, 1958, put Moroccan territory across the Dra River and opened the way to an irredentism that meets no natural or ethnic frontier before the Senegal River, 800 miles farther south. Moroccan irredenta includes all of Spanish Sahara and Mauritania, the northern corner of Mali, and at least the western half of the Algerian Sahara, including areas rich in gas and iron deposits. Ideas of historical and manifest destiny were first preached by al-Fassi of the Istiqlal, who convinced Mohammed V and later Hassan II. By 1962, irredentism had brought about open enmity and sporadic hostilities with Mauritania and Algeria. Only the first 100 miles of the Algerian frontier, starting at the Mediterranean, have been established by treaty. Morocco also hopes to recover the Spanish enclaves of Ceuta and Melilla and associated islands along the Mediterranean coast, which have been owned and peopled by Iberians since the fifteenth century. Moroccan foreign policy preoccupation with irredentism, under the pressure of al-Fassi and the Istiqlal, has led to its isolation in Africa and its absence from international conferences, most notably the African summit meeting in Addis Ababa in May, 1963. It has also detracted attention from the most notable feature of the Moroccan scene, its relatively smooth political evolution, which, for the first seven years at least, has shown up as a rare example among Arab and African kingdoms.

Moroccan government and politics are a combination of tutelary and party systems. The King, with his followers now grouped in a party of his own, and the independence movement, now split into distinct right and left wings, are the two major forces. Of the two, the King is unquestionably more popular, but the parties have assiduously avoided posing their opposition to the King's program or political leadership in openly republican terms. Only by cooperation between the parties and the King can Morocco maintain its progress and stability. The constitution is predicated on this cooperation. However, outside pressures—such as the Algerian revolution or Egyptian republicanism—may aggravate internal disparities—in the cities or, eventually, in the *bled*—and bring about permanent antagonism and finally an open clash between the two. In its great and primordial need of national unity and stability, Morocco may not be able to afford both its party system and its King. But it has them, and the question now is: Can it live with them?

III

ALGERIA

Algeria was the oldest colonial possession in northern Africa and the only one to be considered an integral part of its metropole. Its revolutionary war lasted longer than any other African nation's struggle for independence—seven and a half years (as long as the American Revolution). Today, Algeria is the youngest independent state in Africa north of the Sahara.

Probably the most dramatic aspect of the Algerian rebellion was the way it forged a spirit of national consciousness in the heat of combat, rather than being the product of a nationalism already widely or deeply rooted. When the French took over Algiers in the summer of 1830, they found a country of 2 million people that had been stagnating under three centuries of Turkish rule. Although they promised to liberate, they occupied, beginning first with the coastal regions and gradually extending beyond the limits of the Turkish provinces and the Atlas Mountains barrier into the Sahara. Opposition was led most valiantly by Emir Abdulqader, who succeeded in arousing early ideas of nationalism even after his submission to the French in 1847. Colonialization did not reach its height until the time of the Franco-Prussian War of 1870, but Algerian resistance—particularly in the Kabylia Mountains—continued for at least a decade afterward.

In addition to the Frenchmen who came from Alsace-Lorraine in 1870, others came from southern France and Corsica, and almost as large a number of people immigrated from Spain into the region of Oran, the part of Algeria closest to Spain. (Spaniards in the Oran region outnumbered Frenchmen two to one.) By the end of World War I, the population of Algeria had increased to 6 million, a sixth of whom were European Algerians. The national consciousness that had sparked the rebellions of the previous century was soon engulfed by the influx of the settlers and the economic effects of colonization. Although the official doctrine was one of assimilation, the broadening gap that separated the way of life of the European Algerians from that of the Muslims made the creation of a united society impossible without serious efforts by the government. But the wavering policies of France and the attitudes of the settlers did not produce the needed impetus.

Government was carried out by a governor-general, appointed in Paris. In areas of concentrated European population, the settlers governed themselves autonomously in local affairs, as in France, but the Muslims—who were French subjects, not citizens—had few political rights. As long as they kept their Muslim civil law—as all but about 2,500 did until 1934—Algerians were not eligible for naturalization and were subject to discriminatory laws and police regulations. In 1936, the French Popular Front Government proposed reforms that would have begun the process of granting citizenship to Muslims—starting with about 30,000 of them—but it was defeated by pressure from the settlers.

The interwar years served as the incubation period for conflicting strains of national consciousness among Muslim Algerian intellectuals.[1] On the one hand, a reform movement with a goal of real assimilation arose because of the disparity between the official statements and the practices of discrimination. In a famous statement made in 1936, entitled "France Is Myself," Ferhat Abbas wrote: "If I had discovered an Algerian nation, I would have become a nationalist and would not have been ashamed of it. Six million Muslims live on this soil which has been French for a hundred years. Out of this hungry mass, we shall make a modern society, elevate them to human dignity, so that they may be worthy of the name of Frenchmen." Opposed to the movement of Abbas, which reflected the middle-class nature of both its founder and its followers, was the adamant nationalism of Hajj ben Ahmed Messali, a skilled agitator of poor origins who learned tactics and organization from the French Communist Party. Messali Hajj founded the North African Star among Algerian workers in France as a Communist adjunct in 1923; after it and successor organizations had been outlawed, in 1937, he founded the Algerian People's Party (PPA). By the time that it, too, was outlawed, two years later, the PPA had 10,000 adherents in Algeria and 4,000 in France, and had elected candidates in several elections in Al-

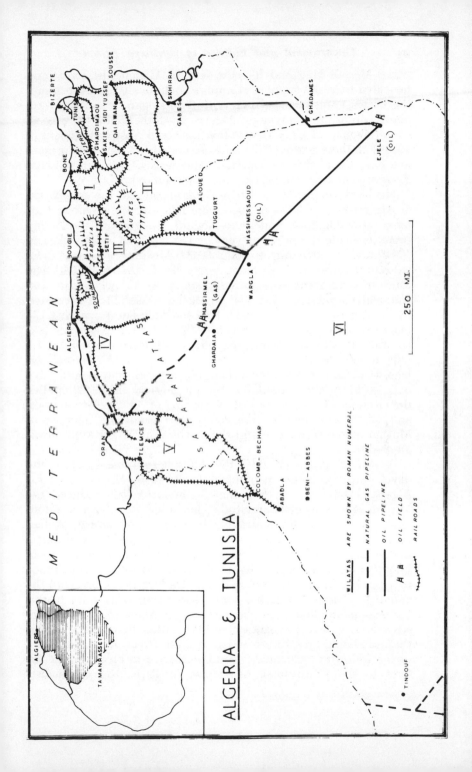

ALGERIA & TUNISIA

WILAYAS ARE SHOWN BY ROMAN NUMERAL

--- NATURAL GAS PIPELINE
─── OIL PIPELINE
А А OIL FIELD
+++ RAILROADS

250 MI.

geria. Messali Hajj had by now left the Communist Party and benefited from the support of a more traditionalist protest group, the Ulema (Muslim scholars), with their slogan "Islam is my religion, Arabic my language, Algeria my fatherland." It was an *alem* (singular of Ulema) who first answered Abbas' statement in 1936 with these words: "We have examined the past and present and have found that an Algerian nation exists. This nation is not France, cannot be France, and does not want to be France."

The harsh regime of the Vichy Government and the occupation of Algeria by the Allies in 1943 were followed by a renewed attempt at assimilation under the label of "integration." Following promises made the previous year by General de Gaulle, a law in 1944 granted citizenship to some 60,000 Muslims, who sent delegates to the French Constituent Assemblies in 1945 and 1946. The Muslims were accorded representation in the French Senate and National Assembly in 1946, and an Algerian Assembly was created by the Algerian Statute of 1947. Half the Algerian Assembly's 120 members were elected by the 530,000 European Algerians and naturalized Muslims, while the other half were elected by 1.3 million male Muslim voters who made up a second electoral college. Had these reforms been honestly applied, they would have gone far to train the population for full political participation. But the elections of 1948 were rigged, for fear of nationalist victories, and other provisions of the reform pertaining to freedom of Muslim religious practice and the teaching of Arabic were never applied.

World War II also provided the atmosphere for new steps in the development of Algerian nationalism. In 1943, Abbas issued his Algerian Manifesto; finding that "assimilation has reduced the Muslim society to utter servitude," he called for Algerian autonomy and full Muslim participation in its government. Abbas' party, the Friends of the Algerian Manifesto (AMA), had half a million members by 1945, a year after its founding. However, in May, 1945, a series of bloody Muslim riots and subsequent French reprisals began in Setif, Abbas' home, leading to the arrest of the nationalist leaders. Algerian nationalists even today refer to this outbreak as the first open manifestation of Algerian national consciousness. It was the clandestine PPA, rather than Abbas' AMA, that was behind the direct action of 1945. Freed by the amnesty of the following year, and given the chance to elect representatives to the Constituent Assemblies in Paris, the nationalists formed new parties reflecting their differing approaches. The original nationalist movement, the PPA, with a program of direct action to attain national sovereignty, was re-established as the Movement for the Triumph of Democratic Liberties (MTLD), but its electoral successes were few. The AMA, whose methods were moderate and whose goal was the association of an Algerian and a French Republic, became the Democratic Union of the Algerian Manifesto (UDMA). Its early successes at the polls, however, brought no more effective results than the moribund Algerian Statute of 1947 and the rigged elections of 1948. In May, 1948, therefore, a new and younger group of direct-action advocates within the MTLD (Mohammed Khider, Ahmed ben Bella, Belqasim Krim) set up an underground Special Organization (OS) to strengthen the Messalist movement among Algerian Muslims and to carry out sabotage against the French.

The arrest of a number of OS leaders in 1950 and the flight of the rest to Cairo seemed to end the possibility of direct action. The Central Committee of the MTLD therefore rallied to the moderation of the UDMA and for a year formed a working pact with the Abbas group, the Algerian Communist Party (PCA), and the Ulema. Messali Hajj, however, remained partisan to harsher measures; his tour of Algeria in 1952, against the advice of the Central Committee, led to his deportation to France and a split within the party. After an abortive attempt to bring unity to the nationalist ranks, those leaders who were determined to embark on a serious campaign of direct action formed a nine-man Revolutionary Committee of Unity and Action (CRUA), with representatives from Cairo (Khider, Mohammed Boudiaf, Ben Bella, Hocein Aït Ahmed) and from each of the PPA's original regions (*wilayas*) of Algeria (Krim). A coordinated attack was finally set for November 1, 1954, at numerous points throughout Algeria, and a "mass" organization, the National Liberation Front (FLN), was organized behind the CRUA, with an initial membership of about 300.

The movement not only had to break up French military control of Algeria—if not by military victory, as was never very likely, at least by Fabian tactics—but also had to weld the Muslim mass into a nationally conscious, organized population. Only in this way could the FLN overcome the disunity which had hitherto weakened the nationalists and create the conditions for the negotiation of independence. A renewed attempt at reconciliation with Messali ended in January, 1955, when the old nationalist formed a rival Algerian National Movement (MNA); during the next seven years, in France more than in Algeria, the FLN and the MNA carried out their own private terrorist campaigns against each other, until finally the strength of the Messalists—along with the prestige of Messali—was, for all practical purposes, destroyed. But most of the Central Committee leaders from the MTLD (Benyussef ben Khedda, Mohammed Yazid, Mohammed Lamine-Debaghine) joined the FLN, either in Algeria or in Cairo. Moderates who had been elected to legislative bodies (Abderrahman Fares, Abbas) were goaded into forming a group called the Sixty-One, which supported the FLN and boycotted the Algerian Assembly. By 1956, Abbas was in Cairo, "at the disposal of the FLN." Some of the Ulema (Tewfiq al-Medani) also joined the FLN in Cairo.

However, the existence of a group of leaders in Cairo and a growing group of militants "in the field" posed new problems of unity between the two groups of the same organization (just as a similar situation was developing in Morocco at the same time). In August, 1956, in the Soummam River valley, some 200 leaders of the interior met to re-examine the FLN's goals. They constituted an Army of National Liberation (ALN) with a general staff, and a five-man Coordination and Execution Committee (CCE), composed of Krim, Ben Khedda, and others; Ben Bella was confirmed in the important position of arms procurer, and the principle of "priority for the interior over the exterior" was established. The Soummam Congress also decreed "the elimination of personal power and the acceptance of collective leadership," and set up a proto-parliament, the National Council of the Algerian Revolution (CNRA) as the "supreme organ of the revolution" and "the sole body authorized in the last resort to make decisions about the country's future." Having established its claim to legitimacy through the CNRA, the FLN declared itself the "only valid spokesman" for Algeria in negotiations with France.

Negotiations had received hesitant encouragement in Paris from time to time since the beginning of the revolutionary war, but the same pressures from the settlers of Algeria that had destroyed hopes of either assimilation or integration had also made impossible any fruitful contacts with the nationalists. In October, 1956, the French Government ventured to make preliminary contacts for discussions, but other members of the same government arranged for the capture of the FLN delegates (Ben Bella, Khider, Boudiaf, Aït Ahmed) en route from Morocco to Tunis. The removal of the original "Cairo group" of the CRUA left Krim as the principal leader of the FLN. Although he favored negotiations, he insisted on recognition of Algerian independence by France before any talks could be carried out on procedural details. Foreign affairs within the FLN were in the hands of Lamine-Debaghine, also a proponent of the hard line on negotiations. In August, 1957, in Cairo, during the second meeting of the CNRA, the CCE was expanded to fourteen members and the CNRA to fifty-four; hard-line supporters were dominant in both bodies, although Abbas and others favorable to an unconditional approach to negotiations were also represented. In January, 1957, a French offer of a cease-fire and free elections was rejected by the FLN.

A rapid series of events on both sides during 1958 prepared the way for the final tedious resolution of the Algerian war. In February, the French Army reacted against increased ALN use of bases and training camps in Tunisia by bombing the Tunisian border village of Sakiet Sidi Yussef; the international reaction pushed the unstable French Government toward openly admitting the possibilities of negotiations. The army and the settlers, showing increasing dissatisfaction with the vacillation of Paris, combined forces on May 13, 1958, overthrew the Fourth Republic, and brought General de Gaulle to power. Faced with a leader who seemed both determined and able to solve the Algerian situation, the FLN in turn strengthened its hand in September by forming a Provisional Government of the Algerian Republic (GPRA) to succeed the CCE; although Lamine-Debaghine was Foreign Minister, Abbas was Premier, and Krim—Vice-Premier and Minister of Armed Forces—had swung his support to the side of unconditional negotiations. On September 28, along with the rest of the French territories, Algeria voted to accept the Fifth French Republic; in reality, the massive vote was an expression of confidence that De Gaulle would find a solution to the rebellion. It took a year, however, before the French President, in September, 1959, announced the possibility of a solution in Algeria by referendum. The following January, Krim replaced Lamine-Debaghine as Foreign Minister and completed his control by heading an Interministerial War Council (with Lakhdar ben Tobbal and Abdelhafid Boussouf). The triumvirate was authorized by the CNRA to carry out negotiations without further instructions.

The first negotiations under the Fifth Republic took place in Melun during June, 1960, and rapidly ended in a deadlock. The next round of negotiations, at Evian and Lugrin between May and July, 1961, at least reached specific points of discussion; in the meantime, De Gaulle had admitted both the representativeness of the GPRA and the future independence of Algeria. Wary of the dangers of another breakdown, both sides continued secret negotiations during the winter of 1961, and the cease-fire agreement was signed at Evian on March 19, 1962. The direct cost of the war was estimated at $5–$10 billion; there were more than 19,000 killed in Algeria and 4,900 in France, over 80 per cent of whom were Muslims.

The settlers' intransigence died slowly. Over 90 per cent of the European Algerians, popularly known as "blackfeet" (*pieds noirs*), had been born in Algeria and were as "Algerian" as the Muslims. In January, 1960, a "week at the barricades" in Algiers showed the opposition of some of the *ultras* (extremists) to the policies of the government that they had put into power on May 13, 1958. In the January, 1961, referendum, the voters in Algeria who approved De Gaulle's policies dropped to 69 per cent, and 43 per cent of the registered voters abstained. In February, a Secret Army Organization (OAS) was formed, and in April the "Putsch of the generals" marked a full-scale revolt against the government of President de Gaulle; although the revolt was rapidly brought under control by the loyal majority of the French Army, a mounting campaign of OAS terrorism against Muslims broke out in the cities, particularly in Oran and Algiers. It was not until June 17, 1962, that an agreement was possible among "Algerians"—European and Muslim—reaffirming the conditions of possible coexistence. On July 1, 1962, 99.7 per cent of the votes in the self-determination referendum were cast in favor of independence.

At the other end of the spectrum were the internal forces of the ALN, which had to be mastered before a state government could be established. During the war, one of the tasks of the nationalist army was to organize the six *wilayas,* or military districts, all of which, by the time of independence, had developed extensive "rotten zones" in which the control of the ALN was uncontested. The colonel in charge of each *wilaya* consolidated his control over his fief after independence and used his influence, when necessary, to support an executive leader or policy that he favored (Mohand Ou al-Hajj [III—Kabylia] supported Krim; Yussef Khatib, alias Si Hassan [IV—around Algiers], supported no one). Communications between the *wilayas* and their sub-units were often faulty, and army groups lived off the country, exacting taxes and occupying public and private buildings, acting in reality as autonomous units within autonomous units. Just as at the time of the Soummam Congress, the FLN at the moment of independence was plagued with a breakdown of external or central control over the internal or local nationalist organs. After nearly two months of anarchy, the FLN leaders forced a showdown with the *wilayas* on August 25, and by September 5 they had reached an agreement with the colonels, permitting the establishment of governmental institutions. The revolutionary war was over, independence had been won, and the revolution was in full swing.[2]

A Powerful Personality Among Collective Leaders

The early judgment of the Soummam Congress in favor of collective leadership still expresses the feeling of many in Algeria. But "collective leadership" is inaccurate to the extent that it suggests a coalition of all political forces in Algeria. In true revolutionary sequence, independent Algeria has gone through an initial period of instability, during which the moderates were replaced by more radical leaders. The result is a tenuous collaboration among several leading figures and their followers, competing as much as cooperating, and often very unsure of their real power. For ultimate power in Algeria still exists at a relatively low level, as well as being relatively dispersed. Probably more than elsewhere in northern Africa, the leaders of Algeria who have emerged from the struggle for power as temporary victors are aware that they are playing to an attentive and critical public.

During the first three months of independence, a number of these shifting groups tried to act as the Algerian Government.[3] The Provisional Government (GPRA) was created by and responsible to the CNRA, which could change its composition; in August, 1961, when lagging negotiations required the presence of a hard-line leader, Abbas was replaced as Premier by Ben Khedda, who had been dropped in the previous governmental change of January, 1960, because he was too widely associated with the group that looked to Communist China for aid. In May, 1962, the CNRA met again in Tripoli and prepared to create a Political Bureau to govern internal affairs. The GPRA, whose members were for the most part not chosen for the Bureau, walked out of the meeting before a plenary vote could be taken, and attempted to continue to function as a government.[4] But at the end of June, when the

GPRA tried to assert its authority over the ALN by retiring its three ranking officers, Ben Bella and the army moved to put the GPRA in its place. After a month of uncertainty and maneuvering, the Provisional Government was left without power, and a radical coalition took over.

However, the GPRA was important after independence as the organ of expression for one nationalist group. Its leader, Krim, was the only one of the remaining six "historic chiefs" of the rebellion—that is, members of the CRUA of 1954—without enough support in the CNRA to be named to the Political Bureau. His opposition to Ben Bella was not merely one of personal or political rivalry; as a guerrilla fighter who had maintained unusually close contact with his home region, the Kabylia Mountains, he wanted, above all, for Algeria a democratic future in which the people would choose their representatives and not be ruled by a single over-riding personality. Around Krim, such leaders as Ben Khedda, Boussouf, Ben Tobbal, and Ou al-Hajj added or borrowed luster.

The second group, which by its very nature was to be the most rapidly forgotten, was the Provisional Executive. Composed of three French Algerians and nine Muslims, it was created under the presidency of Fares by the Evian Accords to govern Algeria until the referendum, which it was to administer. Unhindered by political maneuvering within its midst, it continued to function until the general elections of September, 1962, beyond its provided term, and made a number of decisions of far-reaching importance—on foreign aid, the electoral law, and the army. Instead of being a transitional institution which could become an Algerian government simply by the replacement or addition of members, as anticipated, the Provisional Executive was in the anomalous position of being a government without politics, lacking the means of control over the implementation of its policies and over the political instability that followed independence.

Algerian politics thus rejected the two prototype bodies on hand to take over the role of executive in the new state. In the revolutionary situation in which the nation was born, the new executive needed, above all, a firm basis in the political organisms of the revolution—the FLN and the ALN—rather than institutional purity. The latter would be created afterward; the former could not. The body that replaced the GPRA in the beginning of August, 1962, was therefore the Political Bureau, which the CNRA had suggested and the GPRA had refused at Tripoli three months earlier. The Bureau contained three of the six living "historic chiefs" of the rebellion (Ben Bella, Khider, Rabah Bitat); four of its five members (the three "chiefs" plus Hajj Ben Alla) had been in French prisons since 1956.* The Bureau thus had the political popularity that temporary martyrdom for a national cause imparts. Four of the five (the three "chiefs" plus Said Mohammedi) had been members of the GPRA, and the dominant figure of the Bureau, Ben Bella, occupied the post of coordinator with the Provisional Executive.

The Political Bureau was a skeletal body to handle tremendous tasks. It was charged with "the direction of the country, the reconversion of the ALN and FLN, the organization of the party, the construction of the state, and the preparation of the CNRA meeting before the end of 1962." It hardly ever met in plenary session. It had no post dealing with telecommunications, labor, public works, agriculture, industry, commerce, or any economic function except finances. On the other hand, one member was charged with the organization of the party and the national organizations, while another, handling military affairs, was in reality occupied with the problem of separating military from political functions within the ALN. The Bureau thus had not only governmental but also partisan functions; by a heritage of the rebellion, the construction of an Algerian state was inextricably tied to the reconstruction of the party. When the former task was started, with the establishment of executive and legislative institutions, the Political Bureau concentrated on party and policy problems, acting as a sort of Revolutionary Control Council over the government, as well as reconverting the FLN into a peacetime party.

The group that surrounds Ben Bella differs from the others both in its cohesion and in its composition. Even before it was given formal organization, there was an informal collection of leaders, many of them imprisoned together, working together to take over power. Furthermore, leaders such as Khider and (later) Abbas were associates rather than simply followers of Ben Bella, with

* The Political Bureau originally had seven members. Aït Ahmed, a "historic chief," refused nomination as the seventh member of the Bureau and went into self-imposed exile in Switzerland on July 28, 1962; he returned to lead the opposition in the National Assembly. Boudiaf resigned from the Political Bureau on August 25, considered the general elections illegal, and refused the Assembly seat to which he was elected. The sixth "historic chief," Krim, was not on the Political Bureau, but was an active opposition leader in the Assembly.

popular strength in their own right. Their collaboration with Ben Bella did not always mean similarity of points of view. In April, 1963, Khider resigned as secretary general of the Bureau and a month later Bitat resigned his charge of organization of the party, to be replaced by Ben Bella and Ben Alla respectively. The pair remained members of the Bureau but preferred to give up their jobs rather than run the danger of a costly test of strength with Ben Bella over differing concepts of the role of the party. There is a cult of the personality surrounding Ben Bella, but neither the followers nor the leader have been strong enough to monopolize power; there are too many competing elites and close collaborators. Ben Bella may still gain the support of labor and the young intellectuals, overwhelm the popular but disparate opposition, and develop into a Nasserite figure with an all-powerful position of charismatic leadership. But the instability of 1962 and the vigorous multiplicity of forces still alive in the following year tended to show him that, initially, leadership in Algeria would be collective or would not exist at all.

The ALN also had a national elite of its own, composed of 200 to 300 commissioned and noncommissioned officers, and a General Staff, which was set up in 1959 by the CNRA. This elite was not homogeneous either for it was divided into the officers in the interior, in command of the *wilayas*, and the larger group, including the Staff, standing by in Tunisia and Morocco at the end of the war. It was the GPRA's cashiering of the General Staff (Colonel Houari Boumedienne, Majors Ahmed Qaid [alias Sliman], and Ali Menjli) for insubordination that caused the fall of Ben Khedda, and it was the support of this body against the *wilayas* that kept Ben Bella in power.

The executive institutions established after the September, 1962, general elections were therefore filled by a combination of Ben Bella's group and others. Abbas, the original president of the GPRA, was elected President of the National Assembly.* At the same time, Ben Bella was invested by the Assembly as Prime Minister, at the head of a nineteen-man cabinet. Original plans for a Government of National Unity were abandoned in the face of a number of refusals to participate, and the Prime Minister instead chose his own supporters from divergent and overlapping groups —twelve of them deputies, seven members of the ALN, six for-

* He resigned in August, 1963, and was expelled from the party as he became more and more the spokesman for the dissatisfied middle class.

merly ministers in the GPRA, two members of the Political Bureau. Boumedienne was named Defense Minister, and the General Staff was replaced by a Military Council under Hajj Ben Alla to carry out the reconversion of the army. The government had scarcely served six months before political events caused important changes. Ben Bella took over the Foreign Ministry after the shooting of the Minister, Mohammed Khemisti, in April, 1963. The decline of Khider and Bitat and the increased political importance of Boumedienne led to the replacement of another minister the same month and then in May to the appointment of two additional vice-premiers ahead of Bitat: Boumedienne and Mohammedi. The ALN colonel thus became the number-two man. In September, Ben Bella was elected first president of the Republic and immediately picked a new cabinet. Besides the two vice-premiers, key posts were the Economics and Foreign Ministries (Bashir Boumaza, Abdelazziz Bouteflika).

The overlapping and the evolution visible in the executive institutions also mark the representative bodies and their relation with the executive. The CNRA, created by the Soummam Congress as both a party and a state organ, had seventy-five members by 1962, either nominated by the FLN leaders or co-opted by two-thirds vote of the CNRA itself. In order to ensure minimal representation, local ALN representatives and General Staff members, the GPRA, and leaders of the FLN Federation of France were ex-officio members of the CNRA, and two-thirds of the members had to be from the interior. As a result, the CNRA never met with all its members until after the rebellion was over; no legal quorum was established.

The CNRA was defined as the repository of national sovereignty for the duration of the war and as the provisional constituent body with powers of legislation and control over the government until the liberation of the national territory. Decisions were made by a two-thirds vote, except for the crucial decision on the acceptance of a cease-fire, which required the four-fifths majority given it in the CNRA session at Tripoli in March, 1962. The CNRA met annually (except for 1958 and 1960) in ordinary session and by request of two-thirds of its members or the GPRA in extraordinary session. After the Tripoli meeting, for all practical purposes the CNRA disappeared, despite frequent calls for an extraordinary session; it never met again. It had prepared the revolutionary shift of power by designating a Political Bureau and had established the goals of the Algerian revolution for years to come in a document of great importance, the Tripoli program.

The Algerian National Assembly, whose election was held on September 20, 1962, after having been postponed four times, is to act as the "national conscience" sitting in judgment of the acts of the executive; its powers include legislation, selection (and, presumably, defeat) of a provisional government, and the promulgation of a constitution by September, 1963, when its term expires. As such, its position is slightly different from that of a normal parliament. Of its 196 members, apportioned among the 15 *départements* of Algeria and the Sahara, 16 deputies are European Algerians; geographic, political, and minority representation is calculated on the basis of population. About 60 of the deputies, the largest group, are members of the ALN, and about 25 were members of the CNRA. The opposition could muster 40 to 55 deputies to vote against the investiture of Ben Bella and Abbas. The presence in the Assembly of the same groups that have been seen maneuvering about the executive institutions is testimony to their power, not to democratic idealism. A single list of deputies was nominated by the Political Bureau and submitted to the voters for ratification; between August, when the elections were scheduled, and September, when they were held, 59 nominees susceptible of opposition (Ben Khedda, Boussouf, Ben Tobbal, a dozen ALN officers) were replaced by new names, frequently unknown but more faithful to the Political Bureau. Although reduced in numbers, opposition leaders, through the power of their popularity and their persuasiveness, have already shaped the Assembly into an organ of dialogue instead of an echo chamber for the Political Bureau.

During the rebellion, the various national executives attempted to create their own local organs and to separate political from military power, but until the *wilayas* were brought under control, the central leaders could only "count on the civic spirit of the troops for the immediate application of these decisions."[5] Elections held in May, 1960, under French supervision had filled municipal councils, with a majority of the seats occupied by Muslims, according to law. But many of the councilors were no longer willing or able to serve after independence, and temporary Special Delegations for Administration appointed by the Provisional Executive were again replaced in June, 1963, when local administration was consolidated into 630 communes. New Algerian prefects were also nominated to head the administrative machinery of each of the fifteen *départements* and subprefects were named under them. New communal and *départemental* elections were scheduled before the end of 1962, but have been repeatedly postponed since then.

Like other elites of northern Africa, Algerian leaders are in search of a doctrine. Unlike any of its neighbors, except Egypt, Algeria is in the midst of a revolution in which political, social, and economic realities are completely transformed all at the same time. The pressure for doctrine thus becomes greater than elsewhere; the dangers of haphazard random upheaval are also correspondingly greater. Ben Bella is the most articulate spokesman and the most dynamic leader of the revolution; although Krim, Ben Khedda, Abbas, and others share many of his ideas, under their leadership it is not likely that independence would have been much more than a simple shift of power from one middle class to another, just as it was in Morocco, Tunisia, and Sudan. As early as the CNRA conference of Tripoli in May, 1962, Ben Bella presided over a commission whose report was essentially a critique of the GPRA for "ignoring the profound revolutionary possibilities of the country people" and for seeking only the "traditional nationalist objective—i.e., independence."* Later, he equated this limited nationalist goal in other African countries with "neocolonialism," making a doctrinaire bundle out of Arabism, neutralism, and socialism; the negative side included anticolonialism, latent suspicion of the urban population and the modern city, and opposition to anything, including parts of the Evian Accords, that is believed to obstruct the path to socialism.

Ben Bella seeks to enact a "purely Algerian" form of socialism, not led by the classic proletariat, but based on the peasant majority, "the fundamental revolutionary mass."[6] An agrarian reform is paramount, not simply as a social measure, but as the stimulus to a national revolutionary *élan* and the direct participation of the mass in a hierarchy of popular assemblies. The leading ele-

---

* The policies of the army were less coherent and more revolutionary. The ALN wanted to be the "spearhead of the revolution," combining political and military power in a non-Communist "people's democracy." Although its plans included elected assemblies at the lowest level and a continual appeal to the CNRA to award power at the highest level, its populism was combined with a concept of military government. Boumedienne has also expressed the idea that the Algerian revolution, like the Egyptian, must expand to neighboring countries to succeed in full.

ments of the revolution are to be taken from the ALN's "magnificent cadres, already politically educated," and grouped within a single party "to be created in each city and village, with the youth, women's, and labor associations forming the basic elements." "We need a single party," Ben Bella has said, "[composed of] convinced, clean, pure men, totally free of corruption, controlling but never identifying themselves with power. On this point I will never give in." And on another occasion, "For us, democracy is not only an increase in individual liberties; it is above all the collective expression of popular responsibility." The goal of socialism is described with the same rugged idealism. "Imagine that we are sitting around a plate, one of us eating with a spoon and the other with a ladle. Well, our goal is to have all the Algerians eating with the same spoon." In the last analysis, this drive to socialism, accelerated in practice since April, 1963, becomes an ultimate rationale or a higher law covering all action. In a famous speech, Ben Bella declared, "People cite us texts. We cite our own ethic. If our decisions are not in conformity with the Evian Accords, well, Ben Bella couldn't care less." In this aspect, too, Ben Bella is only expressing the revolutionary mood of Algeria.

The Fundamental Revolutionary Mass

There is often a tendency to consider Algeria as being in a more advanced stage of evolution than its North African neighbors. Because of the large European population, coastal Algeria benefited from a highly modern infrastructure, and the population in general could only profit from contact with it. Algeria has 2,700 miles of railroads and ten times as many miles of roads. Industrialization, although not attaining any importance until after World War II, was increased tenfold over the 1946–57 rate[7] by the $4-billion five-year Constantine Plan launched by De Gaulle in October, 1958; by 1961, industry made up a third of Algeria's $2.2-billion gross national product. In 1962, nearly 3,000 Muslim students were enrolled in institutes of higher education in Algeria, France, and abroad. But these aspects are very selective and, when considered with reference to the Muslim population, concern only a small, favored elite. It is too frequently forgotten that, while Algeria did have an important middle class, estimated in 1955 at 7 per cent of the population,[8] the European minority has tended to pre-empt the upper levels of society. Less than a tenth of this middle class are Muslim; almost three-quarters of the Muslim population are tradition-oriented and live in rural areas. Even in 1961, about 2.5 million Muslims were unemployed, and many more were under-employed. Despite the foresight of the twenty-year education plan of 1944, only a third of the school-age Muslim children were in elementary schools in 1961, although enrollment had been more than doubled since 1954. An estimated four-fifths of the Muslims over six years old are illiterate.

When the Europeans left Algeria in the mass exodus of 1962, what remained was a headless social body, a largely peasant society deprived of upper or middle classes. It had the new advantage of being a more homogeneous society than ever before, and of being governed by leaders who were very much part of the people. But the people were also left culturally disoriented, often physically uprooted, naturally "revolutionized" by the colonial experience and by the dramatic decolonialization that the exodus represented. During the first months of Algerian independence, the leaders recognized this unstable position of the masses and made use of it by playing an irresponsible game of politics over the people's heads—but in the people's name. When they associated the population with their struggle for power, it was not through assemblies and elections but through an appeal to the Forum—Algiers' version of the Middle Eastern "street"—which had in the past played an important role in Algerian politics

But the mass is in a different situation in Algeria than elsewhere in northern Africa, largely because of the long war, the long history of promises of democracy, and the rootlessness and sudden upheaval within the society. During the summer of 1962, when government stood still while politics gathered steam, slogans appeared on Algerian walls saying, "One hero—the Algerian people." The pressure for revolution in Algeria, unlike that in Egypt, comes from below, not from above. Unemployment, the thirst for land, the highly developed social-welfare function of government that France preached and partially practiced, the manifest difference in standards of living between Europeans and Algerians in Algeria, and the impression that power has come to rest in the hands of nationals rather than foreigners—all these make the mass a revolutionary force. The new leaders must not only take account of this feeling but also act responsibly to it, in order to avoid extreme public reactions of either frustration or apathy.

The task of transmitting the wishes of the Algerian mass has been shouldered by the party. The most difficult problem facing the Algerian elite ever since the May, 1962, session of the CNRA has been the "reconversion" of the FLN from a revolutionary nationalist movement to a political party in a single-party system. This task is complicated by the overlapping of party and governmental institutions and by differing concepts within the party leadership. The FLN in itself had neither organization nor unity before independence; its local members were grouped into cells under the control of the ALN *wilaya* leaders, and other members belonged to student and labor organizations. Leaders and followers alike remembered that they had entered the nationalist movement through the PPA, MTLD, UDMA, or ALN. Only the external Federation of France was specifically FLN. The Political Bureau, after independence, undertook to set up similar federations in Algeria, independent of the *wilayas,* each with a regional political bureau including administrative, military, and party auxiliary figures among its members. The basic unit often pre-empted administrative and security as well as political functions. In the absence of a national congress, repeatedly suggested and repeatedly postponed, a conference of some 250 party officials met in Algiers in early April, 1963, to discuss questions of doctrine and organization, and again in August, 1963, to pass a preliminary draft constitution.

In mid-1963, the FLN had 250,000 members, according to Khider's estimate, although Ben Bella, in speaking of the party as a vanguard, has envisaged a membership limited to 100,000. There has always been a tendency to identify the party with the entire population. Party spokesmen use the phrase "nation-party" to describe their concept of the FLN, and explicitly reject any notion of "union of parties"; thus, individual Communists are invited to join, but any attempt to integrate the Communist Party as such or to include PCA representatives among the candidates for the Algerian Assembly has been rejected. Tremendous problems on the nature of the party itself thus face the FLN. Like the Communist Party of the Soviet Union, it must decide if it is to be truly a mass party with a membership including the entire politically conscious population, or if it is to be an elite group in itself. Like the Neo-Destour and the Egyptian National Union, as well as the Soviet Party, it must decide whether it is to double, replace, or remain separate from the governmental hierarchy. These decisions—and the way in which they are made—will shape the future role of the FLN in training the mass to participate in government and in bringing the wishes of the people to the attention of the leaders.

There are a few other parties in Algeria, negligible in size but of special importance; rival parties have been tolerated by the FLN only as long as they are under control and do not pose a major threat to the single-party system. The PPA of Messali Hajj, resurrected to replace the MNA, is seeking to reorganize and reestablish itself in Algeria, but it has few members, is weakened by a dissident faction (Mulay Merbah), is officially ignored by the FLN. The PCA (Bashir Hajj Ali, Henri Alleg), banned in 1955, was established in 1936 as a party of predominantly European workers. Its 1963 membership of 6,000 is 95 per cent Muslim, and it concentrates its efforts particularly among the students and intellectuals, and among labor. However, the PCA was again banned after independence, in November, 1962, although it continues clandestine existence. The Algerian Party has a key position in Communist attitudes throughout northern Africa. Its program, contrary to Communist doctrine, "takes into account the interests of everyone and seeks ground for agreement" instead of class struggle. It has attempted to gain membership by imitating the FLN; its proposals of "union" with the FLN around a minimum program have been rebuffed with a counterproposal of "unity" of Algerian political forces within the FLN.[9] As a result, the Party had no candidates for the Assembly and no role in government; when it tires of its impotence, it may well embark on another shift of tactics and attempt to become the nucleus of all opposition, charging betrayal of the revolution by the single party, the FLN. Finally, a left-wing opposition group, located between the FLN and the PCA and composed of dissatisfied elements of the nationalist movement, was announced in September, 1962, under the name of Party of the Socialist Revolution (PRS). Its strength is as yet undetermined, although it claims roots in the labor unions and the Federation of France. Its leaders (Boudiaf and others) were arrested in July, 1963.

The Europeans have not yet re-emerged in Algerian politics as a group, nor have they found their place in the FLN. European candidates nominated to the Algerian Assembly were for the most part nonentities. The New Algeria Committee, a liberal European group formed to campaign for the referendum, has not sought to act as a political party. The Safeguard Association, set up by the Evian Accords to defend the rights of European Algerians, is specifically precluded from acting as a "political party or group," but it is active in its attempts to protect minority rights. All European Algerians are members, and the association is run by a nine-man committee appointed by church, judicial, and bar associations.

As in Tunisia and Morocco, where strong parties exist, political integration is also carried out by party auxiliaries, the "national organizations" (labor and student unions). The General Union of Algerian Workers (UGTA) was founded in 1956 and immediately affiliated with the ICFTU, replacing the Syndical Union of Algerian Workers (USTA) of Messali Hajj. The UGTA (Rabah Djerman), which claims 300,000 members, began an intensive membership drive after the cease-fire and organized itself on the basis of regional and local unions; all union members are automatically members of the FLN. It seeks to be the sole union of Algeria, corresponding to the single party, and has incorporated European members of French metropolitan unions. In France, the numerous Algerian workers are controlled in either the General Association of Algerian Workers (AGTA), closely associated with the FLN Federation of France and the UGTA, or the Association of Algerians in France, founded in late 1962 by the Political Bureau. The importance of the UGTA (and of the AGTA and the Federation as well) lies not only in its integrative value but in the fact that it formed the mass basis of the "internal" opposition to the FLN. The opposition of the UGTA was both procedural and substantive; it protested its absence from some party councils (Political Bureau) and its small representation on others (National Assembly), and it blamed the Political Bureau for betraying the revolution by acting slowly and permitting chaos. However, during the first congress of the UGTA, held in January, 1963, the Political Bureau took over the union and put it under the control of a seven-man national bureau of its own choosing, with the aim of channeling the activities of the UGTA into the political tasks of the FLN. The other "national organizations" include the National Union of Algerian Students (UNEA), the Algerian Women's Union (UFA), the General Union of Algerian Traders (UGCA), and the FLN Youth.

The most striking disappointment in the progress of Algerian participation in government has been the electoral process. In the first year of independence, no local elections were held, and in the national elections, the only choice has been whether to participate or not; there has been no choice among candidates, nor has there been any popular participation in nominating the single slate. The most valid reason given for this disregard of popular control in developing nations is the need for a cohesive, homogeneous group to take governmental measures rapidly and coherently. But in Algeria, candidatures have reflected some of the divisions and frictions within the nationalist movement, and "the absence of peace" among the leaders was the reason given for postponing the vote. Yet 5,303,661 Algerians, or 81 per cent of the registered voters, went to the polls on September 20, 1962; when the European exodus and the opposition of Wilaya IV are taken into account, participation must be considered quite impressive. In the constitutional referendum a year later, 84 per cent voted.

On the other hand, the most important aspect of popular participation in public affairs is the purely Algerian experiment, the management committee, set up in connection with the expropriations and agrarian reform. By the first anniversary of independence, 3.7 million acres representing half of all European lands in Algeria had been handed over to collective management; the rest of the European lands and 7.5 million acres representing Muslim-owned lands above a 120-acre limit remained to be collectivized. This land—60 per cent of the arable land in Algeria—and numerous factories, hotels, and other enterprises are managed by committees of workers or farmers employed in the particular activity. During 1963, the initial committees, often haphazardly constituted, were to be replaced by a new management committee elected by a "general assembly of workers" in the factory or farm. A national congress of the management committees was also envisaged. Not only was the principle of self-management made an important part of the Algerian socialist doctrine; in practice, too, the committees effectively thrust workers and peasants into positions of responsibility—initially, with both good and bad effects on the production of their particular activity—rapidly elevated a group with a good potential for bridging the social gap, and created numerous local bodies that will doubtless grow to be an important political force.

The Ultimate Rationale of the Revolution

Law in Algeria, as do the elite and the mass, reflects the revolutionary status of the country. Before independence, Algeria lived under two constitutions, both imperfectly applied. In September, 1958, 3.6 million Algerians, representing 97 per cent of those voting and 76 per cent of those registered, accepted the Constitution of the Fifth French Republic. For the first time, Muslim and European communities voted together in absolute equality for a constitution guaranteeing political rights to all. But the gesture came too late to save the constitutional tie between France and Algeria. In December, 1959, in Tripoli, the CNRA voted a Provisional Constitution and Statutes of the FLN. The purpose was more to establish legitimacy than to assure rights, and the revolutionary wartime situation prevented any guarantees from being put into effect. But as the rebellion becomes revolution, the same problems in guaranteeing civil rights and establishing the rule of law continue. It was this matter of concern that was the cause of the Evian Accords; presumably, these agreements were to serve as a basic law or preconstitution. Beginning with an unconditional acceptance of the Universal Declaration of Human Rights and "the principles of democracy and the equality of political rights among all citizens regardless of race, origin, or religion," the Accords and the annexed Declaration of Guarantees proclaim the impunity of all "acts committed in connection with the political events of the cease-fire" and all "words or opinions held in relation to political events prior to the referendum." The Constitution of the Popular and Democratic Republic of Algeria, accepted in a referendum in September, 1963, replaces the earlier documents and reaffirms civil rights, guarantees, and principles. But by the first anniversary of their signature, it had become evident that the Evian Accords were a dead letter. The Accords, written to govern future relations and not simply to end a past situation, had gradually—or, compared with similar situations in Tunisia and Morocco, quickly—fallen victim to the politics of Algeria.[10]

The Evian Accords and the rule of law concern two matters of special importance for Algeria: the courts and the position of minorities. Algeria inherited a court system based on that of France, centered on an Appeals Court in Algiers. Under French rule, the Muslims continued to enjoy separate personal status— long a bar to their French citizenship—and in such cases were under the optional jurisdiction of 107 *qadis* and assistants (a very low number for the large Muslim population). After the GPRA was constituted, the nationalists established summary courts on the authority of their "government" and judged political opponents, often *in absentia,* on charges of treason. Within FLN-controlled sectors, four-man Legal Committees were established "to judge civil disputes and breaches of law." These judgments have been upheld after independence. Breaches of nationalist military law, as embodied in the General Regulations of 1958 and later in a Code of Military Law of 1960, were judged by a hierarchy of ALN military courts, "representing a delicate adjustment between the claims of justice and military efficiency."[11] During 1963, the Algerian Government gradually set up a single integrated court system with a supreme court, 17 appeals courts, and 116 civil tribunals. In criminal jurisdiction, "people's tribunals" inherited from the ALN have brought a sort of jury system to the judicial structure.

The Evian Accords provided for the creation of a Tribunal of Public Order to function during the life of the Provisional Executive and a Court of Guarantees to act as a supreme defense of civil rights, and especially minority rights, without appeal. The latter has never been constituted, although special procedures for Europeans are followed in the new Algerian court system. Because of the need to prevent banditry and private settling of accounts, *wilaya* leaders also felt obliged to enforce law and order with a strong hand, often passing heavy sentences after summary trials. In other cases, "people's tribunals" judged former supporters of the French; in such affairs, intervention by the nationalist leaders and enforcement of the Evian Accords has been politically difficult, whatever may be the legal guarantees. Arbitrary arrests of Europeans increased, instead of diminishing, through mid-1963. Also, more than 3,000 Europeans were kidnaped during the first 15 months after the cease-fire.

In March, 1963, the National Assembly passed the Algerian Nationality Code, which, after modifications on the government bill, created two types of citizenship—original (Muslim) and acquired (European)—with the latter in a less favored position. There are two important minority groups in Algeria, both considered as one under the former French legal structure. Of the 150,000 Algerian Jews, more than 100,000 have joined the exodus to France and another 10,000 have gone to Israel. The Jews were naturalized by decree in 1870, and although probably half of them are descendants of converted Berbers, most are now highly Europeanized. As in Tunisia and Morocco after independence, there has been an effort by the nationalists to reassure the Jews of their place in Algeria. Few incidents marked Arab-Jewish relations during the war for independence, and the Jews are covered by the Evian Accords. One-tenth of the Algerian population before independence was European. Of these, all but 150,000 fled to France during 1962, and a large proportion of the country's capital—over $500 million—went with them. The vast majority of those who remain are concentrated in Algiers. It is likely that the total European population of Algeria will fall to no more than 100,000, or a tenth of the pre-independence figure, in the first half-decade of independence. In many cases, French property has been taken over by Algerians without benefit of legal process, while in other instances, property or usufruct has been expropriated by decree of the Algerian Government. Those who lost apartments, businesses, and farms had received no compensation by the end of the first year of independence, and judicial proceedings, when admissible by the Algerian courts, have been difficult.

Despite a minimum of liberty of expression, the press reflects the revolutionary situation in Algeria. The seven dailies—including the FLN Arabic newspaper *ash-Shaab* and its French translation *Le Peuple*—rally support behind the government, and when they criticize, as does the pro-Communist *Alger républicain,* they are frequently censored. Newspapers from France are often banned. The FLN also publishes an important French-language weekly, *Révolution Africaine,* as well as French and Arabic editions of its former wartime weekly *al-Moujahid.* Radio Algiers is government controlled.

Police functions have been taken over by Algerians, although the security forces have often been divided by the same regional and political differences that have weakened the governmental and judicial machinery. In addition to French-trained police in the cities and a National Gendarmerie created by the Provisional Executive, there were also gendarme, police, and army units belonging to the ALN. Within the French Army, there were some 45,000 *harkis* and 15,000 *mokhaznis,* both Muslim Algerian units; another 60,000 Muslims had been enrolled—by draft or voluntarily —into the regular French Army. More than 350 active officers were Muslims. Theoretically available for integration into the National People's Army (ANP), successor to the ALN, these troops are suspect and thus are often persecuted. At the time of independence, the ALN included 15,000 troops on Algerian soil and larger contingents of 25,000 and 10,000 stationed on the Tunisian and Moroccan frontiers; by the fall of 1962, its numbers had increased to 130,000 as a result of victory and peace, and it had become a burden on Algerian finances and politics. The reconversion of this body into a 50,000-man ANP remains a major task of the government.

The other tasks of the government, and the policies that it puts into legislation, fall into two categories. Over the long run, Algerian leaders seem to envisage a legislated revolution to an extent unmatched in other countries of northern Africa. Beginning with agrarian reform—written into the Evian Accords—and continuing with programs of widespread nationalization and limitation of wealth and property, the government is ready to embark on a socialist program that will take the economic control of Algeria out of the hands of the Europeans and, in the absence of native capital, put it into the hands of the state. In education and cultural matters, plans for Arabization mean recasting schools, teachers, and programs in Arabic. These policies, still unclear in their details, but subject to serious study in Algerian Government circles, are intimately tied to the foreign policy of the state. Caught between a need for foreign aid and an abhorrence of foreign ties, between a commitment to "independence with cooperation" and an aspiration to independence with revolution, between economic and political bonds with France and cultural and sentimental bonds with the Middle East, Algeria—along with much of the developing world—has rationalized its way out of this dilemma by considering foreign aid its due and neutralist leadership its duty. On the other hand, this psychological compulsion to bite the hand that feeds it has also been applied thus far in regard to the Communist world, which gave the FLN more aid than the West before independence and now finds the new state quite devoid of any sense of political indebtedness. Algerian neutralism has had a long history of development; the FLN was represented at the Bandung Conference of 1955, and the GPRA attended the Belgrade Conference of Nonaligned States and the founding conference of the Casablanca Group, in 1961. As a counterweight against both France and the Middle East, Algerian leaders have actively considered the prospects of a United Maghreb. Long before independence, Algeria negotiated with Communist China and Russia, campaigned for support in Europe and Latin America, had "ambassadors" in Africa and Asia, and maintained a delegation at the U.N. This diplomacy was skillfully used to gain international support for the cause of the FLN. The experience gained and the taste acquired for active foreign relations will be put to use in advancing Algeria's position as a neutralist leader.

In the short run, other problems demand immediate attention. Much of the 1962 harvest was lost. Despite the payment of bonuses of more than 50 per cent to French schoolteachers, there was great difficulty in filling the teaching needs for the school year beginning in 1962. Unemployment was extremely high during all of 1963. Kangaroo courts and local police authorities replaced law and order in many regions, and banditry, kidnaping, and vandalism were prevalent in the cities. During the latter half of 1962, for its first half-year of independence, Algeria lived off the French treasury, at the rate of more than $2 million a day; in 1963, the Algerian Government cut its own budget by 60 per cent. The transition from war to independence was thus disastrous for Algerian economic and social life. Much of this, if regrettable, was unavoidable. But in the fast-moving political arena of Algeria today, small delays in solving the problems of simply keeping afloat, let alone moving in a considered direction, can mean important changes among political forces. Just as Ben Bella suddenly became the successor of Ben Khedda, so the alternative to Ben Bella is always present, not in the person of Krim or Abbas, but in the collection of local forces with little experience in governing but much practice in control—the ALN.

Will the revolution produce a wave of creative *élan* or result in disruptive upheaval? Will the advance in development given by the colonial experience be allowed to waste away by inability (for political reasons) to keep the infrastructure in functioning condition? Beneath these two questions is an even more basic one concerning the political structures of the state: Will the FLN be able to give Algeria an effective single-party system, or will a multiparty democracy—of the type compatible with, if not foreseen by, the Evian Accords—come to exist in Algeria? On the other side of the coin, will a single party impose its control over Algeria, or will the country fall to the political infighting of a multiplicity of political groups?

The forces for a multiparty evolution are bolstered by the importance of local organization and the spirit of provincialism, aided by geographic and ethnic differences. They are further supported by the vivid memory of past divisions and rivalries, which have plagued the entire Algerian nationalist movement. There is the individual popularity of Ben Bella's rivals, such as Boudiaf, Krim, and Aït Ahmed, and the corollary fear of a *zaim*, or single leader, shared by practically every nationalist chief. There is also the conglomerate nature of the FLN, and the separate strength of component organisms such as the UGTA. Finally, as real problems and ways of solving them become more pressing, the ideological differences between leaders of manifestly differing backgrounds during the revolutionary war—prisoners in France, political exiles in Cairo and Tunis, organizers and workers in Paris, colonels and guerrillas in the Kabylia, students and labor leaders in Algiers— also work to create factionalism.

A single-party evolution is favored by the widespread popular desire for unity, reinforced by the continual appeals of the divided leaders in the same direction. This unity is also supported by the charismatic figure of Ben Bella, still no *zaim*, but certainly the most popular figure of the nationalists. The myth of unity is also supported by the organization of the FLN, by far the dominant political body, for all its weaknesses. Of the two alternatives, the multiparty future still has the strongest pressures behind it. Yet, paradoxically, the pressures toward multiplicity may possibly lead instead to a variant of the single party—an authoritarian system with few political liberties, the sole political system capable of controlling factionalism and revolution in newly independent Algeria.

IV

TUNISIA

Within the Arab-Berber population of North Africa, the Tunisians are practically a separate nation. Paradoxically, they are more homogeneous than even the Somalis, who are a distinct ethnic group. The difference is instructive. The ethnic unity of Somalia has been broken into regional and tribal rivalries by traditional life and by colonial rule; it needs rebuilding in modern terms to provide a durable reality. The ethnic unity of Tunisia, however, has been recast out of a host of contributing invaders—Phoenicians, Romans, Arabs, Berbers, even French and Italians (through cultural, if not personal, intermingling). This unity is being solidified in a modern society; it is thus preparing itself for durability in a modern world.

Tunisia is a small country, one-twentieth the size of Sudan (Africa's largest). It has a long history, but it has a geographical position that is too important in the Mediterranean world for it to have been permitted peaceful development as a small state. When the French took over, by the treaties of Bardo in 1881 and Mersa in 1883, they found a bankrupt autonomous province of the Ottoman Empire under the Husseini dynasty of beys (governors). In the name of the protectorate, the French gave the country direct colonial administration, modern government (including elected councils), a well-developed economic infrastructure, and the conditions under which a strong nationalist movement could grow—in other words, the take-off stage leading toward political development.

Tunisia did not undergo a period of xenophobia similar to the one that shook the rest of northern Africa at the end of the nineteenth century. The first constitutional movement in the Arab world was formed in Tunisia in 1856, and several nationalist reform groups emerged at the turn of the century. A coherent nationalist movement was organized in 1920, bearing the name of the 1856 reform group, Destour (constitution). Fourteen years later, the younger members of this movement (Habib Bourguiba, Salah ben Yussef, Mongi Slim) revolted against the nationalist intransigence of the Destour and formed a new movement, the Neo-Destour. Its leaders were immediately arrested.

The history of Tunisian nationalism from this time until independence, twenty-two years later, serves to exemplify and explain the current Tunisian tactics known as "Bourguibism."[1] By 1936, the Popular Front was in power in France, and Bourguiba was out of prison, negotiating with Paris for reforms and building up party sections in Tunisia. The elements of negotiations and pressure, characteristic of Bourguibism, were already operating concurrently. By 1938, French policy had hardened and so had that of the nationalists; after a bloody riot in Tunis, Bourguiba and more than 1,000 nationalists were again arrested. Bourguiba was not freed until the end of 1942, when the Germans handed him over to Italy in order to have him make a propaganda statement. He refused. A pro-nationalist government formed under the new Bey, Munsif, also preferred to trust in France rather than capitalize on the wartime instability with an opportunistic move, such as declaring independence or siding with the Axis.

However, the defeat of the Axis in North Africa in 1943 brought about the replacement of Munsif by Mohammed al-Amin Bey and the installation of a government obedient to France. The deposed Bey died in exile, but his martyrdom could not compete with the growing popularity of Bourguiba. Finding official ears closed to his attempts to negotiate "constitutional co-sovereignty," Bourguiba went to Cairo in 1945, while Ben Yussef rebuilt the party. Egypt disappointed, even wearied, Bourguiba, and after four years he returned home. He found a Resident General determined to weaken the nationalists by favoring the moderates. Bourguiba vigorously pushed his demands for a Tunisian government and constitution. In 1950, France offered autonomy and eventual independence by stages; Ben Yussef represented the Neo-Destour in a new government with increased powers. In December, 1951, however, Paris, pressured by the French colony in Tunisia, refused to go any further with its reforms. The next month, Bourguiba was again arrested, along with most of the Neo-Destour leadership. Ben Yussef succeeded in finding refuge in Cairo, where he soon gained support from the military regime of Nasser. The nationalist movement then turned to terrorist action.

By 1954, Paris again shifted, and Premier Mendès-France, in a declaration in Carthage, announced complete autonomy for Tunisia. The Neo-Destour formed the new government under Tahar ben Ammar, and Bourguiba was again freed to negotiate in Paris. The result was the Conventions of Autonomy, finally proclaimed in June, 1955. But this time opposition came from within the movement. Ben Yussef, returning from Cairo, attacked the agreements for the close ties with France that they imposed on Tunisia. But the Neo-Destour upheld Bourguiba. Ben Yussef's supporters then took to the maquis in the desolate southern part of the country, and Ben Yussef himself, deprived of his party position, was chased into Libya and then back to Cairo.

The agreements in the fall of 1955 that promised independence to Morocco put pressure on Bourguiba to increase his demands. Again, negotiations were begun, and on March 20, 1956, Tunisia attained independence. Within a week, a Constituent Assembly was elected, and Bourguiba was chosen Prime Minister.

Independence thus found Tunisia with a strong nationalist movement united around a single charismatic figure. Dissident nationalist elements were out of power, and their leaders were out of the country. Most important, however, was the character of the movement. Its lower echelon was well rooted in the Tunisian people, and its leading elements were part of an important modern middle class. More than any other country in northern Africa, Tunisia has enjoyed a middle-class development that brings it close to the national evolution of the nation-states of Europe. A commercial tradition, dating from Phoenician times, gave a historical basis to this group; the colonial period gave it its modernistic character. A high degree of urbanization, also dating from Carthage, precluded the existence of a dominantly rural society such as that found in Morocco, and the semi-urban development of villages kept a rural-urban split from developing, increased the contact between middle class and peasants, and strengthened the bourgeoisie. The result has been less of a social gap and more of an integrated society than elsewhere in northern Africa, and this characteristic is reflected in the nationalist movement. Yet, despite these factors of uniqueness and development, a perspicacious student of modern Tunisia is still able to ask, "Can the bourgeoisie of a country more bourgeois than many others answer to the needs of all categories of the population?"[2]

The Supreme Combatant and His Lieutenants

Tunisia, like Egypt, has its personality cult. Bourguiba's official position, his party leadership, his general popularity, and his political acumen make him the undisputed leader of his country. As with Nasser, events and rivalries that would have shaken an ordinary leader have provided an opportunity for him to show his skill and power and have left him stronger than before. Indeed, the very nature of Bourguibism is to keep a flexible control on both the hot and cold "spigots" and to adapt tactics to the flow of events. Bourguiba was re-elected President of the Neo-Destour in November, 1955, and was elected President of the Constituent Assembly and then Premier the following April. In July, 1957, he was named President of the Republic by the Constituent Assembly, a position which was confirmed for a five-year term by national election in November, 1959. Of the electorate, 91 per cent participated, and 90 per cent voted for Bourguiba, who ran unopposed.

As chief executive in a presidential regime, Bourguiba exercises great power. He is guardian of the constitution; he appoints his government, which is responsible to him; and he "draws up the general policy of the country and controls its execution." He is commander-in-chief of the army and makes military appointments, and he ratifies treaties, declares war, and makes peace, with the agreement of the National Assembly. His initiative in legislation has priority over that of the members of parliament. He also ratifies legislation and has the power of veto, subject to a two-thirds overriding majority. He convenes special sessions of the Assembly, may issue orders in council (subject to subsequent ratification) when the Assembly is in recess, and may take exceptional measures in times of crisis. As head of the party, Bourguiba's contact with his people—and particularly with the politically conscious quarter of the male population who are party members—is also great.

He has at his disposition both a hierarchical party organization for mobilizing the nation and a political cabinet for deciding policy. There is no question but that his cabinet members are assistants, advisers, and collaborators. Their anonymity is encouraged alongside of Bourguiba's public personality, and those who cast aspersions on the cult of the personality, such as former Information Secretary Mohammed Masmoudi, are quickly disciplined.

Bourguiba presents a small but dynamic figure, impassioned in speech and flexible in action.[3] Since Bourguibism puts a high premium on pragmatism, rationality, and tactics in any situation, it is hard to pin down much more than the salient guideposts within which it operates; apparently, there is no complex philosophy. Bourguiba has answered critics with: "My task is to free the country from French colonization. It will then be the task of others to study, analyze, and, if necessary, work out a theory adapted to Tunisia." Paramount among the guideposts are the complete achievement of Tunisian independence, the development of Tunisian personality, and a process of evolution through steps wherein each attainment becomes a new jumping-off place.

The build-up of Tunisia is Bourguiba's prime preoccupation. "I am creating a nation," he has said. "Liberty must be suppressed until the end of the war in Algeria [and] until the nation becomes homogeneous. The state and its existence are essential before everything else." Yet the state remains a means, not an end in itself. Although human liberties may be limited in a particular instance, the need for their suppression in Tunisia has been rare. It is, in fact, the dignity of the Tunisian—"the feeling of human dignity," "a dignified life," "to perceive the level of man and take part in it"—that is the present and ultimate goal.

Essentially, such an aim means political, economic, and social development under the tutelage of a strong government that can enlarge, rather than narrow, possibilities of action. "The Tunisian plan is socialist, if socialism means the formation of a society that works for the benefit of the majority and is based on an economy whose interest is the respect of man, ensuring balanced development that responds to his needs and possibilities within the framework of justice and equality." The strong government is conceived of in terms of dynamic political leadership, not simply of technical or bureaucratic control and administration.

The duality of diplomacy and force have become famous as the tenets of Bourguibism in foreign policy. There is, however, a further step, which is also part of the process, and that is the return to "comprehension and conciliation" when the resistance phase can be dispensed with. The struggle to remove French military and economic control from Tunisian territory, which has brought so much bitterness between the two nations, has been kept quite distinct from the Tunisian attitude toward French residents and teachers, and "once the battle is over, we will return to our conciliatory position." In domestic affairs, too, this dual approach is visible in Bourguiba's use of persuasion mixed with firm leadership. In matters of religious tradition, he has been remarkably outspoken, and sharp reforms of social and economic customs have been legislated, yet his speeches are larded with apt quotes from the Koran, and he increases the penetration of his audience by frequently arguing in religious terms.

The effective use of tactics, in Bourguiba's mind, depends on the coordinated action of elite and mass. "Success depends only on the sound administration of our leaders and the actions of our citizens." The agents of leadership are the party and the government, acting under Bourguiba's personal direction. "We need strong power which does not dissipate in multiple ramifications. We need cohesion and discipline to increase efficiency. It is indispensable that the two structures [party and administration] reinforce each other and evolve harmoniously."

The role of the people is instrumental; it often involves sacrifices, and the parallel of the soldier who "gives up freedom which, if he were a civilian, he would consider inseparable from his dignity" is often evoked in speeches and mirrored in action. Limitation—but by no means abolition—of private property is another aspect of Bourguiba's socialization, justified in the name of individual sacrifices for the common good. The role of the people, however, also leads to greater integration in public life. The preferred "way to achieve success is to obtain the backing of our citizens, giving them even more reasons to understand that Bourguiba proposes only what is reasonable and perfectly acceptable. The people must take part at all stages in working out the plan, so that they feel really involved." Again, the party backs up the government to this end. The Assembly is not enough; its deliberations must be echoed "at different levels of popular representation: with national organizations, party cells, professional associations, and trade unions."

Above all, leadership means Bourguiba. His position is much less one based on Nasserite mysticism than it is that of the Supreme Combatant (as he is known), pushed by an inner drive and a national responsibility. "My conscience compels me to use my authority." There is a profound egotism in Bourguiba's view of his role; put another way, there is devotion to a mission that is incarnate in one person. Sometimes, even to his colleagues, Bourguiba seems to confuse the person and the mission; the Supreme Combatant is not gentle with criticism of his dominant position. "Government policies are my policies; members of the cabinet are my secretaries of state, not independent ministers, and they will carry out my policies," he said when he assumed the Presidency.*

Bourguiba's collaborators are more than administrative heads of their departments or executors of the President's will. They meet with the President to form policy, and they include within their number an inner circle of Bourguiba's close advisers. When Bourguiba was chosen President, the post of Premier was abolished, and the ministers were demoted in name to secretaries of state. Individual secretaries have been changed several times since then, but the government as a whole has remained stable. It meets as a cabinet only infrequently, but the President more often calls interministerial councils or private ministerial conferences. The first cabinet contained nine Neo-Destourians, six party-affiliated labor-union leaders, and one independent; since 1957, all secretaries of state have been party members. There was a major shift in the government in December, 1958, involving five secretaries, but the years of independent government have not seen any sweeping change in the ruling elite. Although there is no premier, a Secretary of State for Coordination effectively occupies his duties under the President; the post is held by Bourguiba's closest collaborator, Bahi Ladgham, also Defense Secretary. The cabinet administers a small but quite efficient civil service.

The other policy-making body, approximately the same size, has been the Political Bureau of the Neo-Destour Party.[4] It contained Bourguiba, the party Secretary-General (Ladgham) and four other ministers, three ambassadors, the governor of the Central Bank, one businessman and two labor leaders, and a director of the Political Bureau. Not all members of the Bureau have had the same importance, and the Party Bureau did not dominate the government, although it met before the cabinet in times of crisis. There has been rather an interaction between the two and an

* In terms of Tunisian foreign policy, it often appears that Bourguiba is holding his own against some of his closest associates—Masmoudi, former Foreign Secretary and now Paris Ambassador Saddok Mokaddem, and former Justice and Finance Secretary and now Algiers Ambassador Ahmed Mestiri—whose pronouncements on various occasions have been intransigent and even favorable to the Soviet Union.

overlapping membership that has allowed the inner circle to have a role in both groups. In both groups, too, the tendency has been toward centralization of power under Bourguiba's surveillance. These characteristics of centralization and concentration were made formal in the proposals of the party's National Council in March, 1963. The Political Bureau was to be succeeded by a thirty-member Central Committee, from which Bourguiba would pick a five- or six-member Presidium, corresponding to the inner circle, where the essential decisions are now made.

In general, there has been unity on national goals among this political elite, but there has been disagreement over tactics and over the role of the elite organs. It is instructive to look at prominent cases when this disagreement occurred, for it reveals much about the power relations within the Tunisian Government and also about the practice of Bourguibism in domestic politics. In late 1956, Ahmed ben Salah, whose General Union of Tunisian Workers (UGTT) had helped Bourguiba oust Ben Yussef the previous year, threatened to form a left-wing opposition party and to advocate a doctrinaire socialist line through its ministers in the government. Middle-class members of the Neo-Destour were alarmed, a rival trade-union federation was promoted, Ben Salah was replaced by a Neo-Destourian (Ahmed Tlili), and the reunified labor union was restored to its proper place in the political forces. But in January, 1961, Ben Salah was in a position of greater power—under Bourguiba's control—as Secretary of State for Planning and Finance, and in March, 1963, Tlili lost his job as UGTT head, presumably for having criticized the lack of democracy in the government.

In mid-1958, Ben Ammar, Premier at the time of independence and still a member of the Constituent Assembly, was brought before the political High Court of Justice on charges of having hidden the Bey's family jewels; the semiofficial weekly, *L'Action,* criticized the trial and the court as demeaning to the Tunisian image abroad.* The editor (Bashir ben Yahmed), a former Neo-Destour Secretary of State for Information who had resigned in protest against Bourguiba's control, was censured, and the paper was closed. Masmoudi, who was a stockholder in the paper, was expelled from the party's Political Bureau, which had voted the censure, and was dismissed from his post as Ambassador to Paris.

* The High Court of Justice was abolished in October, 1959, when all its work in settling accounts was accomplished.

But in December, 1958, Masmoudi was in the government—under Bourguiba's control—as Ben Yahmed's successor, and he was soon back on the Political Bureau.

The third incident also involves Masmoudi and *L'Action*'s successor, *Afrique-Action*, which he directed. In October, 1961, a year after its founding, the weekly ran an article generally criticizing strong personal regimes. Masmoudi was again expelled from the Political Bureau and also from the party; Bourguiba maintained that he should have expressed his views in party council rather than in public print.* There is thus a good deal of collective leadership, but it must fall within the framework established by the President. Those who wander outside these bounds are placed outside the leadership group, in penitence, until they can be rehabilitated under the President's control. Defeat and reintegration are as much a part of Bourguibism as diplomacy and force.†

As the institutional circles become ever more distant from the center of power, they lose their importance in government. The next governmental organ in the hierarchy is the unicameral National Assembly. The ninety-eight-member Constituent Assembly elected on March 25, 1956, was composed exclusively of National Front (Neo-Destour–sponsored) deputies. It complicated its task in July, 1957, by declaring Tunisia a republic, and so was unable to finish its work before mid-1959; however, after 1957, it also served as a legislative body. In November, 1959, the first National Assembly was elected for a five-year period. Again, the ninety candidates of the Neo-Destour were all successful; there was competition, however, among party militants for nomination as candidates.

Although there are electoral districts, the constitution provides that "every deputy is considered as representing the whole country." The Assembly is the legislative body, and its members have a power of initiative second only to that of the President; it "ratifies" the budget, which it may amend. In fact, however, the Assembly has fallen in importance, meets only briefly in its semi-

* To complete the circle, he was replaced by Ben Salah.

† When dealing with his enemies, the *irrécupérables,* Bourguiba is inexorable and thorough. Al-Amin Bey gradually lost all his power and was then deposed; Ben Ammar was rendered politically impotent and then subjected to a humiliating trial. After the latest Yussefist plot against his life, in December, 1962, Bourguiba had eleven death sentences carried out against those involved. Bourguiba does not spare the *coup de grâce,* although there is nothing very gracious about it.

annual sessions, and leaves much legislation to its permanent commissions or to Presidential decrees.

The corresponding body in the party circles is the Neo-Destour's National Congress. Since its 1955 meeting, it has convened only once, in March, 1959, but it went through the motions of thoroughly reviewing government as well as party policy before it gave its approval. The National Congress can interpellate ministers and debate openly; it elects the Central Committee in a free vote, and in 1959 it replaced one of Bourguiba's close collaborators on the Political Bureau. The President himself is never criticized directly, and, despite the generally democratic atmosphere, the Congress follows the broad lines of Bourguiba's wishes. As in the Political Bureau and its successor, the Central Committee, there is democratic exercise within a well-established framework. The next party Congress is scheduled for March, 1964. In the interim a National Council of ninety-six members reviewed decisions of the party leadership.

Local government is centralized, carried out by mixed elective and appointive institutions on the provincial, municipal, and *sheikhat* (rural administrative) levels. An appointive governor and secretary-general represent the central authority in the thirteen provinces; the mayor of Tunis is also appointed. Appointed government councils vote the provincial budgets; 116 municipalities run their own affairs through an elected council and a mayor chosen by it. Rural *sheikhs* are appointed after consultation with the governor and the local population. Women voted for the first time in northern Africa in the Tunisian municipal elections of May, 1957; in some towns, independents were elected councilors and mayors over party candidates. Municipal councils were again elected in May, 1960, and 1963, with only the Social Improvement (Neo-Destour–sponsored) lists presenting candidates, although many of the victorious independents from 1957 were included in these lists in 1960.

In the party reorganization of 1958, commissioners were appointed in each of the provinces to supervise party activity at the base and to coordinate popular efforts and desires with the needs and programs of the governor. Bimonthly meetings of party leaders on the provincial level have been among the most outspoken exercises of critical contact between national and local leadership in Tunisia; problems at all levels were discussed, and important answers and grievances were cranked into the party machinery eventually to become action. However, in the reorganization of 1963, each governor was made the party commissioner for his province, and regional coordination committees were set up, with members elected by the labor and agriculture unions and the party cells. Thus the party and state organizations are now closely intertwined.

The Party Among the People

Tunisia's 4 million people are increasing at a rate variously estimated at between 2 and 3 per cent. A third of them now live in municipalities, and half of this number are in Tunis and its suburbs. The principal centers of population are the ports along the coast; extended railways and roads tie these cities together and reach into the interior. Tunis, however, is truly the center of national life, benefiting from its important port and air facilities, its position at the head of the rich Mejerda valley, and its population (ten times that of any of the other towns). More than half the Tunisian people are under the voting age of twenty. Despite the efforts of the government to increase education, illiteracy in Tunisia is still in the 80 per cent bracket. Thus, except for its characteristic urbanization, the Tunisian population is in a position similar to that of the other countries of northern Africa.

However, in Tunisia more than in any other country of northern Africa, there are institutions that bridge the gap between the mass and its leaders, beyond the simple facts of urbanization and the existence of a middle class. The most effective of these is the Neo-Destour Party, with its highly developed organization at the lowest level. In recent years, the party has cut back its membership, but it still includes more than 250,000 members, mostly men. Since the party reorganization decreed by Bourguiba in 1958, the number of sections has also been reduced, to about 1,000, with widely varying membership. They meet openly several times a year.

"The Neo-Destour cell is more a vehicle for the mobilization and education of the masses than a forum for discussing national issues or proposing national policies."[5] National matters are the subject of slogans distributed at section meetings; rarely are they the subject of discussion. But local problems are given great attention. The National Congress of 1959 called on each section to come up with a local development project of its own; such activities increase both the coordination between government and party groups at the lowest level and also the role of the section in initiating action. Section officers look over local matters of welfare; candidates' nominations must be approved by the Political Bureau, but their election is open and often contested. Through the officers it trains and the members it develops, the section becomes a recruiting office for government employment—so much so that one of the reasons for the reduction in sections in 1958 was the lack of local leadership. In its personnel and its programs, the party is the political ground from which new growth springs—a point that distinguishes Tunisia sharply from the U.A.R. In fact, the Neo-Destour, with its contested elections, its local-national interaction, and its training in civic responsibility and participation, is probably more democratic than is Tunisia itself.

The party is everywhere, and this is the secret of its effective control. A number of auxiliary organizations have been created by the Neo-Destour to organize special segments of society. As groups having a monopoly on organization in special sectors of the society, these auxiliaries are powerful forces of social mobilization and of party control. The most important of these is the UGTT, founded in 1945 as a nationalist labor union. Its able leader, Ferhat Hached, who did much to organize Tunisian resistance, was assassinated by French counterterrorists in 1953. The UGTT took part in the first independent government, but tended to develop its own ideology in the early years of independence. After the replacement of Ben Salah by Tlili, the UGTT again fell under the control of the party, thus avoiding the kind of split that separated the Moroccan UMT from the Istiqlal; the replacement of Tlili by Habib Achour in 1963 tightened party control even further. The UGTT has about 80,000 members and meets in biennial national congress. It also runs evening classes and sporting events. It is affiliated with the ICFTU, of which Tlili is still vice-president, and has been a prime mover in the establishment of the African Trade Union Congress (ATUC), of which Tlili is President. The UGTT's control over the labor movement is unchallenged; all past attempts at labor separatism have failed.

Two other party auxiliaries were founded in 1946: the Tunisian Artisan and Commercial Union (UTAC) of artisans, small businessmen, and their employees; and the National Union of Tunisian Agriculture (UNAT), originally established as the General Union of Tunisian Agriculture. There is also a student organization, the General Union of the Students of Tunisia (UGET), which dates from 1953, and a women's organization of 45,000 members, the National Union of Tunisian Women (UNFT), founded in 1957. Youths are enrolled in the Association of Tunisian Boy Scouts, which has a membership of 22,000, under party control, and in the Neo-Destour Youth, numbering about 80,000. The latter has been kept from the irresponsibility of many nationalist student groups by not being allowed to pass resolutions; however, since it lacked both excitement and useful occupation, the Neo-Destour Youth lost momentum in recent years, until the 1961 Bizerte incident afforded its members an opportunity to volunteer for the evacuation battle. While under the political control of the party, all these groups are organizationally independent and are useful for civic education, political indoctrination, and training in electoral procedures.

Tunisia also has a well-developed press, publishing in Arabic and French, and adequate postal and telephone networks. Some of the dailies and weeklies are party-controlled. Even those which are not are subject to suspension if they stray too far from appreciation of the regime. *L'Action* is one important example; a major morning paper was suspended for half a year in 1957 for opposing the government; and two pro-Communist papers were banned in January, 1963. As with the political organizations, there are limits outside which freedom of expression may not wander; within these limits, the mass-communication media serve a useful educational service. Probably the most important aspect of mass communication, unique in northern Africa, was the weekly address to the nation that Bourguiba used to broadcast on Thursdays. Often in a haranguing tone, often repetitious, these addresses nevertheless served well both his popularity and his desire to increase the political awareness of his people.

It must not be forgotten, as political control and restricted expression come up again and again, that Bourguiba is extremely popular among his people as well as his colleagues. As the Supreme Combatant, he incarnates Tunisian nationalism. Opposition is kept in check by his political power, but it is, above all, kept impotent by its own lack of support.* Salah ben Yussef was assas-

---

* A National Tunisian Democratic Front was organized in Morocco in early 1962 in opposition to "six years of Tunisian despotism." Its spokesman is Mohammed Abdelkafi, and it includes some former followers of Ben Yussef. At the present stage, it is more an element of Tunisian-Moroccan friction than a factor of Tunisian politics.

sinated in exile in August, 1961, but he had long ceased to be a nuisance to the government; some of his followers planned to assassinate Bourguiba in December, 1962, with more sympathy, however, from Algeria than from within Tunisia. The "old Destour" is still heard from sporadically, but it has lost all contact with the people. The Tunisian Communist Party was banned in 1962, but until then was the only party to oppose the Neo-Destour in elections. It won 1,693 votes in 1956, and 3,461 in 1959—not enough in either case to elect anyone or to register a significant protest; its clandestine membership is about 1,000. On the other hand, by establishing its National Front and Social Improvement lists for elections, the Neo-Destour is able to include acceptable nonparty candidates—particularly trade unionists and conservative businessmen—under party tutelage. This tactic increases the representativeness of the single slate, and it also keeps under control elements that might be the source of dissatisfaction and opposition.

Another remarkable indication of Bourguiba's popularity with his people—even greater than Nasser's place in the heart of Egypt —is found in the elections. Many countries are able to claim 99 per cent of the votes cast for their ruling elite (Egypt and Algeria are examples in northern Africa). But few countries indeed, where voting is not compulsory, can claim, as can Tunisia, such participation as 90 per cent (1959), 84 per cent (1956, when Ben Yussef's call for abstention was partially heeded in the south and Tunis, and 1960 and 1963 municipal elections) or 67 per cent (1957 municipal elections, when women first voted)—particularly when there is no choice of candidates. Elections are thus usually popularity contests, not occasions for choosing, but they testify to the political homogeneity of the nation.

Government programs to increase the integration of the mass have gone beyond political action. As in Egypt, there has been a direct attempt to change traditional social ways, with varying degrees of success. Legislation has outlawed polygamy and bettered the status of women. In the municipal elections, the women's vote rose from 80,000 in 1957 to 134,000 in 1960; in the national election of 1959, it reached 210,000. The *habous*, church property usually only inadequately exploited, has been nationalized and put to work. Traditional clothing—the veil for women and the burnoose for men—has been criticized by Bourguiba in his speeches and limited by legislation, although here he is striking at folkways that do not change rapidly. Cactus hedges, which breed a harmful fly and harbor rodents, and goat herds, effective agents of deforestation, are two typical characteristics of the Tunisian countryside that have been attacked by legislation with a good deal of success.

Probably the most notable of these attacks on traditional social institutions is the campaign Bourguiba began in February, 1960, against the Muslim month of daytime fasting, Ramadan. The fast is one of the "Five Pillars of Islam," but it brings daylight activity almost to a standstill; in its place, Bourguiba suggested an extra hour of work and a "holy war" against misery and poverty. Although he announced his opinion as a layman's *fetwa* (interpretive pronouncement) and was supported by the Mufti (religious leader) of Tunisia,* the President met stubborn resistance from the population. Bourguiba saw to it that Boy Scouts and soldiers were fed at noon, cafés were closed at midnight, and regular office hours were enforced. This "battle" between Bourguiba and his people goes on every year at Ramadan, with the President making slow inroads as the younger generation of Tunisians grow up.

Tunisia, too, has public projects that help integrate, train, and modernize the mass. The most important of these have been used at the same time to combat the major economic problem of unemployment. Youth Work Groups enroll some 3,000 young men in part-time work and part-time civic and character education. In 1958, a new offensive against unemployment was launched, and a program of Work Camps utilizes 100,000 to 200,000 unemployed (varying according to the season) to build up the economic infrastructure of the country. A National Labor Service was established at the same time, and twenty-year-olds who have not had military service are enrolled for a year's work. In the countryside, the cooperative movement and agricultural communal projects are widely developed, and in May, 1963, a gradual land reform program was passed, providing for cooperative farming, technical guidance, and acreage limits.

Law, Economy, and Foreign Policies

The Tunisian constitution was promulgated on June 1, 1959, the fourth anniversary of Bourguiba's return from his last imprison-

---

* Significantly, the Grand Mufti is attached to the Office of the President. The post was created in March, 1957, as titular head and guardian of Islamic affairs in Tunisia, in preparation for the deposition of the Bey.

ment. It had been finished in mid-1957, but the Constituent Assembly's decision to depose the Bey, who had played an equivocal role in the ten years preceding independence, caused a complete revision of the constitutional framework. Ironically, the legal status of the Constituent Assembly was provided by the Bey whom it deposed, who had charged the body with its task; all property of the Bey was confiscated as debt to the state.

The constitution declares that "a republican regime is the best guarantee of human rights and of equality among citizens in rights and duties." An ample list of civil rights is guaranteed—above all, equality before the law—although there is little restriction on laws that might limit civil rights. Notable guarantees include political asylum, free movement within the country, prohibition of exile, and the right of property. Judges are independent under the law, and a unified judicial and legal system has been established since independence. The court hierarchy contains a High Court of Appeals, three additional courts of appeals, twelve courts of the first instance, and fifty-four local courts of justice. There is no judicial review. The legal system is based on an amalgamation of French and Muslim principles, reformed and unified into three major codes covering personal, criminal, and commercial matters. *Shariaa* (Muslim law) courts, which used to govern all personal relations, are integrated into the national system of justice, and the *shariaa* itself has been modified according to the needs of modernization.

Personal liberties are effectively enjoyed by the Tunisian citizens, although their political exercise is limited by the regime, as has been seen. Party control of public organizations and popular support of the government preclude serious strikes and civil disorder. In early 1961, a public demonstration against the government over a social-religious issue took place in Qairwan, and National Guard units were called in to fire on the mob; this has been the only incident of its kind since independence—except for the 1956 political dissidence of Ben Yussef in southern Tunisia. Normally, the hand of the police is light. The Army was recently increased to 20,000. At times of national emergency, such as the Bizerte and Saharan crises in mid-1961, the state is able to call on several thousand volunteers to augment these military forces.

There are no national minorities of major significance within the Tunisian population. A small Jewish population—about 1 per cent of the total—has enjoyed an egalitarian status rare in the Arab world, although incidents and emigration have increased since 1961. A large French minority of about 50,000 and an Italian population of 40,000 still stay in Tunisia, although the granting of independence and the Bizerte crisis, with a number of political incidents in between, have persuaded many others to return to Europe. Those who remain find life pleasant, if uncertain, and their relations with Tunisians good. A number have had their farmlands and businesses confiscated by the state, with the promise to pay still filed away in the dossiers of interminable Franco-Tunisian negotiations. One important group of Frenchmen is made up of the 3,000 schoolteachers, one-fourth of Tunisia's teaching staff.

Tunisia's strength is its national and political unity; its weakness is its economic system. Since independence, Tunisia has been struggling for economic independence and development, two goals that are both interdependent and contradictory. France, which started Tunisia on the take-off stage of economic development, removed the forces of continued expansion when the French colony withdrew after independence. The high productivity and consumption of the European community are now lacking in the Tunisian economy. On the other hand, Tunisia has aided this outflux by taking over French economic enterprise and by requiring 50 per cent Tunisian capital participation in foreign commercial activities. An attempt to recapture momentum is found in the ten-year development cycle that began in 1960 under the direction of the National Planning Council. The goal is to raise the national income 80 per cent by the end of the period. But, except for a few areas, principally the Mejerda valley, farmland in Tunisia is poor and resources are mediocre. There are signs of barely enough oil to take care of present needs, but there is little promise of other natural resources, except for the presently exploited deposits of phosphates, iron, lead, and zinc. The greatest resource is manpower, three-quarters of which is still engaged in agriculture; some 350,000 of the population are regularly unemployed or underemployed.

Bourguiba maintains that problems in the foreign field have kept the leadership from focusing full attention on domestic development. Many of these problems stem from Tunisia's special relation to Algeria, for the FLN maintained important bases and training camps on Tunisian soil, supplied troops across the Tunisian frontier, and made Tunis its provisional capital. Such activity was an open temptation to French violation of Tunisian territory, of which the most famous incident was the February, 1958, attack on Sakiet Sidi Yussef. Foreign problems have therefore occupied much of Bourguiba's time, for he attempted to convince the FLN of a "Bourguibist solution" to the Algerian war. The final 1961–62 negotiations that led to the Evian Accords were to a large extent the result of his preparations with Paris. In perspective, given the Algerian war, it is a testimony to French and Tunisian *sang-froid* that relations between the two countries have not been worse. By the same token, considering Bourguiba's increasing advocacy of a united Maghreb, it is surprising that relations with independent Algeria have not been better. Between January and June, 1963, diplomatic relations between the two countries were totally interrupted in protest against Algerian protection of the authors of the December plot. The main problem is that Algeria's revolutionary government looks with scorn on Tunisia's evolutionary progress.

Foreign problems also arose out of Tunisia's own incomplete independence. French troops were not evacuated from Tunisian soil until 1958, and even after that the great naval-air-base complex at Bizerte remained in French hands. In 1958 and 1961, Bourguiba mobilized his people against the French bases; success was more notable the first time than the second. France has claimed that Bizerte is of strategic necessity in the Cold War and that its evacuation would set a bad precedent for similar installations in Algeria; however, Bizerte is now to be evacuated during 1963. Bourguiba has spoken of these problems in the usual anticolonialist vocabulary, but he has also affirmed his affinity for the West and for the United States, "his ally." After the Bizerte crisis, he disavowed these ties, patched up a long-standing conflict with Egypt, and attended the Conference of Nonaligned Nations in Belgrade. But the apparent change of policy was only temporary.

All the problems with the Western world are real and demand attention, but they do not overshadow Tunisia's need for internal development. Bourguiba has built a strong tutelary system around his person and party, and has wielded this political force against domestic and foreign problems in accordance with a tactical doctrine. The strength of the system lies in its unity and its methods; the tactics of "Bourguibism" alone, with its demands and concessions, force and persuasion, are sufficient to explain the need to control the population completely, to manipulate it and hold it in check as the tactics may demand. By concentrating on domestic development, Bourguiba has offered his people rational hopes instead of irrational hates. It has taken strength—and a bit of help from abroad as a unifying distraction—to adhere to this line; it will take strength to continue it. The alternatives are dangerous. As the people develop, they may take both demands and tactics in their own hands and reject the flexibility of concessions. Doctrinaire anticolonialism, or more extreme neutralist opportunism, is always available to the leaders as more potent ways of capturing public imagination if moderation fails. Even more dangerous is the possibility that Bourguiba may not be able quickly to fulfill enough of the domestic hopes that he arouses throughout his developing nation.

V

LIBYA

Libya is the fourth largest country in Africa, but its population is the smallest of all the northern African states. There is little national consciousness; until the discovery of oil the per capita income of $35 was one of Africa's lowest; and 85 per cent of the people are concentrated in 7 per cent of the area. Indeed, Libya is not one country but three, loosely held together for eleven years in a federation; the unification of the three provinces into a centralized monarchy in 1963 did not remove the spirit of provincialism. Yet, on December 24, 1951 (a week before the United Nations deadline), it attained independence—more as a result of contemporary sympathy for the principle of self-determination and long-standing Great Power disagreement over who should rule it than because of any realistic promise of viability.

Libya has weaknesses common to many other northern African countries. Like Somalia, it has been kept alive by foreign aid. Like Ethiopia, it tries to contain a traditional monarchy within the framework of a modern constitution. Like Egypt, it is mostly desert. Like Sudan, it has major problems of national unity. But unlike any other northern African country except Algeria, Libya has vast underground deposits of petroleum, which, given its other characteristics, may make its future development resemble that of states outside the African area, such as Saudi Arabia or Kuwait, more closely than that of its own neighbors.

Libya fell under colonial domination in 642 and so remained for exactly thirteen centuries. The Arabs who drove across North Africa in the seventh century ruled for 900 years, interrupted by the Normans, the Spaniards, and the Knights of St. John. They were finally replaced in 1551 by the Turks. When the Ottoman Empire fell apart, in 1911, Italy moved in to pick up the pieces.

The Italian conquest was not accomplished without difficulty, and it provided the impetus for a xenophobic opposition similar to contemporary manifestations in Morocco and Somalia and to outbreaks in Sudan, Egypt, and Ethiopia during the preceding decades. During the previous century, in 1843, Mohammed Ali as-Sanussi had founded a puritanical Islamic sect (*tariqa*) opposed to Turkish rule;* during World War I, the Sanussis were led against Italy by the founder's grandson (Mohammed Idris as-Sanussi), using Turkish support. Sanussi strength centered in Cyrenaica, the eastern region, about the family home of Jaghbub near the Egyptian border. In the western coastal area around Tripoli, military resistance to Italy was led by the more advanced and urbanized segment of the population.

At the end of World War I, the Tripolitanian leaders proclaimed Libya a republic. After lengthy negotiations with Italy, elected parliaments were established in Cyrenaica and Tripolitania under Italian governors, and the Emirate of a united Libya was offered to Idris. Italian policy was changed radically in 1921–22 by the newly appointed governor and military commander, who turned to military conquest before these reforms could be implemented. By 1932, Fascist rule had subdued all opposition, even among the nomads in the interior. Conquest of the coastal area was consolidated in 1938–39 by settlement of some 30,000 peasants on agricultural reserves in Tripolitania and Cyrenaica. The war interrupted further plans, and by the end of 1942, the British from the east and the French from the south had swept the Italians out of Libya. Idris returned to Cyrenaica from his exile in Egypt.

Except for some after-battle scrap, 600,000 acres of colonial farmlands, war-damaged communications lines, and some new city buildings which survived the war, the Italians left very little. Education had been neglected before the war and stopped after 1940; Libyan participation in government had been discouraged, and economic and civic training ignored. However, Idris and his *tariqa* had sided with the British and were promised at least freedom from Italy. The form this freedom should take, however, was

---

* The Sanussi sect is not the only one in Libya. Along the Algerian border, the *tariqa* is the Ibadiya, equally strict but regarded as heterodox by the Sanussi.

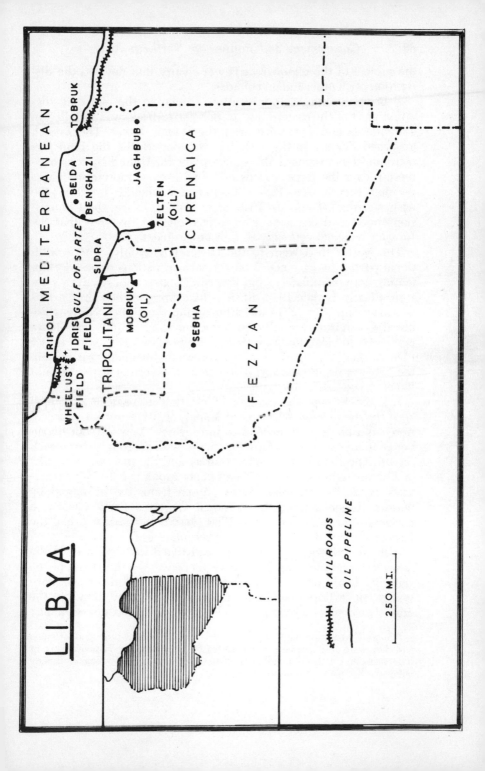

the subject of the same Great Power rivalry that delayed the disposition of all other Italian colonies.

A British military administration, similar to the one that governed most of the eastern part of northern Africa, was installed in Tripolitania and Cyrenaica after the Italian defeat. The French governed Fezzan. In the early postwar period, the Big Four foreign ministers proposed alternative plans for United Nations trusteeship over the three regions of Libya. As a compromise, it was decided that a Four-Power Commission should ascertain the wishes of the Libyans. In 1948, after visiting Libya, the Commission ended in disagreement on everything but the view that the Libyans were not yet ready for self-government.

The matter then went to the General Assembly, where additional parties had a voice; Latin American nations opposed eliminating Italy completely, and the Arab states opposed Italy's return. Finally, by late 1949, all sides had dropped their pretensions at trusteeship over Libya or its parts, and the United Nations Political Committee was able to agree on Libyan unity and independence, to be attained by 1952. A United Nations Commissioner (Dr. Adrian Pelt), aided by an international council, was to help the Libyans decide the sort of union and government they would have.

Differences over the manner of electing a constituent council kept the democratic selection of leaders waiting until a constitution could be drafted, instead of the reverse. A twenty-one–member committee was therefore appointed, with seven men from each region. The Emir of Cyrenaica (Idris) and the paramount *sheikh* of Fezzan (Ahmed Seif an-Nasr) each appointed his representatives, while Tripolitanians were chosen from lists presented by political organizations; the National Congress Party (NCP), a nationalist coalition formed in 1949 (Bashir as-Saadawi), had the largest number of Tripolitanian representatives.

Although all representatives agreed that Idris should head the new country, there was sharp disagreement over the shape of the state he should head. Tripolitanians strongly opted for a unitary system, since Tripolitania had the bulk of the population, but the other two regions successfully advocated a federal government.*

---

* Some Cyrenaicans had, in fact, pressed for their own independent state, and they were only induced to join Libya by a promise, by Tripolitanians, of federalism and a Sanussi monarch. After World War II, Cyrenaica already enjoyed self-government under the British.

A National Assembly of three twenty-member delegations was appointed by the Emir, the Sheikh, and the Mufti of Tripolitania (Sheikh Abu al-Asad al-Alim) to accept the constitution, and the United Kingdom of Libya, under Idris I, was born.

The unity of the kingdom is its most dubious heritage. Population is concentrated in three areas. Two-thirds of the people (800,000) live on the coastal strip within a radius of 200 miles of Tripoli, while another fourth (320,000) live on the Cyrenaican hump around Benghazi and Beida. Between these two populations, each concentrated on coastal strips less than 50 miles deep, the Gulf of Sirte deeply dents the coastline and meets the desert, creating a barren gap of 300 to 400 miles (by camel and by car, respectively). The remaining 100,000 Libyans are oasis dwellers in the interior, half of them living in the string of villages which make up the Fezzan, 400 miles south of Tripoli. Nowhere are transportation channels or migratory habits sufficient to tie the three regions together and give a sense of unity.

The King and His Councils

The sovereignty of Libya's kingdom, constitutionally vested in God, is entrusted to the Sanussi dynasty of Idris I.[1] The position of the King is strongly entrenched in the clauses of the constitution. He exercises executive power through his ministers and legislative power in conjunction with parliament, which he convenes and may adjourn (for thirty days) or dissolve. He promulgates all laws and may issue decrees in the absence of parliament, to be examined when parliament reconvenes; he also makes "the necessary regulations for carrying out laws" within the framework of existing legislation. The King may veto legislation and be overridden only by a two-thirds vote of both houses. He can proclaim a state of emergency and also martial law with the ratification of parliament. He chooses and removes ministers and governors, and appoints all senators, judges, senior civil servants, and diplomatic representatives. In all his functions, the King is inviolable and without legal responsibility. His hand is heavy and is frequently felt in the direction of state affairs.

Born in 1890, Idris is an old but vigorous man. His long experience as the head of the Sanussi has given him a position of veneration throughout the nation, and he is wily in the ways of Libyan politics. But for all his popularity, the politics he knows is centered in the palace and not in the populace; Libya lacks dynamic popular leadership. Furthermore, he retains the post of Emir of Cyrenaica, and thus has special ties to one region. His position as a traditional monarch further separates him from the small modernizing urban society of Tripolitania.

The King has not been very vocal about his view of government. He has expressed interest in improvements in health and education, and he has attempted to keep the palace and the government under firm control and free of corruption. But his primary interest still lies in Cyrenaica, although he spends more and more time in Tripoli and in 1963 he led the campaign for the unification of the three provinces. His thorough understanding of the country he rules has not led him to any original thinking on methods of modernizing his system of government, or of integrating the largely traditional society and bringing it into close contact with its government.

One of the uncertainties raised by the age of the King is the problem of succession. Four wives produced the King no offspring until 1953, when a premature son born to his latest wife (and cousin), Fatima, lived only a day. A fifth marriage, to a girl from Egypt in 1955, ended in childless divorce in 1958. The heir to the throne, Idris' brother, Mohammed ar-Rida, died in 1954, leaving his second son, Hassan ar-Rida as-Sanussi, next in line. Hassan has married a daughter of the Governor of Tripolitania and was well received in a state visit to Tripoli, thus strengthening royal ties with the most populous section of the country. Politically, he is an unknown quantity, although socially he is quiet but well liked. Unlike Hassan II of Morocco or Crown Prince Wosen of Ethiopia, he is only the second in a dynasty that is new and unassayed, despite its traditional character.

There are thirty-eight royal princes, but only six of them are from the King's branch of the royal family. Following the murder of a trusted adviser, the Controller of the Royal Household, by a member of a rival branch of the royal family* in 1954, seven younger members of the royal family were exiled to a desert oasis, and all the family except those in direct succession were divested of their titles and their right to hold government office. The Royal Household was restricted to the royal couple, their children, and the Crown Prince. Busairi Shalhi, son of the murdered man, was appointed to succeed his father. His influence and authority re-

* A young nephew of Queen Fatima and, more important, grandson of Idris' predecessor as head of the Sanussis.

main great, and relations within the immediate family have been more stable since then.

Even outside the royal family, palace politics rather than popular responsibility still governs the country. According to the constitution, the ministers are collectively and individually responsible to the lower house of parliament. In fact, the cabinet is dependent on the King and is caught between these two political forces on the issue of legislation by royal decree, which has at least thrice caused the cabinet's resignation. As King and parliament grow used to their roles in government, and as the boundaries of authority grow clear with time, the cabinet, too, may grow into its constitutional position of bridge between the two legislative organs. Now it is an unstable body between an institution of traditional authority and an institution of modern representative responsibility.

Ministers have come from either parliamentary or provincial seats (which they must resign) or from business or technical positions that have brought them to the attention of the King. Since, until 1963, there were two dozen provincial ministries in addition to the fifteen in the federal government, there has been a continual training ground and source of candidates for rotation. But there is also a tendency to shift ministers one or more times a year, a practice that brings in new blood but also promotes ministerial instability. There have been only five premiers, but there have been over a dozen governmental changes involving some fifty ministers in only eleven years.

The first Premier was Mahmud al-Muntassar, a Tripolitanian businessman who presided over a shifting cabinet until February, 1954, when he resigned over a clash of power between the government and the King's appointees, the governors. He was succeeded for less than two months by Mohammed as-Saqizli, former governor of Cyrenaica and chief of the Royal Cabinet, who resigned over the question of legislation by the King. His Commerce Minister, Mustafa ben Halim, another Cyrenaican, headed for thirty-seven months a government that he reshuffled at least once a year; he finally resigned over the same legislative dispute.

In May, 1957, Abdulmajid Kubar, who had been President of the Chamber of Deputies since independence, became Premier. He lasted forty months, although his ministers were changed at least three times during this period and his attention to the possibilities and problems of Libya in the oil age was scarcely energetic. Interpenetration of government and business increased under Kubar, but his cabinet was brought down by parliament over a road-construction scandal involving at least one minister. For the first time, parliament exercised its control over a government and insisted on collective responsibility; for the first time, too, Tripolitanian and Cyrenaican deputies called a special parliamentary session and voted together for a political purpose.

Kubar was succeeded in October, 1960, by a Fezzani, Mohammed ben Othman as-Sed, who held the record of having been in all except two of the previous cabinets (as Health Minister and once as Finance Minister). His government was also reshuffled at least once a year. In March, 1963, Othman resigned and was replaced by Muhiaddin al-Fikini, formerly Ambassador to Cairo and then to Washington. The cabinet has been growing as it faces new responsibility. Under Kubar, two new Ministries, of Agriculture and of Labor and Social Affairs, were added; Othman created five new Ministries, of Industry, of Petroleum Affairs, of Information, of Development, and of Interior.*

Ministerial instability is a debilitating experience and one that a young country can ill afford. Changes take place not because of individual incompetence in a specialized post—as its constitution suggests should happen—or because of shifting party support (since there are virtually no parties); they occur because of political maneuvering among politicians, with little sense of responsibility to any constituency, but frequently with an overdeveloped sense of regional particularism. At best, ministers turn out to be no more than administrators, lacking in leadership or insight into the specialized problems of their ministries.

In such a situation, the civil service frequently performs the real functions of government. Libya has a large staff of government employees, totaling 40,000 in the federal and the three former provincial administrations. The latter governments were far more complex than the national administration, and the two coastal provinces each had a civil service several times the size of the federal government's; the cost and inefficiency of this system was one reason for its abolition, but most of the provincial civil servants are likely to be absorbed into the central government. Government service is often acquired through political patronage or family ties. Yet good civil servants are poorly paid. The result is

* Interior affairs were reserved for the provincial governments prior to 1963.

either poor morale or administrative instability, as civil servants leave to go into business. Furthermore, there has been little central control over policy, another reason for the abolition of the provinces. Even though the constitution provided a detailed list of matters to be executed by the provinces, the provinces often acted without any legislative guidance from the capital, according to widely divergent policies.

The same provincialism has been evident in the Libyan parliament. The House of Representatives has fifty-five members, directly elected every four years and formerly apportioned by population to the three provinces of Tripolitania (thirty-five), Cyrenaica (fifteen) and Fezzan (five); by the end of 1963, the House is expected to have over sixty members, two-thirds of whom are to come from the Tripoli region. The Senate is composed of twenty-four members appointed by the King; formerly, four Senators were elected by each provincial legislative council, and twelve were royal appointees. The Senate sits for eight years, but half of its membership is replaced at each election for the House. The two bodies have equal powers, except in matters of tax and fiscal legislation, which can only be initiated in the House. Initiation of all other matters is shared by the King and both houses of parliament. Parliament is scheduled to meet at the beginning of each November, opening its session with a "Speech from the Throne," usually read by the Prime Minister.

Like the other leadership groups in Libya, parliament is only growing into its role. The part it played in the collapse of Kubar's government demonstrated increased attention to national affairs and momentary disregard for regional politics. The example is still exceptional. Parliamentary members are still delegates from tribal hierarchies and business firms, more skilled in defending parochial interests than in attending to responsible government. Interaction between the representatives and their constituencies is slight, except at election time.

Until the end of 1962, provincial government exercised all powers not assigned to the federal government by the constitution through royally appointed governors (*walis*), executive councils made up of provincial ministers (*nazirs*) and their departments, and elected provincial councils. All of these offices and bodies, including the elected councils, disappeared in April, 1963, when the provinces were abolished. Liaison between federal and provincial ministers was cumbersome, although there was greater homogeneity in government and familiarity with problems on the provincial level than on the national level. However, there was no greater contact between the *nazirs* and the local village units than there is between the national government and lower levels. The country is now centrally governed, and is divided for administrative purposes into ten districts. Whether at the provincial or the federal level, government remains an elite function with little popular participation—and for the most part a traditionalist elite function at that.

A People Who Do Not Participate

The ruling elite presents an often paradoxical picture, since it is growing into a governing role that in many instances has never been defined, despite the good intentions and compromises of the constitution-makers. The sociopolitical picture of the general population is also full of paradoxes. In many ways, Libya presents the typical scene of a traditional, underdeveloped society. Its literacy rate is 15 per cent. Its rural society is tribally dominated, and economic activity in many such areas is deprived of security and incentive by tribal ownership of both land and water. In other areas, water rights, trade, and transportation are the monopoly of private individuals, with an almost feudal relation resulting. Even including the growing urban population, the people are ruled—with little or no participation in government and little readiness for political integration.

Yet there are elements of atypicality, signs of both progress and backwardness. One such is the rate of population increase, which has not yet entered the explosion stage. Because of poor health and hygienic practices, total annual growth is about 1.5 per cent, despite a high birth rate. As a result, in spite of the desert, which occupies 400 million of the country's 435 million acres, the amount of arable land per person is higher than in most Arab countries; some 3 million acres are suitable for cultivation, and 30 million for grazing. Another element, which can easily lend itself to political and social progress, is the high degree of urbanization and the surprisingly low percentage of nomadism in this desert society. The only two cities with more than 50,000 inhabitants, Tripoli (200,000) and Benghazi (85,000), hold a fifth of the population. Another tenth are settled in many small towns, but nearly half the population live in rural areas. As a result, only 8 per cent of the Libyans are nomads, and another 18 per cent seminomads. The oases of the Fezzan have the smallest number of wandering inhabitants (fewer than 10 per cent), while half of Cyrenaica is nomadic or seminomadic.[2]

The population of the Fezzan and the oases is dropping noticeably, while migration to the cities and to settled coastal farm areas —particularly by the young—is increasing. Even the discovery of oil in at least half a dozen major points in the interior will not reopen the desert to reclamation and resettlement; although there is a current drain on labor away from traditional agriculture to wage-earning employment in the oil business, it is estimated that the industry cannot absorb much more than 5 per cent of Libya's labor force. Moreover, the absence of modern means of transportation into the interior, with the exception of the one road (the subject of scandal during its construction) from Sebha (the Fezzani capital) to the coast, is of much less importance than a map would suggest. There is simply not enough population and economic potential to justify a developed road system, when camels and desert trucks and—paradoxically—light air traffic will do just as well.

Such population characteristics do not aid the modern state in carrying out some of its duties, such as border defense, exploitation of national territory, or development of natural resources. But they can lend themselves to social modernization in areas of population concentration, to an increase in political integration, and to a gradual collapse of divisive tribal provincialism. Libyan national consciousness did not arise as a force leading to independence, as in most other countries of northern Africa; rather, it is now growing as a result of living together under newly granted sovereignty. In the early years of independence, "an awakening of indigenous interest in national politics" was discerned in many small ways[3]—public discussions, business groups, national pride, small intellectual followings, interaction and cooperation among the cities of the two coastal regions.

This subtle process has continued, more strongly in the cities than elsewhere. Urban society is a mobile society, leading away from many traditional patterns of Libyan social life. There is a growing wealthy class, becoming richer in individual businesses. There is an important wage-earning proletariat, earning more than most of the people in Libya and envied by all those who stream in from the oases to find no jobs. Wage-earners are employed primarily by the oil companies and by the British and American military installations; total employment before the oil boom was about 75,000. There is even a middle class, composed largely of civil servants. In between, there are plenty of sources of unrest—in the tin-can slums of the unemployed, among many oilworkers who have been highly trained in skills soon to fall out of demand, among the air-base workers who have been accustomed to fixed employment that will disappear when the military installations are withdrawn.

Unfortunately, there are as yet few instruments of political integration to channel the interest and unrest of the changing society. Political parties are banned, largely as a result of a bad experience with one in Tripolitania at the time of independence. During the constitutional debates, the NCP expressed with vehemence the Tripolitanian predilection for a unitary state. In the first parliamentary elections of February 19, 1952, it added to this message pro-Egyptian Pan-Arabism and attracted Communist, xenophobic, and labor support. The NCP won only seven seats against forty-six pro-government independents, but it carried Tripoli and surrounding areas and led its followers into violent riots after the vote. Saadawi was exiled, and he died in Egypt. The Communist leader (Enrico Cibelli) was deported to Italy at the end of 1951, and there is no Communist Party left. However, in 1963, parliament was to reconsider the question of legalizing political parties.

Unlike movements in those countries which have had to fight for independence, Libya's nationalist movement—which existed in regional splinters in Cyrenaica and Tripolitania—withered away instead of reorganizing after independence. Subsequent parliamentary elections have been held on January 7, 1956, and, by secret ballot for the first time, on January 17, 1960. They have been nonpartisan, although sometimes hotly contested. Family ties and personal influence are the decisive criteria for voting; and the number of those voting has habitually been kept low by franchise restrictions and by apathy. Voters must be adults, free of debt; in 1952, about 140,000 Libyans, or one-eighth of the population, voted. Suffrage was opened to women for the first time by a constitutional amendment in 1963.

Libyan trade unions are as underdeveloped as the economy. In Tripoli there are three competing federations. The Libyan General Workers Federation (LGWF) (Salem Shita) has had a membership of some 6,000 and until recently was affiliated with the ICFTU. Petroleum workers formerly federated in the LGWF have withdrawn to form their own federation. A more radically oriented Libyan Federation of Labor and Professional Unions has 1,500 members. There is also a Cyrenaican Workers' Federation, but there is no nation-wide union. However, business still has the upper hand in dealing with labor, and Shita and other leaders were arrested by the government in September, 1961, following union-led strikes. Minimum wages and some social insurance have been established by federal legislation.

There are two Arabic newspapers in Tripolitania, four in Cyrenaica, and one in the Fezzan; Tripoli also has an English-language and an Italian-language newspaper. The constitution guarantees freedom of the press "within the limits of the law," and there is domestic control of news. A new ministry, with the curious full name of the Ministry of Information and Guidance, was set up in 1960. Newspaper circulation is very small. Libya also has two small broadcasting stations in Benghazi (5 kilowatts) and Tripoli (50 kilowatts), and is served by Arabic and English programs from the British and American bases. As in Somalia, by far the strongest radio broadcasts come from Cairo's Voice of the Arabs. Apart from the dominant position of Radio Egypt, information and public-opinion formation are still in an unorganized stage, depending most of all on village criers, readers, discussions, and rumors.

The World Bank mission to Libya in 1959 suggested the creation of "national advisory councils in agriculture, industry, and transport . . . through which outside advance can be obtained and information exchanged."[4] Although the integrative and informational value of such a step would be great, no comparable body exists at any level. The nearest thing, a Development Council for the elaboration of Five-Year Plans, has been simply an arena for provincial politics. Nor are there any development projects involving rural or urban community councils. Some 6,000 farmers are members of agricultural cooperatives, but they are only starting to expand beyond limited credit functions into cooperative planning, purchase of machinery and supplies, and marketing.

Probably the basic difficulty in the political position of the mass is not the channeling of wishes, but their formulation. The rural dweller is mostly interested in avoiding drought, feeding his family, and holding on to his accustomed way of life; little else matters, and his experiences are narrow enough to keep him from conceiving of much else. This is less true in the cities, where experiences are broader at least, even if demands are no better formulated. Since the intermingled economic and political elite seem to be generally satisfied with present conditions, articulation of popular aspirations is not likely to receive much attention in the near future.

The Growth of Law and Policies

Libya's constitution existed before Libya's independence.[5] It was obviously not a description of existing practices, but a list of rules and goals that the new government would have to "try on" and "fit into." The major characteristic of the government during its decade of existence is its development, as it tries to settle into its functions. There have been amendments to the constitution, in December, 1962, and April, 1963, abolishing the provinces. There have also been both strains in and re-evaluations of the constitutional framework. There will be more. It is impossible to graft a developed nation's constitution—Libya's resembles that of the United States in many ways—onto a traditional society and expect it to fit. Changes are most likely in the definition and division of responsibility among the monarchy, parliament, and government.

It is in this area that the most prominent clashes have already taken place. In January, 1954, the King dissolved the Tripolitanian legislative council, and in March the Supreme Court, in its first judgment since its creation, declared the royal decree unconstitutional. Informal conciliation (by an Egyptian) between the court and provincial officials brought about an understanding on the question, after new elections had already been held. In May, the Cassation Branch of the court declared all previous decisions invalid because an advocate general had not yet been appointed. In fact, the King's apparently unconstitutional action stood; in law, the matter remained unsettled.

The constitution does provide a lengthy list of civil liberties, based on Western bills of rights. It also includes some rather progressive guarantees protecting marriage, labor, an appropriate standard of living, and freedom of language. One of the most striking examples of the prescriptive nature of the constitution is its provision for compulsory elementary education, which is still short of being met even halfway.

Libyan law is a mixture of Italian and Egyptian ingredients. The judiciary is independent, and its hierarchical organization, which formerly followed the federal-provincial system, is now centralized. Supreme Court justices are appointed for life by the King. The court exercises judicial review and is the highest court of appeals; it formerly heard cases between the provinces or between the provinces and the federal government. Under the Supreme Court are courts of appeal, courts of the first instance, and, at the lowest level, magistrate courts. An unusual aspect of this modern court system is the high percentage of foreign judges who rule on Libya's laws. An American and an Englishman join three Libyans on the Supreme Court, and many other Arab and European nationals sit as members of the lower courts.

Until 1954, *shariaa* courts regulated the largest body of litigation, concerning the personal affairs of Muslims. Then an attempt was made to integrate them into the modern court system. It failed, and the government is still trying to work out some arrangement by which the law of custom and local reality may be taken into account in judicial proceedings. In law, as in institutions, the country still has to grow into its prefabricated framework.

Minority rights are the subject of constitutional guarantees. For the most part, the population is a mixture of Arab and Berber stock in varying proportions. Jews, Greeks, and Maltese constitute small national minorities. The Jewish population has been sharply reduced by emigration to Israel, although there has been no persecution since independence. A larger problem is that posed by nearly 40,000 Italians. Italians were cleared out of Cyrenaica during the war, but they still occupy an important position in Tripolitanian agriculture and business. Although an agreement with Italy provided for ownership rights for the Italians remaining on 1,400 farms after 1960, present Libyan policy is rather to encourage repatriation of this foreign population.

Law-enforcement agencies include an army of 3,000 and efficient police forces of twice that size. The army is British-trained and equipped, and has received arms from the United States, Turkey, and Egypt as well. Its capability is possibly even less than that of the police force, which in Cyrenaica, at least, has had military experience in the Sanussi resistance allied with England during World War II, and is kept up in arms and training. Policing is a prestigious occupation, and the army's greatest importance is probably as a source of national pride.

As with many of its neighbors, troubles both outside and in are intertwined in Libya. Firm lines of Arab solidarity and Maghreb unity stand out in foreign-policy statements, but the shading is blurred in implementation. Libya accepted the resolutions of the Maghreb Unity Conference at Tangier in 1958, but did not attend; it attended the Casablanca Conference of African states in 1961, but did not subscribe to the cooperative plans established.

The Provisional Algerian Government on occasion sat in Tripoli, and Libya strongly supported its cause. Relations with France have therefore been touchy; after the French evacuation of Fezzan, the treaty of "friendship and good neighborliness" of 1955 with France was only ratified on French insistence, and a battle between French and Algerian forces on the Libyan frontier in October, 1957, further troubled relations for a brief period. During this incident, Libya called on Britain for assistance in accordance with the Anglo-Libyan treaty of 1953. The treaty gives Britain a twenty-year lease on facilities at Idris Field, near Tripoli, and at al-Adem Field, near Tobruk, and provides the right to conduct military maneuvers in specific areas in Libya. Britain, in return, has annually given more than $9 million to Libya in aid.

In 1956, Libya requested Britain not to use its Libyan bases in connection with the Suez campaign. At the same time, however, an Egyptian plot against the King was discovered, the Egyptian military attaché was expelled, and the Cyrenaican frontier was armed. Of the two, Britain has probably enjoyed more stable relations with Libya than has Egypt, despite Libyan sympathy on the question of Israel and other Arab causes. Egypt has a dominant hand in Libyan education, with an estimated 500 out of some 2,500 teachers, and Nasser has great popularity in Tripoli and the surrounding region. But in the province along the Egyptian frontier, the King and the Sanussi—dominant political forces in Cyrenaica —are extremely wary of Egyptian penetration.

Until the discovery of oil in 1959 and its serious exploitation after 1960, sympathies and foreign policies were two different things. The latter were decided by the country's need of foreign subsidies. The American aid program, set up by the 1954 treaty, which also provided for the lease of Wheelus Field near Tripoli, at least until 1970, is nearly double the British subsidy; in 1958, the government pressed for substantial increases in American aid. The U.S.S.R., which since 1955 has had embassies in Tripoli and. Benghazi, has also offered aid. During the Suez crisis, Egypt promised to underwrite the Libyan budget if Anglo-American aid failed, but the Egyptian performance on a similar promise to Jordan the following year and a Libyan distrust of economic colonialization by its neighbor have kept Libya's bank account in the West.

There is evident strain in this relationship. Total economic dependence does not go well with the goal of political independence. It is not likely that Libya will turn to Cairo or Moscow, but it is possible that it will threaten to bank in the East in order to get bigger deposits from the West. There is even greater likelihood that, as the annual predicted oil-production increase of 50 per cent above the 1962 level (150,000 barrels per day) raises oil revenues, Libya might try to find economic independence to go along with its second decade of self-government.

In this eventuality, Libya will need more than ever to modernize its government, increase the ties between the public and the politician, and train its population in civic exercise. Libyan government today is remarkably expensive. The luxury of three capitals alone—Tripoli and Benghazi for two years each, to assuage provincial rivalries, and Beida as the newly constructed administrative center—takes up nearly $300,000 every time the government moves, and the construction of Beida cost $20 million and is not finished. Weakening of provincialism may in time eliminate this expense, but the large civil service shows no signs of ceasing to grow. Popular participation and leadership responsibility are two sides of the same coin that is too little in circulation. The law and the elite in Libya are growing into their roles, shaping the political process as they find their way. However, the even more difficult task—that of bringing the people along with them—must not be forgotten.

VI

UNITED ARAB REPUBLIC (EGYPT)

President Nasser has dated the beginnings of Egyptian national consciousness from the British occupation in 1882, although the roots of modern nationalism in Egypt probably go as far back as the Napoleonic invasion, nearly a century earlier. The French experience was only a brief interruption in centuries of nominal Turkish suzerainty over Egypt. But the British remained there for thirty years as an occupying power and then declared Egypt a British protectorate when Turkey entered World War I in 1914. At the end of the war, in 1918, Egyptian nationalism emerged under the leadership of Saad Zaghlul; his Wafd (Delegation) Party—its methods and its struggles for independence—was quite similar to nationalist movements in the other northern African countries at the end of World War II. Britain granted Egypt formal independence in 1922, when the rest of northern Africa was only entering into the height of its colonial history and when the brief colonial period of Ethiopia had not yet even begun. This very characteristic of Egypt's history—its attainment of independence "one war ahead" of its neighbors—does much to account for the considerable difference of its evolution from that of the other northern African countries.

It was not until 1936, when the evacuation of British troops (except from the Suez Canal Zone) was obtained, and the Anglo-Egyptian Alliance was signed, that independence began to mean anything more than internal autonomy.[1] Even then, the fact that independence came between the wars rather than after World War II meant that Egypt could be satisfied with an essentially conservative change of government, and England could still make sure that the change was only a legal, and not a social, manifestation. The Wafd, dominant in Parliament since the first elections of 1924, remained a large, ambiguous, factional nationalist movement; it united the upper classes (who were later to be called the "feudals") and the peasant mass with the restive youth and other, more ideologically aware elements. The last King, Farouk, ascended the throne of the Pharaohs in the same year, 1936, and during the sixteen years of his reign he showed himself to be decreasingly interested in either reform or responsibility.

At the outbreak of World War II, Egypt had a government that was as pro-Axis as it could be without denouncing the Anglo-Egyptian Alliance of 1936. When the national territory was threatened and then invaded by the Axis in 1942, the British had to resort to a show of military power and threats to depose the King in order to force the formation of a government that would give its full cooperation to the Allies. For the next three years, the exigencies of the war, which was far from popular with the Egyptians, made necessary active British interference in Egyptian affairs, thus producing a situation that was barely distinguishable from the protectorate, which had been manifestly unpopular. During and after the war, Egyptian businessmen prospered, but corruption spread within the government. The bureaucracy, which long years of Turkish rule had left as a powerful force, grew in size to a quarter-million without growing in honesty, efficiency, or responsibility.

Anglophobia in the country was compounded by violent resentment of British policies in Palestine. But the weak and corrupt Egyptian Government was powerless to organize any effective policy, and the army was sent by the King to shameful defeat in the Palestine War of 1948 without preparation or support from Cairo. By this act, the King and the government deprived themselves of the loyalty of many of the military; in 1949, on returning from the Palestine War, a group of eleven young officers in the middle ranks started a Society of Free Officers, which dabbled in terrorism and directed more serious efforts at propaganda and planning against the government.[2] Other manifestations of dissatisfaction appeared, in the spread of intellectual, socialist, and Communist groups and parties and, perhaps most important, the Muslim Brotherhood, which sought answers to the current governmental impotence by returning to the classic principles of Islam.

The government attempted to regain popular support in Octo-

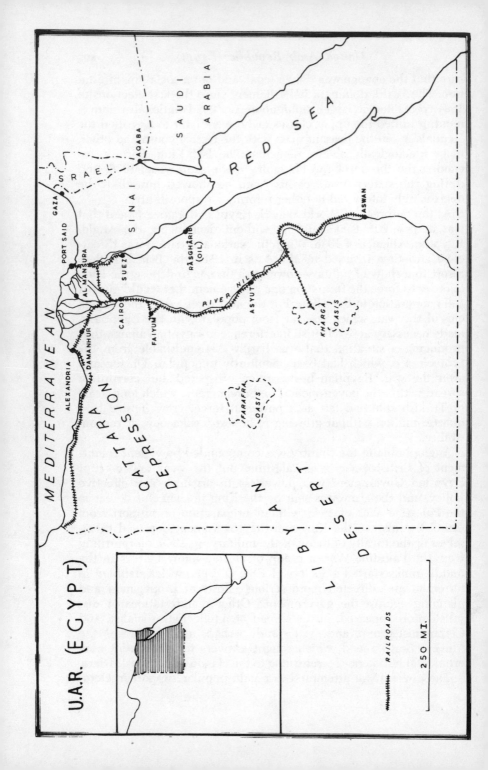

ber, 1951, by denouncing the Anglo-Egyptian Alliance and calling for immediate evacuation of the British forces remaining in the Suez Canal Zone. Instead, the reaction of the country was to fall into the anarchy of the "street"; in January of the following year, an uncontrolled mob systematically burned out the heart of Cairo, while the King "fiddled away" his time and his control at a state banquet and the Prime Minister waited outside in an antechamber, unable to mobilize the organs of government. All available evidence points to the hand of the Muslim Brotherhood in the organizing of the riots, but the inaction of the government and the pent-up dissatisfaction of the urban population were also elements of the anarchical outburst.

Unhappy with his government's attempt to oust the only army committed to his support—the British—Farouk tried to use the government's complicity in the riots to buy its silence on both his own inaction and on the Suez Canal problem. For half a year, the King held the government hostage, and the country waited in restive expectation of the revolution. This period was marked by increasingly frequent strikes and even peasant revolts on the large landholdings. The King himself saw his fate, and in July he signed one of his letters "F.F." ("Finished Farouk"). In June, he dismissed his government, and the ensuing crisis lasted a full month. During the early morning of July 23, 1952, as Farouk attempted to install the last members of the new cabinet, the revolution came.

Three days after the Society of Free Officers took over, King Farouk abdicated in favor of his infant son, Ahmed Fuad. In September, Ali Maher resigned as Premier of the revolutionary government, and was replaced by General Mohammed Nagib. In June, 1953, the republic was declared, and Nagib was chosen President as well as Premier. He was replaced in February, 1954, and then reinstated two days later as head of the government, but the next month Gamal Abdel Nasser took over as Premier; following sedition trials of Muslim Brotherhood leaders in November, Nagib was impeached as President and put under house arrest for six years. In June, 1956, when a constitution was submitted to the voters, Nasser was elected President with 99.9 per cent of the 5.5 million votes.

The government of contemporary Egypt can be divided into three periods.[3] From 1953 to 1958, the republic existed under Nasser's consolidating control; in February, 1958, the United Arab Republic (U.A.R.) was proclaimed, uniting Egypt and Syria into a federated state until September 28, 1961, when Syria withdrew; thereafter, the name U.A.R. has continued to be used in reference to Egypt alone.* The politics of Egypt also can be divided into three phases. Between 1952 and 1955, the three-year "transition period," domestic politics and particularly the need to define relations among the governing elite absorbed most of the government's attention; foreign policy was formulated largely to solve outstanding problems. Between 1955 and 1961, Nasser adopted an active foreign policy, which occupied most of his attention; even efforts toward internal consolidation of the U.A.R. spring from a concern with Pan-Arabism. However, just as the introduction of socialist measures into Syria helped to split the original U.A.R., so the secession of Syria helped to bring about an acceleration of socialism in Egypt and the turning of governmental attention to domestic policies. Since, in this third period, Egyptian governmental and political evolution coincides—and because of this book's limited space and the fact that Syria lies outside this study's geographical area of attention—emphasis will be concentrated on the present period of government and politics in Egypt.

The Cult of the Personality

Egyptian government is firmly in the hands of a small elite—the remaining Free Officers and their civilian associates—and this group is dominated by one man, Nasser. A man of words and action, emotion and purpose, although scarcely a philosopher of the revolution,[4] Nasser rose rapidly from behind-the-scenes leadership of the junta to Prime Minister and then President of the republic. His charismatic leadership and organizational control have kept the reins of politics and government in his hands without any serious challenges or defections in Egypt since the removal of Nagib. Even in defeat, in the Suez in 1956 or in Syria in 1961, his popularity has been great enough to carry him through the crisis, and his political skill inventive enough to make reversals give birth to renewed energy or sudden advantage. The secession of Syria has left him in complete control of Egypt, under a provisional constitution that gives him almost unlimited power.

* This review of government and politics in Egypt does not treat the renewed attempts at creating a united Arab state, following the 1963 *coups d'état* in Syria and Iraq; as of mid-1963, these attempts brought no changes in Egyptian government and politics, and little hope of change beyond renewed declarations of intentions.

Beneath this cult of the personality, there has been some semblance of collective leadership. The original leadership structure was hierarchical and military. About the *raïs* (chief) was the Revolutionary Control Council (RCC)—a "politburo" of the Free Officers with twelve members (the original Free Officers plus Nagib). The RCC was a collegial organism, but it was not immune to political differences, and it expelled several members of its own left wing between 1954 and 1956. Nasser won his support from the RCC by winning over its members to his ideas and actions, and particularly by securing a majority against those who supported Nagib, but he also relied on the ideas and counsel of its members. The RCC was what its name suggested— a revolutionary organism of control—and made no pretense at being a popular representative body. In July, 1957, after the Legislative Assembly was elected, the RCC was dissolved, but its members remained in positions of importance in the government. The twelve-man Presidential Council, highest executive body of the state, formed in September, 1962, was composed of six of the original RCC members, including Nasser, plus later additions to the inner circle. The group is no longer a council of equals, but a team under Nasser's leadership.

Under the RCC was the Society of Free Officers, composed of about 250 officers (mostly colonels and majors). In the coup, it provided the military leadership used in the actual takeover; during the republic, it provided group support for the RCC. Beyond this second circle is an ever-expanding number of army officers (about 500 in 1963), who have been assigned to key government, administrative, and diplomatic posts. Personally loyal to Nasser, they use their organizational ability to assure both political control and efficient functioning of the ever-growing political and economic machinery of the state.

The Executive Council, or cabinet, is responsible to the Presidential Council and its President, who appoints and dismisses it. In the early years after the revolution, a civilian cabinet was chosen to administer and execute the Free Officers' wishes, and was responsible to the RCC. Thus, Nagib's first government, of September, 1952, was all civilian, made up largely of technicians, and his second government, of June, 1953, had only four military members. Nasser's first government, of April, 1954, was dominated by eight ministers who were members of the RCC. Following the creation of the U.A.R., in March, 1958, the Egyptian cabinet was replaced with a triple federal cabinet. It was composed of four vice-presidents (two Syrians and two of the original RCC, Abdulhakim Amer and Abdullatif al-Boghdadi), eight Union ministers (including three of the original RCC, the 1952 Foreign Minister Mahmud Fawzi, and only one Syrian), and two eleven-man cabinets for the Egyptian and Syrian sectors, covering affairs internal to each region.

Although this arrangement was to change several times during the following three years, the instability reflected the difficulty of integrating Syria into an Egyptian-dominated union, rather than changes within the Egyptian sector. In October, 1958, the government was revised to facilitate efficient and centralized controls; it now included an enlarged Union cabinet of twenty-three members (of whom fifteen were Egyptians, eight of them Free Officers), and two Regional Executive Councils of fifteen members for Egypt and fourteen for Syria. Five new Egyptian regional ministers were officers. Changes were made in the Syrian membership in 1959 and in 1960; finally, in August, 1961, in an attempt further to centralize control and to meet some of the problems that were to cause the defection of Syria two months later, the regional councils were abolished and a new central government created with thirty-seven members (including twenty-one Egyptians).

After the breakup of the U.A.R. in October, 1961, the cabinet was again reconstituted. It included the President and five vice-presidents, all of them former members of the RCC and all but Nasser also holding ministerial posts, plus eighteen ministers and three deputies; of the twenty-one ministers and deputies, at least six more were old Free Officers, and Fawzi was still Foreign Minister. New professional men were also added to head ministries. A year later, the cabinet was again modified, a Prime Minister (Ali Sabri) installed, and a National Defense Council created, with sixteen members drawn from the General Staff and the Presidential Council. Over the years, the government has thus shown flexibility in its membership, centered around a core of six of the original collective leaders of the RCC (Nasser, Amer, Boghdadi, Zakaria Mohiaddin, Hussein ash-Shafei, Kamaladdin Hussein) and personal military friends of the President (Sabri, Anwar as-Sadat), who still hold the key positions. However, the trend has also been toward greater, not less, military participation in government.

The reorganization decree of October, 1958, also set up four major interministerial committees, some with subcommittees, to act as the central policy organs. The ministers legislate through decrees implementing policy established in the committees. The working relationship between the Presidential, Executive, and National Defense Councils is still unclear: the second is mainly administrative, and the first can change or cancel its decisions before promulgating them as law. Executive and administrative functions are thus muddled, in a partial return to the system of the RCC.

The holding of free elections was one of the major dreams of the revolution, but in practical application it clashed with the more immediate aim of removing the politicians and parties of the old regime from power. Despite sporadic promises of elections, the idea of a representative parliament fared badly during the first years of the republic. By the time Nagib was finally removed from governmental power, in March, 1954, parliamentary government was firmly rejected. Not until a constitution was adopted (June, 1956) and the National Union created to replace political parties (May, 1957) was Nasser ready for an elected parliament.

Elections were held in July, 1957. The 350-member National Assembly had little real power, although it went through the formal motions of listening to lectures on laws submitted to it by the cabinet, and passing them. The Assembly lasted only until the formation of the U.A.R., when it was to be replaced by a unicameral union parliament. Again, plans moved slowly. In July, 1959, voters chose 4,000 village councils of the National Union; these in turn elected provincial councils, which then chose regional congresses in the Egyptian and Syrian regions. The Egyptian Congress had 3,814 members (of whom 1,164 were appointed by the President), and the Syrian Congress had 1,800 (of whom 360 were appointed). In July, 1960, the first General Congress of the two regional bodies was held to elect 300 members to a parliament; the President appointed an equal number of members from the former membership of the Egyptian and Syrian assemblies. The main function of the new National Assembly was to review the budget, which it could not amend, and pass it (or, inconceivably, reject it) as presented. This body, too, collapsed with the withdrawal of its 200 Syrian members in September, 1961.

As happened in other fields, the collapse of the U.A.R. brought significant changes to Nasser's parliamentary ideas. The third attempt at a representative body was no longer along the usual lines of geographic representation, but was based on functional membership. Fifteen hundred members of a new National Congress of Popular Powers (or Forces) were to be elected to represent farmers (375), labor (300), professional men (225), nationalized industry (150), women, professors, and students (105 each), and others (135); this composition was in sharp contrast with the 1957 Assembly, one-third of whose members were businessmen, one-third high government officials, and scarcely any farmers or workers. By purposely keeping out the "reactionary millionaires," Nasser was capitalizing on the broad base of popular support which was his, despite the defection of the "reactionary element" in Syria.

The most important segment of the National Congress was a 250-member group appointed by Nasser in November, 1961, to draw up a pre-election report defining the role of the Congress, and then to serve as its elite after it was constituted. The preparatory committee included the U.A.R. vice-presidents, ministers and deputy ministers, provincial governors, and spokesmen for labor, professions, universities, and cooperatives. The remaining members of the National Congress were elected during February, 1962.

The entire 1,750 members of the National Congress first met from May to July, 1962, to approve Nasser's National Action Charter, in which he explained his program for Arab socialism. It was to meet six months later to approve the final constitution. Plans included the establishment of partially elected councils "at all levels, above the authority of the executive machinery." However, at the beginning of the second decade after the revolution, a channel through which popular needs and wishes could be expressed had still not been created. The representative elite and the executive elite in Egypt are intermingled, and the real power in both politics and government lies in the small group at the top, surrounded by 1,750 of its closest followers. The new group basis of organization, leading to representation that is functional rather than geographical, reflects the junta's new approach in its third attempt at representation, along the lines of an "Arab socialist" society.

The philosophy of the revolution has frequently been articulated, although, like any statement of principles, it often has remained beyond the reach of both precision and reality.[5] One reason appears to be that the junta has never been very clear as to where it was leading the country or how long its services would be required. Early estimates were for a six-month stay in power or for a spontaneous rallying and revitalization of the national political forces. The officers have not been wrong in finding that there was a continuing need for their leadership.

The army considered itself not a force of military occupation imposed on the nation, but the vanguard of the people and the best interpreter of its will. "The army is of the people and for the people." The result of a decade of populism is that the junta has had its own thoughts pushed again and again—with frequent failures in between—toward an implementation of its slogans on the concrete level. From this the idea of Arab socialism has sprung. The cause of the revolution, in Nasser's words, was "the enslavement of the people by the imperialists and their lackeys, the Egyptian feudal lords and politicians"; the task is, therefore, "to liberate the slaves, that is, the people, and to put them in the place of their masters in the government of the country." The six principles of the revolution, stated in 1955 and reaffirmed after the defection of Syria, therefore begin with a purge of the old elites: "elimination of imperialism, elimination of feudalism and domination of capitalism, elimination of monopolies." To these must be added the abolition of two other groups considered harmful: the political parties and the bureaucracy. Obviously, with these negative aims in mind, the revolution means a complete reversal of governing, social, and economic elites.

On the other hand, the position of the new popular elites and the masses—particularly the "oppressed classes"—is to be raised. The final three principles of the revolution are "establishment of sound social justice, establishment of a strong national army, establishment of a sound democratic life." Since 1955 and his experience at the Bandung Conference of Independent African and Asian Countries, Nasser has proclaimed that socialism is the way of attaining social justice. He has defined socialism as the closing of the gap between classes. However, his ideas of classes are scarcely Communist, any more than dislike of masters and slaves *per se* is Communist. The concept, to the extent that it can be pinned down, is rather one of bettering the condition of the farmer and urban worker (through agrarian reform and "socialist" dividends), creating national unity on a socio-economic basis rather than through class struggle (by destroying the social gap that makes Egypt an underdeveloped society), and erasing the distinctions that make for classes rather than perpetuating the dominance of any one class (through "the peoples' control over all production and over the distribution of the surplus according to a definite plan"). So far, these ideas have been rather constant. The turning of attention to domestic affairs which followed the Syrian secession has only intensified Nasser's attachment to the philosophy of Arab socialism and his search for ways of implementing it.

One final note of constancy has been the junta's attachment to Islamic principles, or at least mythology, in an attempt to justify the search for social justice. Contrary to the atavistic attitudes of the Muslim Brotherhood, Nasser seeks to find support in Islam for his modern ways, and has even succeeded in finding traces of socialism among the Companions of the Prophet. Islamic principles also reinforce the predominance of dignity and destiny in Nasser's ideas. The content, however, is modernized; the Egyptian is told that dignity means the shaping of his own destiny, free not only of colonialism but also of control by the upper-class minority.

The most fluctuating element in this array of values concerns the goal of democracy and, ultimately, the entire political shape of the revolution. Since the secession of Syria, ideas on democracy have been revived and sharpened along closely reasoned lines. Nasser set the stage for the argument in November, 1961, in announcing plans for the National Congress: "The political revolution [of 1952–56] has achieved the liberation of the homeland. The duty of the social revolution is to liberate the people." The needs of the social revolution require the existence of genuine popular representation, in the current view. "These genuine representatives should be united in action by uniform ideology," for the social revolution must remove the negative and harmful attitudes that centuries have baked into the hearts of the people. The battle, therefore, takes place within the hearts and minds of the people, and the only thing that can move the people to change is a feeling within themselves of responsibility in government and participation in shaping their destiny.

Responsibility is only possible in an atmosphere of freedom—debate, criticism, and self-criticism. But at the same time, radical controls are necessary, for the uncongenial mixture of a moneyed minority that opposes the revolution on the one hand, and the great majority that supports it but has never before been able to express its support on the other, has always in the past been one of the main obstacles to freedom. Therefore, the policy of "isolation" has been applied to that part of the minority "whose reform is hopeless"; the economic power of the upper class has been reduced, and adherence to the Charter of National Action is a precondition for franchise.

Confiscation and economic limitations, and even nationalization, are not only measures of "correction"; they are also designed to unite the society into a homogeneous economic unit, more readily amenable to a uniform ideology. "Domestically we seek democracy, not only in elections, but as participation in the national economic revolution to increase production, achieve equality in distribution, equalize opportunities, and melt differences between citizens." Ideology, participation, and socio-economic homogenization of society are therefore three wings of the same phalanx, and the army leadership marches simultaneously on all fronts. Having found a technique of revolution, Nasser is still looking for a technique of government.

A People Controlled but Unorganized

In the coup of 1952, a new stratum of society, almost a class, came to power. The new elite was only one, or at most two generations away from the *fellah;* it was the nascent middle class. Behind this group stand about 2.5 million Egyptians who can also be considered urban middle class, but beneath them are 14 million landless peasants and 4.5 million urban lower class and unemployed—the bulk of the population.[6]

Nasser's consciousness of the social gap and his professed desire to increase popular participation in government are reinforced by the high degree of urbanization in Egypt and by the presence of integrating organizations. Cairo, with 3.5 million people, and Alexandria, half that size, are the largest cities in Africa; 30 per cent of the Egyptian population live in urban areas with more than 200,000 inhabitants, and there are also some 5,000 smaller villages strung along the narrow Nile oasis. The concentration of 27 million Egyptians on 3.5 per cent of the country's territory— 2,300 per square mile—increases their susceptibility to organization and social communication, and has created a population which for millennia has been amenable to strong centralized governmental control.

The most direct attempt to organize the masses and facilitate public participation is found in a series of official political parties. The National Union was a hierarchical mass organization founded in May, 1957, "to watch over the realization of the aims of the revolution and over the reconstruction of a sound national life." It was the successor to the Liberation Rally, which on paper replaced all parties in 1953. The National Union took three years to construct. Not until July, 1960, did its first General Congress meet, and then its only responsibility was to elect the new parliament.* Although the General Congress included members from Syria, political leadership was still in the hands of a five-man Supreme Council (Amer, Boghdadi, Hussein, and the Syrian Abdelhamid Sarraj, with Nasser as President). After the defection of Syria, the National Union fell into disuse, and in May, 1962, Nasser launched the idea of replacing it with a similar Arab Socialist Union. A year later, the Union had some five million carefully screened members, but its organization was slow in taking shape.

It is hard to consider any of these bodies political parties, although they were formed to replace the prerevolutionary parties of Egypt and Syria. Their role as parliamentary-type institutions is one point of confusion. Another—more serious—is their real lack of responsibility and participation in government. Leadership remains firmly in the hands of the junta, and no new faces have yet risen from its broad popular base. The National Union was accompanied by florid proclamations of popular participation and included 29,000 elected positions in its hierarchy, but in fact it only went through the forms and motions of public political activity. The promise of responsibility is present, and has been present for a decade; there is no reason to write off this promise for the future. But there is the present danger that the new Arab Socialist Union may continue to be only a popularistic sop to the masses, deceiving them into thinking that they participate in the matters of state.

The seventeen parties of the *ancien régime* were told, in the early pronouncements of the junta, to purge themselves and reorganize, and their internal rivalries and confusion in the revolutionary situation were used by the new leaders of Egypt to weaken their organization. In January, 1953, the parties were finally outlawed. Total control by the junta, and arrests and confiscations in 1954, destroyed the former parties. By 1959, however, the junta's purpose had been achieved, some political restrictions were relaxed, and a few Wafdists were even elected to the National Union.

Two movements of deeper roots and tighter organization continue to exist clandestinely. One is the Muslim Brotherhood,

* It also passed 502 resolutions calling on the government to continue its policies.

founded in 1929 and still powerful as late as 1953 and 1954, after the dissolution of the other parties. The Brotherhood was hit severely by its legal dissolution in January, 1954, and by the treason trials that followed the attempt on Nasser's life in October of the same year. The Brotherhood's fanatical devotion to a return to traditional Islamic rules of government and its clandestine organization throughout the Arab world are bases of some continuing strength, although not of influence in the present government.

The other group is the Communist Party, founded in 1919 (the oldest in Africa). Attacked through the legal arm of the state in 1953, and split into many competing factions, it rallied to Nasser in 1956, defected in 1958 on the formation of the U.A.R. and the Iraqi coup of July, 1958, and has been the subject of severe repression ever since. Its remaining leaders are still kept in the Libyan Desert oasis of Kharga. In 1960 and 1961, worsening relations with the U.S.S.R. were both the cause and the result of an intensified anti-Communist campaign, and cogent state propaganda has been issued showing the incompatibility of Islam and Nasserism with Communism. The ideas of the junta owe much to Marxism, but Nasser continues to proclaim that he "will not tolerate a Communist Party which receives instructions from a foreign country."

Elections and candidacy in 1957 were under the close control of a three-officer board of the National Union, which rejected half the candidates before they ever reached the voters. Voting, however, was compulsory for the 6 million registered voters (a very low percentage of the voting-age population). In 1959, candidatures for the National Union village councils were controlled by the Interior Minister. The institution of functional representation encouraged the centralized organization of social groups in Egyptian society, but these efforts were in the domain of the National Union, and its committees have had strict control over access to functional organizations. In 1958, before reorganization under the National Union, about 200 student, economic, and professional groups existed. Within the National Union, these groups took active part in the February, 1962, elections to the National Congress, discussing national issues and contributing to the increased interest in national affairs that Nasser seeks to promote. After the creation of the Arab Socialist Union, 11,400 members of regional sections were elected in May, 1963, and half of these seats were reserved for workers and peasants.

Labor organization, too, has lost its diversity and its independent powers, and has become a centralized arm of government under the National Union. The first unions were formed in 1910, and after the revolution the junta tried several times to bring them together in a national congress. The Egyptian Federation of Labor was founded in 1957 and is affiliated with both the International Confederation of Arab Unions and the All-African Trade Union Federation. Its members enjoy liberal benefits, but the unions themselves have no right to strike. Union leadership is strictly controlled by the government, and union views on policy are strained through the military oligarchy before they reach any level of influence. In state-controlled industries, selected workers sit with government and management on the board of directors.

The agglutination of a mass of urbanized nomads does not in itself mean progress, nor does it even bring immediate change to a sharply stratified society, other than "converting old indolence into new aimlessness."[7] One drawback of the urbanized society of Egypt is found in the importance of the "street" and the facility with which anomic public demonstrations can begin and get out of hand. The Cairo riot in January, 1952, was worse than any similar manifestations since the revolution, but in the early years of the republic—encouraged by the confusion of the revolution itself—other public outbursts among townsfolk, students, workers, and even farmers occurred. Nasser has attempted to use, and at the same time control, such public outbursts, and organizes frequent student and worker demonstrations. In his public harangues at crucial moments, such as the nationalization of the Suez Canal or the secession of Syria from the U.A.R., he plays to massed throngs of highly emotional supporters; but he has succeeded in directing their furor largely against external scapegoats.

The Egyptian press, television, and radio are all nationalized. For Nasser, the radio has proved to be a major weapon against illiteracy and has revolutionized government.[8] Radio Cairo's many broadcasts are widely followed throughout the Arab and African world. They are also an active arm of the government's internal political-education program, and Egyptians are avid and regular listeners. Television, introduced in July, 1960, has attracted a broad audience in the Cairo area. The publicly televised series of debates of the Preparatory Committee and the National Congress, in which Nasser played a patient and instructive role as members rose to challenge and debate the ideas of the President, brought government to the level of the urban population. This new exercise in freedom evoked avid public discussion in the cafés and wide interest among the spectators.

The newspapers reach a greater audience than the literate 18 per cent of the population or their 500,000 daily circulation, for they are publicly read aloud and commented on. In the editors of Cairo's leading papers (Mustafa Amin of *al-Akhbar,* Ali Amin of the *Dar al-Hilal* weeklies, and Nasser's unofficial spokesman and commentator, Mohammed Hassanein Heikal of *al-Ahram*) the government finds able and diligent propagandists of the revolution.

Egypt also benefits from economic projects that bring segments of the population, particularly the farmers, in contact with modernization and governmental activity. One-eighth of Egypt's 6 million arable acres have been distributed since the Agrarian Reform Law of September, 1952 (one of the priority measures of the revolution).[9] Two-thirds of these lands were made available for 150,000 families by the limitation of land ownership to 200 acres; in July, 1961, the limit was dropped to 100 acres, and another 250,000 acres were thus added to the distributable land. Plans are also under study to make more land available by reclamation. A farmer who accepts redistributed land is obliged to become a member of one of the 344 paternalistic agrarian-reform cooperatives, which take seeding, water, and management problems out of his hands. The farmer, however, does participate in the selection of the cooperative board, which works with the official of the Agrarian Reform Ministry to see that the reform decrees are carried out. The favored position of the "reformed" farmers is shown by the fact that they alone among the farmers were allowed to elect agricultural representatives to the National Congress. This group, however, represents only about 6 per cent of the 18 million *fellahin.*

Finally, the government has used its legal power to change the social ways of the population and to prepare them for life in a modern society, although its progress has actually been slow. In various laws, the government has attacked the cafés, Muslim laws on easy divorce, multiple jobs, belly dancers, *galabias* (cloak-like robes), beggars, and other "undesirable" (to Nasser) features of traditional Egyptian society. While adopting Muslim appeals and using the Friday sermon to strengthen its position, the junta has regulated the activities of the *tariqas* in order to weaken their control over their 3 million followers.

The government touches the life of the Egyptian as it never has before, making economic decisions for him and changing even his daily life and ways. That is its aim. Much is done in the name of the people; the people have not yet taken much part in the process of government, except to give a Nasserite ticket infrequent, if wholehearted, support. Yet there are problems of the past and future that must be solved before the people can effectively participate in government. One is the political lethargy of the Egyptians—the centuries-old habit of being governed. Recognition of this weakness is a frequent theme in Nasser's *Philosophy of the Revolution* and his subsequent speeches. The other is the booming population, which has increased by 5 million in the last ten years. Plans for social democracy, which are to permit effective participation in a political democratic system, hinge on doubling the national income during the decade of the 1960's and then, during the 1970's, reclaiming new land and making electricity available throughout the country with power produced by the Aswan High Dam. Yet both of these projects, which put heavy strains on the efforts of the people, government, and economy, will only amount to running hard to stand still if the current population increase of 2.5 per cent continues. In such a situation, political and social democracy may remain as elusive in the future as it has been in the past.

Nasser's Laws and Policies

Egypt has been through two constitutions since the revolution and is starting on its third.* An early proposal for a constitution, drawn up by a body of fifty jurists and providing for parliamentary government, was rejected by the members of the RCC, who then drew up the 1956 constitution themselves. This document proclaimed Egypt an Arab nation with a socialist system and a Muslim state religion. Government was organized on a presidential system, with legislative powers and political control in the hands of the President. The 1958 constitution proclaimed the U.A.R. as an "Arab, constitutional, democratic republic," consisting of Egypt and Syria and open to membership of other Arab states. Freedom was guaranteed within the law; election was declared the right of citizens within the law, and participation in public life their patriotic duty. The rule of law was proclaimed, the right of private property safeguarded, and an independent judiciary guaranteed.

* The last prerevolutionary constitution was adopted in 1923.

Legislative powers were to be given to a National Council, executive powers to the President. In fact, institutional implementation of this document was only being planned when the U.A.R. fell apart, and the rights and duties of citizens had reality only as goals and not as reflections of a going system. The National Action Charter of 1962 is equally bold as a statement of principles, but the same gaps between future goals and present practice remain. A "final" constitution is in preparation for application in 1963. Provision will be made for a parliament "with the highest authority," and a President with a fixed term; a cabinet with a Prime Minister has already been created. As yet, however, Egypt is still under the rule of men rather than of law.

The position of law-enforcement agencies in Egypt still reflects the revolutionary situation. The courts are in the process of being reformed; customary courts judging civil cases according to the *shariaa* have been abolished, and the many judicial bodies inherited by the junta are being standardized on a single national system. Judges are nominated by the Interior Minister and appointed by Nasser. A number of military and special courts have sat to try enemies of the regime. Probably the most notorious among these were the Muslim Brotherhood trials of 1954, the conspiracy trials of 1957, and the trials of French diplomats in 1961–62. Justice of this type reflects the views of the regime on democracy. In 1957, Mohiaddin stated, "All citizens are equal before the law and the government. . . . When we speak of freedom, we speak of freedom for sincere citizens, not of freedom for conspirators and reactionary citizens." There is no judicial review; Egyptian law is still based on the Napoleonic Code.

The police, too, are agents of the regime. In daily life, their hand is not heavy, but they are assisted by a well-developed organization of secret police. The six-year disappearance of Nagib in comfortable house arrest is the most famous example of political detention, but many other political prisoners remain in jail for long periods awaiting trial. To the average Egyptian, despite Nasser's broad political control and his deep regulation of social customs, Egypt is still far from a regime of totalitarian terror. Yet power has only changed hands; the clearly stated liberal aims of the revolution have not been implemented.

Probably the most publicized breach of civil liberties—as generally construed to include property as well as life and liberty—has been the series of confiscations which, since mid-1961, have struck the old Egyptian aristocracy, Levantine merchants, and foreigners. Confiscation actually began in 1953 with the first agrarian reform, and extended to certain foreign properties in 1956 after the Suez crisis. However, it was not until July, 1961, when the program of Arab socialism went into high gear, that banks, insurance companies, transportation lines, the cotton export industry, pharmaceutical distributors, utilities, some hotels, and other "essential enterprises" were nationalized. Compensation was made in each case by fifteen-year government bonds bearing 4 per cent interest. The government decides in individual cases how much personal wealth, up to a limit of $40,000 annually, may be retained by original owners. Stock ownership is limited to $29,000. Other industries —commerce, textiles, fertilizers, construction, oil, and cotton—have been reorganized with the controlling ownership in government hands.

Efforts to homogenize society have left minority groups out in the cold in more than just economic matters. The xenophobia that has welled up in Egypt in the past is now primarily directed at the French, who have largely left Egypt; but other European minorities—the British and even the 70,000 Greek and 30,000 Italian residents of cosmopolitan cities such as Alexandria—are also feeling pressure to leave. Arrests of Jews for espionage during the Suez crisis and an inhospitable atmosphere have encouraged the disappearance of the Egyptian Jewish colony. Even the Christian Copts, who comprise about 7 per cent of the Egyptian population, are implicitly ignored in growing discussions of an Islamic community. Egyptian businessmen provided the glitter of Cairo and Alexandria and the strength of the Egyptian economy—but also the support for the monarchy and the opposition to Arab socialism; they are therefore specific targets of the new mood of austerity.

The 100,000-man army, supplied with Russian and Czech arms, and its 2,000 officers in the biennial parades in Cairo are still a regular reminder that the regime rests on power more constant than that of the "street." The army remains the privileged class, and has been criticized by Nasser for showing class-conscious superiority. Nasser's own austere army life, reflected even today in his personal habits, governs his expectations for his fellow officers. The Egyptian Army is nationalistic, religious, and loyal—in most cases, devotedly so. Yet, following the defection of Syria, there were signs of unrest even among some army units. Anti-regime literature, particularly critical of socialism and Syria, circulated among officers of old middle-class families, and the army was subjected to security checks, enforced rotation and retirement, and even rumored arrests. Military figures are not always pleased with the civilian and police tasks that they have been assigned, although sporadic dissatisfaction is far from open unrest.

Domestic policies dominate the government's attention and center on the creation of Arab socialism with the greatest possible speed. Some of these policies are designed to speed industrialization and liberate the economy from its dependence on cotton. In recent years, the cotton crop has been mortgaged to Russia to pay for costly arms purchases and other assistance. The 1961 crop, however, was struck by—ironically—an army worm invasion,* and Egypt was for the first time forced to turn to the United States to supplement its major crop. Industrial production, growing at the annual rate of 7 per cent, rose to over $3 million in 1961 (thus passing the agricultural sector) and is supposed to double by 1970.[10] European firms and an aid program from both the United States and the U.S.S.R. have helped industrialization and agricultural needs. The proudest spot in the present economy is the Suez Canal, which nets $12 million annually and in 1961 grossed $152 million; an annual 5 per cent increase in gross receipts has been the trend since nationalization in July, 1956.

The policy of Arab socialism also brings with it problems that both foreign observers and, to an extent, the Egyptian regime have recognized. Nasser has always been wary of the huge Egyptian bureaucracy, and yet his plans for government control of the growing economy demand an expanding bureaucratic machine. Civilian management has often been kept on the job in nationalized industries, and the army, too, has been pressed into service. However, Egypt continues to lack the foreign exchange necessary for its programs, and capital and businessmen continue to leave the country. Another drain on the economy is the unnecessarily high military budget, which has cost Egypt over $2 billion since the revolution.

The hope of the future is the 300-foot-high, 3-mile-long Aswan High Dam. Since 1958, the Soviet Union has been lending the first $400 million of this $1 billion project, and work has continued at an uneven pace. When finished in the early 1970's, the dam will per-

---

* The bureaucratic worm also worsened the affair, through the "Toxafine scandal." Three-quarters of the budget for insecticide disappeared in 1961, and the spray was watered down. Nasser, as a result, called for a law that would provide the death penalty for the crime of negligence.

mit the irrigation of 1 million new acres and the year-round cultivation of 700,000 acres now only seasonally farmed; however, the
250-mile-long reservoir behind the dam will not be full before an
additional five years have passed. Three rising figures race against
each other: the Nile, the dam, and the population.

In foreign policy, Nasser has been the leading neutralist figure
on the African continent, with fortunes and policies closely tied
to the milestones of neutralism.[11] He was the major African leader
at Bandung in 1955, where his warm reception and contact with
other leaders infused him with new ideas and ambitions. As a
newcomer to neutralist leadership, he was the most eager participant in the Brioni talks the next year, associating with Tito and
Nehru, already established spokesmen for a nonaligned policy. In
the Suez affair of October, 1956, he capitalized on his rescue by
the United States, the U.S.S.R., and the United Nations from the
hands of the British, French, and Israelis, and thereby increased
his prestige. Similarly, his ability to win aid from the Communist
bloc—from the Czech arms of 1955, through the Russian 20-kilo-
watt reactor, to the renewed Russian arms shipments of 1961—
without compromising his independence or weakening his internal
campaign against the Egyptian (and Syrian) Communists made
him a living proof of the success of neutralism. In September, 1961,
he was a sponsoring participant in the Belgrade Conference of
Nonaligned States, and since then he has increased his contacts
with Tito, to the encouragement of state socialism and of neutralism.

After the secession of Syria, Nasser pulled in the horns of his
Pan-Arab foreign policy and broke relations with Yemen, Saudi
Arabia, Turkey, Syria, and Jordan, in moves in most cases dictated
by a socialist dislike for traditional monarchies instead of a neutralist dislike for Cold War moderates. When the imamate was
overthrown in Yemen in October, 1962, and the secessionist government was replaced in Syria the following March, Nasser took
quick advantage of the new situation, and extended recognition
and active support. The overthrow of the Iraqi government by
Arab unionists, in February, 1963, opened the possibility of unity
among ideologically compatible partners, and in April a declaration of constitutional principles, largely inspired by Nasser's ideas,
was signed by Egyptian, Syrian, and Iraqi representatives. The
new tripartite U.A.R. was to become reality after a referendum to
be held no later than September, 1963; but in the months that fol-

lowed the initial declaration, serious differences arose among the three countries. More significant has been the mutual admiration and cooperation that has grown up between Algeria and Egypt. Although Ben Bella has refused for the moment to join an Arab Union, Nasser's influence in Algeria is a strong, new element in northern African politics.

Little has been new in Nasser's decade of domestic policies. There is scarcely a measure—including agrarian reform, the High Dam, and parliamentary elections—that had not been discussed or even tried before the revolution. The junta's contribution up to 1961—besides the destruction of the monarchy and the creation of the U.A.R.—was to bring to these plans an *élan* and energy that carried them toward fruition. But by 1961, the revolution was in danger of being spent in the vigorous energies of foreign policy, from which the Egyptian people benefited not at all.

The renewal of the revolution in 1961, with its attention directed to Egypt's pressing domestic problems, showed responsiveness to a number of pressures. There was general criticism, inside and outside Egypt, that the revolution up till then had not amounted to much. There was a sudden awareness by Nasser—probably upon studying the 1960 census—that a doubling of national income in the decade of the 1960's would be impossible at the present economic and population growth rates, and that something would have to be done. Increased contacts with Tito also appear to have influenced Nasser to adopt a policy that pays more attention to domestic problems.

Nasser's policies—foreign and domestic—have been extremely popular among the Egyptians, and Nasser, with his renewal of the revolution, has returned the favor by paying attention to the condition of the people. Nasser's speeches and actions do strike a responsive chord in the hearts of his people. On the other hand, the population does not know specifically what it wants, and knows only generally what it wants corrected;* it only knows that it wants Nasser. And Nasser is by no means content to ride aimlessly on the wave of popularity; he wants to harness and channel it. Nasser's self-appointed task is thus immense; his greatest asset

---

* Sheikh Mohammed al-Ghazali, a member of the National Congress, discussed the shame of women going unveiled, and told the Congress, "This must not be permitted in a socialist state"—a striking example of the uncomprehending use of modern symbols by a traditionalist figure (*The New York Times,* June 3, 1962).

is that he is aware of its complexity. He must bring economic, social, and political development to the people as a whole, so that they can conceive of their wants and needs in realistic terms. He must develop the capacities of his government so that he can fulfill these needs and wants and make "dignity" a reality. He must build up the bridges between government and people, so that popular wishes and needs can be transmitted to the elite and results can ensue. So far, Nasser has been successful in divining those things "written on the hearts of the Arab people," but he goes about this by guess and feel. The revolution has only begun.

VII

SUDAN

The Republic of Sudan was born on New Year's Day, 1956, but a turning point of greater importance in the country's political life was the military *coup d'état* of November 17, 1958. Since that time, government in Sudan has borne superficial and misleading similarities to the neighboring Nasserite regime. Comparison with Egypt is as irksome to the Sudanese as it is deceptive. Essentially, Nasser controls both the government and the politics of Egypt; in Sudan, Marshal Abboud controls his government, but only the promised return to parliamentarianism will reveal how effective has been his attempt to reshape Sudanese politics. Furthermore, the military has never been an intellectual elite in Sudan, as it has in Egypt. For this reason, the junta's attempt to create an ideology has met with only amused contempt from the Sudanese intelligentsia.*

The development of national consciousness in Sudan has greater similarities to other northern African countries who achieved independence the same year. Like Morocco, Sudan had been plunged into a xenophobic religious revolt at the end of the nineteenth century, resulting in foreign occupation. The messianic movement of Mohammed Ahmed al-Mahdi in 1881 set up the Mahdist state, which was not overthrown until seventeen years later.[1] As in Morocco and Tunisia, new and modern elites were in training during more than half a century of colonial presence. But the comparison ends there. The theocratic succession of the Mahdi and the institutions of his state were immediately suppressed by the colonial power; paradoxically though, the underlying social

* I am grateful to P. M. Holt for calling this point to my attention.

forces of the last century—the religious sects—continued to dominate Sudanese politics with greater tenacity than traditional forces
in the Maghreb.

Although the Anglo-Egyptian Condominium Agreement of 1899
provided for equal governing responsibility of Sudan by the two
powers, this arrangement was possible only as long as one power
agreed with or dominated the other. After Egyptian independence
in 1922, the example of Egypt and differences between the colonial
policies of the two powers led to a rupture of the condominium in
all except name within two years' time. An early Sudanese nationalist movement which had turned to Egypt for support was
crushed by the British in 1924. Thereafter, Egypt had the luxury
of a double role: It was the dispossessed ruler of Sudan, and it was
a convenient source of support for purely Sudanese nationalism
against Britain.

The expulsion of Egyptians from Sudan's administration after
1924 left an increased number of posts open to Sudanese graduates
of secondary and higher schools, and in 1938 they formed an
alumni association of civil servants, dedicated to vague civic aims.
By 1942, this association, the Graduates' General Congress, had
dropped its political modesty and demanded self-determination
for Sudan after the war. Brusque rejection of this demand by
Britain sent the new nationalist middle class scattering in different directions for allies. One group (Ismail al-Azhari) founded the
first open political party—Ashiqqa (Full Brothers)—the following
year, and looked to Egypt for support. A more moderate group
(Abdullah Khalil) turned for support to the 1.5-million-member
Ansar religious sect that the Mahdi had founded, and formed a
second party—Umma (Islamic Community)—with the Mahdi's
grandson (Siddiq al-Mahdi) as its President and the Mahdi's son
(Abderrahman al-Mahdi) as its active patron. The Ashiqqa then
sought association with the rival 1.5-million-member Khatmiya
sect (Ali al-Mirghani), which had been the dominant influence
under the Egypto-Turkish rule, before the Mahdist revolt. From
the start, nationalism brought to Sudan not the awakening of a
sense of national unity, but the factionalization of politics along
old religious lines and even over the matter of national independence itself; while the Umma looked to the creation of a national
state, the Ashiqqa ostensibly advocated Nilic unity with Egypt.

In the following years, the Umma cooperated with the British,
while the Ashiqqa turned toward Egypt. Continued disagreement

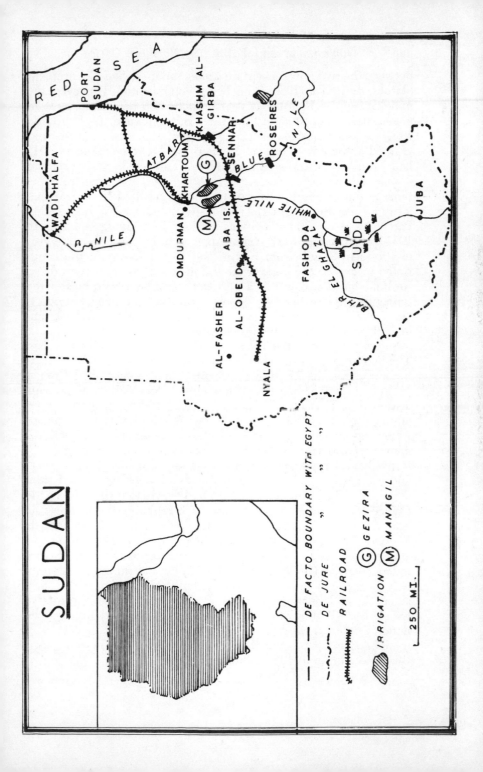

SUDAN

DE FACTO BOUNDARY WITH EGYPT
DE JURE   "   "   "
RAILROAD
IRRIGATION   G GEZIRA
             M MANAGIL
250 MI.

between the two powers kept an Anglo-Sudanese Self-Government Statute, drafted in 1952, from being implemented. However, the military coup in Egypt that year brought into being an Egyptian government interested in Sudanese independence. In February, 1953, a joint agreement accepted the amended Statute and granted autonomy to Sudan. Limited legislative elections in 1948 had been boycotted by the unionists, resulting in a government dominated by the Umma; now, in November, 1953, general elections to the first full-powered parliament resulted in a clear majority for the reconstituted Ashiqqa—renamed the National Union Party (NUP). Factionalism was not long in bringing violence. In 1954 and 1955, followers of the Umma rioted against the state visit of President Nagib from Egypt, and Negro troops in the south rioted to protest the imposition of national unity on a centralized Arab model. It was in this atmosphere, and largely to bolster the falling prestige of the NUP government, that the former supporters of Nilic union passed a resolution in parliament in mid-December, 1955, declaring Sudan independent.

Sudan came to independence in the midst of a political crisis. The main forces in the country included a weakened NUP, drifting away from its Khatmiya supporters, and a continued Umma-Ansar cooperation that left little room for non-Mahdist opponents of the NUP. There was no common coin of national unity—either ethnic, socio-economic, or psychological. There was no leader of stature to serve as a national symbol; the top religious and political figures were personifications of sectarianism rather than of unity. Radicals and gradualists, unionists and nationalists, northerners and southerners, Khatmiya and Ansar—all were "separated from one another by so broad an intellectual divide that there was little chance of any traffic moving across it."[2] Probably the most stable group was the Sudanese civil service, which had grown into its job since 1924. During the 1940's, the process of Sudanization was accelerated, and it was nearly completed in the two years before independence. The effectiveness of education among a narrow elite gave the civil service stability, but it also widened the characteristic gap between the ruling class and the still primitive tribes. For all these forces, independence changed little of the nation's political life.[3] It was merely one—and not the last—of a number of regularly spaced steps of governmental evolution across the uneven ground of factionalism.

Military and Political Leaders

The newly independent Sudanese state was headed by a five-member Supreme Commission, appointed by parliament and presided over by a monthly rotating chairmanship. Leadership of government was vested in a Prime Minister chosen by parliament and responsible for his cabinet, along the classic lines of British parliamentary tradition. But since the rise and fall of governments depended not on changing electoral fortunes but on changing political constellations revolving about rival personalities, the parliamentary system was a system of elite maneuvering, not of popular responsibility. Scarcely had independence been won when Azhari was forced to broaden his coalition to include important opposition leaders, and in July, 1956, a new coalition government replaced him entirely and put the NUP in the opposition. The uneasy alliance that reigned between 1956 and 1958 under Khalil gave a superficial semblance of stability. Underneath, serious differences in foreign policy and personal rivalries made governing difficult and serious programs unlikely. Apparent stability fostered corruption. The profits of political power flowed uphill into the hands of the ruling coalition, instead of benefiting the nation. When negotiations began in 1958 for a broader coalition, former unionists reverted to the pre-independence tactic of seeking Egyptian support; in August, 1958, a military coup under Khalil was forestalled.* In this situation, governing was not so much the work of a cabinet of ministers or a parliament of politicians as it was the work of the civil service, a small group of some 6,000, relatively free of corruption, who neither guided nor represented the country, but administered it.

In time, the political elite might have worked itself out of this situation of irresponsible maneuvering on its own initiative, and in fact, during November, 1958, agreement was reached among Umma-NUP leaders for the creation of a broad coalition. But the role of Egypt in this *rapprochement* was still suspect, the basis for cooperation within the coalition was uncertain, and its promise of government responsive to the Sudanese people was unassured. Before the new coalition could be announced, a bloodless *coup d'état* was carried out by the Sudanese Army, and all parliamentary institutions were dissolved.[4]

* Khalil was a former colleague of Abboud's in the officers' corps and the first Sudanese to attain the rank of general.

The powers of the disbanded Supreme Commission as head of state were assumed by the Supreme Council of the Armed Forces, made up of senior officers, with General Ibrahim Abboud, the commander-in-chief, as its President. The Supreme Council delegated all executive, legislative, judicial, and military powers to Abboud, and created a Council of Ministers to assist him. As seven of the ministers are also members of the Supreme Council, there is permanent liaison between the two councils. The Supreme Council is the organ for the formulation of policy, which the Council of Ministers implements through legislation. Both act as collegial bodies, although ministers can pass decrees without cabinet approval if they follow Supreme Council policy. Ministers who are not members of the Supreme Council tend to be simply department heads; one element of strength of the regime is still the efficient administration.

Abboud has not acted with the autocracy or the assurance of a military dictator, and, as frequently happens among collective leaders, the ruling junta has not been free of internal changes and divisions. The initial Council of Ministers was almost evenly split between Ansar and Khatmiya, and at least three officers (Abboud; his uncle, Interior Minister Ahmed Abdulwahab; and Presidential Affairs Minister Hassan Bashir Nasr) had large enough personal followings within the junta to be considered potential strong men. Less than six months after the army coup, in March, 1959, two other officers used the same tactics of military pressure to gain entry into the junta and to eliminate Abdulwahab.* However, before the end of the year, a renewed attempt by the same pair to use military pressure against the remaining conservative leadership failed; the two officers were themselves eliminated and given life imprisonment, and the Supreme Council was reduced to its present size of seven. The incipient tradition of military pressure was brought to an abrupt halt in December, 1959, when another attempted coup ended in the trial and execution of five officers. Since then, the junta has been stable. A cabinet change in December, 1962, brought only a reshuffling of portfolios, not a change of personnel.

---

* This group, rather than the generals' junta, could be compared in some respects to the liberal *bikbashis* (colonels) of Nasser's regime, whom they resembled. Although presently well under control, the large number (400) of rapidly trained junior officers poses a potential threat to the junta if its success wanes.

The forms of parliamentarianism were highly developed in Sudan when the military coup wiped out representative government. The first partially elected Assembly, with a parliamentary cabinet as its offspring, came into existence as a result of Britain's usual practice of gradually introducing parliamentary institutions to its colonial dependencies. The Self-Government Statute of 1953 brought in the second step with the creation of the bicameral parliament, elected with the participation of all parties. Three-quarters of the House of Representatives' ninety-seven seats were filled by direct election; members from the least developed areas were elected by their provincial assemblies. This initiation of parliamentary government also marked the nearly total disappearance of traditional leaders of the northern tribes from the national political leadership.

The first parliament dominated Sudanese politics for five years. Its first session, in 1954, was calm and businesslike; its second session, scheduled for the same year, was postponed because of the state of emergency occasioned by the riots against President Nagib's visit. The following year, the parliament played a decisive role in the adoption of a transitional constitution and in setting up conditions for the transfer of power to an independent Sudan, taking time off from these problems in the fall of 1955 to defeat, and then quickly reinstate, Azhari's government. In the process, Azhari succeeded in having parliament revoke its old orders; instead of holding a referendum on independence and at the same time an election of a Constituent Assembly, the existing House and Senate under Azhari's regime would both declare independence by vote and rule the country.

The second parliament, elected in February and March, 1958, had a lower house of 173 seats, nearly twice as large as its predecessor; the 20 (out of 50) appointed members of the Senate were chosen by the Supreme Commission on nomination by the parties. The House of Representatives' regional composition was also altered to give greater representation to the populous center of the country, and the increased number of seats theoretically provided for closer contact between representative and constituency (averaging 60,000). To avoid renewed problems over the formation of a Constituent Assembly, parliament itself was to pass on the newly proposed constitution. The life of the second parliament was short and complex. An economic crisis, a controversy over a U.S. economic and technical aid agreement, a fundamental clash of conceptions on the constitution, and shifting party alliances over all these issues ended with the ratification of the aid agreement and suspension of parliament to avoid a no-confidence vote in July, 1958. It was this maneuvering among the parties in the six months following the elections that led to the formation of a new governing coalition and, before it could take office, to the military coup.

After two and a half years in which no representative institutions were permitted, the government has again been attempting to build up an understanding of republican government—this time on the intermediate level. In late 1960, a Provincial Act decentralized local government by giving health, education, and welfare powers to the provinces. In June, 1961, the nine provincial councils—appointed bodies that had their origins in the condominium —were given deliberative powers to govern the provinces with the military governor, who is also chairman of the council. A year and a half later, on the fourth anniversary of the revolution, Abboud announced the creation of a similar Central Council for a fixed term of two years, with 24 appointed members and 48 members elected by the provincial councils. Ministers are automatically members. The Central Council has the power to debate and suggest laws, authorize ratification of treaties, review the budget, and, eventually, approve the constitution. Elections have also been promised for the future selection of provincial councils, but as yet, all governing power is in the hands of the junta and its appointees. The idea behind the plans is to create unity and awareness of civic problems on the provincial level, before bridging the gap between local individuals and national institutions, rather than to create a superficial semblance of republicanism that would, in fact, be only an opportunity for factionalism among a small isolated elite.

Meanwhile, the now unemployed representative elite has been restive. Ten of the leading parliamentary figures, including Azhari and Khalil, were detained in comfortable seclusion from June, 1961, to January, 1962, in Juba, far to the south, where they had little opportunity for political work or press contact. Their arrest was occasioned by a campaign for restoration of parliamentarianism that began in November, 1960, with a petition by nineteen political leaders for the return of the state to democracy and the officers to their barracks. The removal of the political leaders from the scene helped limit their influence, although they still retain some of their following.

The ideas of the military leadership, as expressed by Abboud, are clearly oriented toward preparing the country for democracy and returning government to civilian hands when "all the revolution's aims are fulfilled." In the meantime, the government considers itself not an order imposed on the people, but an expression of popular will against partisan corruption, a frequently found use of populism to rationalize tutelary regimes. The President has said: "A good government is one which can realize the aspirations of the citizens for social justice, economic revival, internal stability, complete union of all national sectors, and maintenance of good relations with all countries. . . . Sudan is a democratic republic with full sovereignty of the people." The day of the revolution, November 17—rather than the anniversary of independence —is the major national holiday, and the junta has attempted to give "the revolution" importance as a national symbol. In its public pronouncements, the junta identifies itself with the people, and speeches by its commander-in-chief have officially been called "a true expression of the voice of the Sudanese people and indeed the voice of the Arab nation and the African continent"—a rather substantial claim. A minister has said, "The revolution will crush anyone who tries to hinder its progress, since it is the will of the people."

Another important theme in the junta's governmental views is the lengthy process of preparing the people for democratic participation—"the transformation of our different and backward regions until we eradicate all trace of the past and until they develop sufficiently to participate with us in building the future. We shall always be worried as long as an important segment of the population remains nomadic, remote from the centers of education and health." As a result, the junta views its role in terms of concrete aims and real problems in the nature of the Sudanese nation. Perhaps the most serious of these is the social gap that was the ultimate sanction, if not cause, of the corrupt and factional system of government before the coup. "Our economic development should be directed to the welfare of the people as a whole and not just to the benefit of a few," the President has said. "Foreign aid should be limited to serving as a propelling force to revitalize stagnant factors of production and awaken dormant resources for the take-off. . . . It should fill a temporary gap in our economy and not become a permanent substitute for our own efforts." Rather than encourage a hasty return to representative government, the regime seeks to present itself as the embodiment of a redefined and superior brand of democracy—as the correct interpretation of both popular needs and desires.

Parties Without Participation

There is as yet no open channel for public participation in Sudanese government. The basic obstacle lies in the primitive nature of the population, but also there has never been much attention given to preparing the people for participation in political life or to developing any institution to act as a responsible mouthpiece for the people. Tribal society still predominates in the desert west and north and in the tropical south. An extensive rail network is in continual expansion, but roads are few and bad; yet Sudan is the largest country in Africa. Of the 11.6 million people, 4 per cent are literate, and fewer than 4 per cent live in urban areas of more than 100,000 population. As a whole, in the present state of things, the people seem content to let the revolution run its course, for it is doing more for the people in terms of socio-economic well-being than did the parliamentary regime.

The best-organized segment of the population is urban labor, grouped into more than 150 unions covering all types of trades. The first union was formed in 1946 among the railway workers, and the Sudan Workers Trade Union Federation (SWTUF) was created by the railway union in 1950. By the time of independence, half the wage earners were organized. The SWTUF, cooperating with the Communist-dominated World Federation of Trade Unions (WFTU), but a member of the Egypt-dominated International Confederation of Arab Trade Unions (ICATU) and the All-African Trade Union Federation, has been the controlling factor of nearly three-quarters of Sudanese labor. A rival Sudan Government Workers Trade Union Federation (SGWTUF) was formed in 1956 under government sponsorship, and in 1958 it joined the International Confederation of Free Trade Unions. All unions were suspended after the coup, and SWTUF leaders were imprisoned, although liberal legislation on labor welfare benefits, begun under the British, was continued by the junta. However, in areas of SWTUF penetration, and particularly among the railway workers, there is growing criticism of the government, stemming either from labor's past radical nationalist stand or from disruptive Communist tactics.

In June, 1961, a serious railworkers' strike was called to protest against the junta's rejection of the memorandum appealing for a return to civilian government. This was only one manifestation of a weapon that has been widely used and even respected in the past as a means of bringing direct pressure on the government.* In addition to the strike, public marches on Khartoum are a time-honored means of showing strength in the absence of democratic processes. On the deposition of General Abdulwahab, the Ansar marched from the Mahdist center on Abba island to the capital, and were received by Abderrahman al-Mahdi and recognized by the Interior Minister—although to no avail. The small degree of urbanization, however, has kept Sudanese demonstrations from having the power of the "street" in the Middle East.

There are other groups that claim or, for limited segments of the population, act to bridge the gap between government leaders and the mass. The most vocal of these are still the political parties. Although they have all been legally dissolved, they continue to do their best to be heard. The great weakness of the parties lies in their attempt to reach the population through the intermediary of the religious leaders—al-Mahdi and al-Mirghani—thus putting modern instruments of political participation in the hands of traditional groups and leaders.

Only Azhari, with his personal support in the towns, has been able to establish an independent following; he even made cabinet changes between 1953 and 1956, against the wishes of the religious leaders. In the 1958 elections, however, Azhari's NUP won 45 seats in the 173-member House (as opposed to 51 out of 97 in 1953) and 5 (compared with 21) of the 30 elected seats in the Senate. Azhari continued his pro-Egyptian appeals, at least outwardly, and met with Nasser in October, 1958; at the same time, however, negotiations with the Umma over a new coalition were reaching fruition. The military coup which prevented Azhari from coming back to power was naturally a target of his criticism. After the November, 1960, memorandum calling for a return to democracy, Azhari was deported with other politicians to Juba, and the temporary passing of the party's leadership was not openly protested in the atmosphere of government control.

* An average of 30,000 man-days per month were lost in strikes between 1952 and 1954 (see *Africa Report*, IV, No. 1 [January, 1959], 12). It should be noted that violence in Sudan has not had the anticolonial character common to Egypt or the Maghreb, but has generally been a factor of intra-Sudanese politics.

The faction of the party that left the NUP in 1956 was made up of parliamentary elements jealous of Azhari's power and sympathetic to the Khatmiya sect, which had formerly supported him. The dissident representatives formed the Peoples Democratic Party (PDP) under the leadership of Ali al-Mirghani, head of the Khatmiya, and joined forces with the Umma to form the new government. Its *raison d'être* was personal, and its policies followed the pro-Egyptian and anti-Western attitudes of the NUP. In 1958, the PDP won twenty-seven seats in the House (which, added to the forty-five of the NUP, indicated a drop in popular support since 1953) and four of the elected Senate seats. The Khatmiya are numerous in northern and eastern Sudan. In the subsequent maneuvering, two PDP ministers also met with Nasser in October, 1958, but seemed to be outside the impending Umma-NUP coalition. The coup was therefore welcomed by al-Mirghani, but at least one leader who had talked to Nasser (Ali Abderrahman) was among the deportees after the 1960 memorandum. The sect remains, but the party has lost its influence, at least for the moment.

The Umma Party has remained the most constant element in Sudanese politics. It benefits from its close ties with the Ansar sect, strong in the region of the White Nile and in the western part of the country; the Mahdi's grandson (al-Hadi al-Mahdi, half-brother of Siddiq) is head of the party and of the sect. Although the Umma won only twenty-two seats in the House and three elected seats in the Senate in 1953—largely because of Egyptian propaganda and the party's association with Britain in the public mind —Khalil created a coalition with the PDP after independence and ruled until the military coup. In the 1958 elections, his policy was vindicated; the Umma won sixty-three seats in the House and fourteen elected seats in the Senate. But his coalition was one of political expediency only, and it took great maneuvering to reconcile the Umma's pro-Western stand with the ideas of the PDP. The same problems would have been evident in the projected Umma-NUP coalition, and Khalil's place was not secure in the proposed 1958 government. At the same time, the Umma's reliance on the Ansar led it to advocate a position of life presidency of the republic for Abderrahman al-Mahdi (which the Khatmiya-affiliated PDP rejected) and a unitary constitution (which the southerners rejected). There is reasonable evidence that Khalil and General Abdulwahab worked together to plan the military coup and save the country from "chaos" and "the aggressor in the

Middle East"—Egypt. Siddiq and Khalil were outspokenly critical of the junta's policies, and joined in the November, 1960, manifesto. Siddiq died in September, 1961; al-Hadi has thus far been circumspect in his politics, and in November, 1961, he pledged his "cooperation and confidence" to Abboud.

The Southern Liberal Party (SLP) was a regional-interest group whose freewheeling politics made and broke governments without offering a program for stability. It was founded in 1953 among politicians from the southern provinces, with little agreement even on its own leader. It helped unseat Azhari and put Khalil into power in 1956, won twenty seats in the House and a few in the Senate in 1958 (other southerners won eighteen in the House and a few more Senate seats), but was subsequently passed over in favor of the dissident southerners when cabinet posts were distributed. The SLP then joined in a federal bloc with other southerners to push local interests in the opposition. Although it represented its region, it had no grass-roots organization as a party, even in the south.

The best-organized party, even after the coup, has been the Communists' Sudanese Movement for National Liberation. Founded in 1944 among Sudanese students in Egypt, it has been outlawed since the condominium, but is still active among students and labor. On the Anti-Imperialist Front ticket, the Communists elected one member in the special graduates' constituency[5] in 1953 and none in 1958, but their organizational skill—despite the ban on parties and the arrest of Communist leaders—has given them influence in clubs, groups, unions, and associations. The Communists were accused of complicity in the last attempted coup, in 1959, but by 1961 their diminished importance was shown by the government's disparagement of their role in the railworkers' strike of that year.

The press is another influence that serves to bridge the social gap. There are about three dozen newspapers in Sudan, but illiteracy limits their circulation, the government limits their freedom, and their area of contact is extremely small. Charges by Khalil and Abboud that the press was Egyptian-controlled and heavily partisan before the coup go far to justify the tight restrictions under which it currently operates.

Elections are also a means of bringing about public participation in government, but the two national elections in Sudan did little to foster this aim. Voting was carried on in primitive conditions in the tribal areas; constituencies favored tribal interests by often following tribal boundaries. Only adult males were enfranchised. Trading votes for cloth, money, and food was common, and much voting was done simply on the basis of personalities or religious sects. There was little appeal to the population in terms of programs.

In the socio-economic field, Sudan's imaginative and successful irrigation project, the 1.5-million-acre Gezira Scheme,[6] has in recent times provided more than half of the government revenue (the government and the tenants each own 42 per cent of the cotton crop) and has produced some progress in civic education. Management is left in the hands of the Sudan Gezira Board, a nationalized planning company which also has a 10-per-cent share in the crop, and the farmers are left to follow instructions. However, the fact that 500,000 people are supported by work in a modernizing sector of agriculture under competent management is already a sign of progress among what is normally the most backward economic group. The addition of side benefits, such as cinemas, cooperatives, schools, and newspapers, and, above all, the creation of village councils, has brought training in responsibility and participation to the cotton growers of central Sudan. The balance of cotton-sales proceeds is allocated to social development, the local councils, and a tenants' reserve fund.

Law in a Benevolent Dictatorship

Sudan has stepped back into the statutory stage of legal evolution, but the rule of law still exists. Just before independence, the parliament adopted a transitional constitution, based largely on the Self-Government Statute of 1953. The transitional constitution provided for a parliamentary cabinet, the Supreme Commission as head of state, and a new constitution to be submitted to the parliament elected in 1958. In September, 1956, a National Constitutional Committee was appointed to work out a constitution providing for a unitary state with an elected head and a continuation of the British-modeled cabinet system, with the government appointed by the head of state but responsible to the lower house of a bicameral parliament. Southerners' demands for consideration of a federal system were given little heed, but some northerners' desires to establish an Islamic republic based on the *shariaa* were likewise rejected, along with Ansar demands for a hereditary position for the Mahdi's descendant.

The military coup suspended the constitution and the Committee, and the Supreme Council of the Armed Forces immediately fulfilled its functions as new head of state by issuing three "constitutional decrees." The second and third named the composition of the Supreme Council and the Council of Ministers, and the first declared that the "Sudan is a democratic republic in which all legislation is promulgated in the name of the sovereign people" and "the Supreme Council is the supreme constitutional organism of the state." It was only on the third anniversary of the revolution, however, that Abboud announced that the creation of the Central Council would be followed by "a national committee to draw up a constitution . . . embodying the basic principles and rights to strengthen the creation of a true parliamentary life after general elections. By this we shall attain our true aim of building the foundations of true democracy after having insulated it from the mistakes of the past."

The legal system in Sudan is dual. Modern law is based on British codes and ordinances from 1900. The modern court system is headed by a chief justice and judges of the High Court, a Court of Appeal, district courts in civil matters, and major and minor courts in criminal affairs. The *shariaa* is the civil law of the Muslim north, and the *shariaa* court system is headed by a Grand Qadi and administered by *qadis* (judges) trained in Muslim law. The judiciary is independent and apolitical. Military tribunals have also been used since the coup to judge offenders of the junta's regulations.

Civil liberties are largely in suspension under the military junta. When the coup took place, all newspapers, public gatherings, demonstrations, and associations were banned, and similar emergency decrees have been reapplied at frequent intervals since then. Travel outside Sudan was made subject to authorization by the Interior Ministry in December, 1959. Although there has been very little loss of life for political reasons during or since the coup, most important political leaders, and even some high military figures, have been summarily retired on pension or put under house arrest from time to time. An unlimited detention act is part of the emergency regulations in force since 1958. Newspapers have occasionally been suspended for violating the Interior Ministry's press regulations, and the radio is government-controlled. Through its control and guidance of public demonstrations, associations, and communication media, the government hopes to provide the educational function that the partisan regime lacked. None of the suspensions appears to have been arbitrary or long-lasting, and all government control action has a legal basis. But the arrests of politicians are justified only in terms of the "general interest" as opposed to "dark conspiracies, fabricating lies, and distorting facts"—a charge that is credible, even if broad, in the current context.

Sudan's major minorities problem is not so much one of a suppressed group with unequal rights as one of an ethnic segment that wishes to maintain its own identity. Out of the 12 million Sudanese, some 3.5 million are southern Negroes who are neither Muslim nor Arab, neither townsmen nor tribal nomads, as are the people of the north. The southerner protests against administration by northerners, against the creation of a unitary state under a dominant Muslim legal and social tradition, and against his own lack of representation in local and national government. However, since the coup, talk of federalism and general southern demands have been silenced, several southerners have been imprisoned for threatening violence in the name of federalism, and Christian missionaries have been expelled. Secessionist movements have set up offices in Tanganyika and London since 1961, and opposition has increased. There is one southerner (Santino Deng, Minister of Animal Resources) in the government, although the custom in the past was to have three. The military government has sought to increase the economic development of the south through the Gezira-like Equatoria Project Board, and is carrying out a rapid takeover of missionary schools in the south for integration into the national Arabic language system. The "Sudanization" of the south means, in fact, the Arabization of Sudan and is consistent with government aims to foster national unity and identification as an Arab nation. It will, however, continue to evoke resentment among the subjects of the policy, until it finally attains a point of success.

Among the security forces, the police act as an apolitical instrument of the Interior Ministry. The position of the 8,000-man, British-trained and British-, Egyptian-, Russian-, and American-equipped army is very much more important. It is not only the ruling caste, but also a force that, four times in 1958 and 1959, decided the outcome of military leaders' challenges to governmental power. Sixty officers, including two generals, were dismissed and eighteen imprisoned through 1959. Since that time, there appear to have been no rifts in army leadership, and control of the military has been an effective dissuasion to violence and demonstrations by sectarian or partisan groups.

Within the framework of the rule of law, Abboud and the junta have tried to win over popular confidence through policies designed to overcome the weaknesses of Sudanese society, economy, and politics. The President has created the impression of providing disinterested government, responsible for its own strict standards of performance, but responsive to the evident problems of the country. The economic position of Sudan, which fell in the two years after independence partially through the fault of the government sales policy, has been stabilized; long-staple cotton, by far the dominant marketable product, is now again finding hard-currency markets, and since the *coup d'état*, over a hundred new industrial plants have been established to reduce the need to import. An Improved Enterprises Act was passed in 1956 to attract private-investment capital, but it was the junta that liberalized the trade policy in 1959 by removing quantitative controls.

The new regime's greatest triumph has been the Nile Waters Agreement of November, 1959, which allocates the lifeblood of Egypt and Sudan on a revised 75-25 per cent basis, with an additional margin for evaporation, an eighteen-year "loan" of unused Sudanese water to Egypt, and a complementary trade agreement. By this compact, which took five years to negotiate, work has been allowed to progress on the 830,000-acre Managil extension of the Gezira project, giving profitable employment to 50,000 more farmers' families since 1962. The Managil project, using water from the Sennar Dam, was supported by a $15 million loan by the World Bank in 1960; the next year, a $32 million loan from the Bank and the International Development Association made possible work on the Roseires Dam provided for in the Nile Waters Agreement, which will increase present yields and permit irrigation of 870,000 more acres when it is completed in 1968. Also in 1961, construction was begun on the Khashm al-Girba Dam, to irrigate 1 million new acres by 1963. Such projects lead to a dramatic extension of Sudanese agriculture, which in 1961 covered only 5 per cent of the 250 million potentially arable acres; it can also help to extend the benefits of political and economic development to a growing segment of the population.

In foreign policy, the junta has attempted to develop the concept of national interest, rather than to make foreign relations a servant of partisan maneuvering. This approach responds at least to analyses of popular dissatisfaction with the civilian government. There is, if anything, increased identification with Arab causes,* but greater independence from the policies of Egypt. Abboud has developed a policy of careful neutralism, and has exchanged state visits with Washington, Moscow, Cairo, and Belgrade. Sudan was represented at the Bandung Conference in 1955 and at the Belgrade Conference in 1961. In addition to accepting Western aid, Abboud has negotiated barter, trade, and technical-assistance agreements with the U.S.S.R., including a $22 million loan for factories and education in August, 1961.

Sudan's relations with neighbors other than Egypt are correct and uneventful. Following the Fashoda incident of 1898, the Nile-Congo watershed was established as Sudan's southwestern boundary, and this ragged line was extended north in a further Anglo-French convention in 1919. The boundary with the Congo was fixed at King Leopold's death in 1910, and the frontier with Kenya and Uganda in 1913–14. After independence was restored to Ethiopia, a boundary that had long been the scene of troubles was re-established along a line set up in 1902. In the north, the Condominium Agreement had put the frontier at 22°, modified subsequently in practice to allow Sudan to maintain a low-water steamer station north of Wadi Halfa on the Nile, and to allow Egyptian and Sudanese nomads to wander north and south of the line in two other places. This arrangement has worked for nearly half a century. The lake that will back up into Sudan behind the Aswan High Dam will obviate any problems over the Wadi Halfa enclave by submerging the entire area. However, during the U.A.R. referendum and Sudanese elections of February, 1958, Egypt moved in with troops to restore the straight-line boundary. When Sudan protested to the United Nations, the affair suddenly "blew away," without any definitive settlement.

Sudan is not democratically ruled, and never really has been. Under the parliamentary regime, it went through the motions of parliamentarianism; under the junta, this routine has ceased. On the other hand, there is little doubt that the present regime has been more beneficial to the country than its parliamentary predecessor. Some of its measures have been popular, while others—such as the continued Sudanization of the south—have been carried out in the best tradition of a benevolent dictatorship "for the good of the people." The regime has lasted longer than the politicians—

* Sudan joined the Arab League in 1956.

even those who claimed to be aware of preparations for the coup —expected or approve; yet it continues to proclaim, with a sincerity that can only be judged on the surface, that it has no desire to remain in power for long. There is nothing to indicate that the people are tired of being governed or are in any more hurry than the junta to return to democracy. Certainly, national unity and an awareness of national needs, desires, and responsibilities must be instilled before representation (on the elite level) or democracy (on the mass level) can have meaning. It is to the junta's greatest credit that it seems particularly aware of this. When elections are brought back to Sudanese life, the political parties will return, even if the present restrictions continue. Perhaps the greatest test of the junta's work will be to see whether the parties return in their old form of isolated elite groups, or whether enough integration of the masses into national life will have been accomplished to force responsiveness on the old parties or to create new groups with a popular, nonsectarian base.

VIII

ETHIOPIA

The oldest independent kingdom in Africa, the only surviving Christian nation outside the Western world, the country with the briefest colonial experience (outside of those who have had none at all), the only non-Arab, non-Muslim state in northern Africa— all these unique characteristics apply to Ethiopia and do much to determine its paradoxical position. A final element of uniqueness— and even of irony—is that Ethiopia is consciously trying to achieve development under the leadership of a traditional monarchy.

The beginnings of modern Ethiopian history go back to the reign of Menelik II (1889–1913), who pulled his country out of its internecine rivalries and united it by force into roughly its present shape. Menelik defeated the Italians at Adowa in 1896; annulled the Treaty of Ucciali (signed by him in 1889 to guarantee the integrity of Ethiopia), by which Italy had sought to make Ethiopia a protectorate; limited the position of the *rases* (dukes) to local governors; and commissioned the construction of Ethiopia's main railroad, linking the capital of Addis Ababa with Djibouti in French Somaliland. Three years after Menelik's death, his nephew, Tafari Makonnen, overthrew the successor regime and assumed the position of regent for Menelik's daughter, Zauditu. When Zauditu died in 1930, the regent ascended the throne and was crowned Haile Selassie I. One of his first actions, only a year later, was to grant Ethiopia its first constitution, setting up a constitutional monarchy with appointive advisory organs. The development of modern Ethiopia has been the history of his reign.[1]

The Italians had taken over Eritrea as a colony between 1882 and 1885. In 1935, the Fascist state reopened its attack against

144

Ethiopia, and within a year conquered it. But the colonial period lasted only five years; in 1941, the British liberated the empire, and the Emperor returned from exile in Britain, enriched by this period of contact with the modern world.

Short as it was, the colonial period nevertheless had its impact. The nature of the Fascist rule accentuated the material advances associated with colonialism, but it also produced its ill effects in the human field. Roads, communications, urbanization, minor industrialization, mining, and agricultural production were prime sectors of Italian attention. But at the same time, intellectual and governmental leaders were killed, schooling stopped, health uncared for, and political evolution ignored. On the other hand, wage labor was introduced, and the population came in contact with new political, social, and economic ways. European contact of a more helpful sort was continued between 1941 and 1944 through Ethiopia's cooperation with the British Military Administration and British advisers.

In Eritrea, the British Administration had full responsibility for government until 1952, and made frequent use of Italians left over from the longer colonial regime. District and municipal advisory councils, first made up of traditional chiefs, were appointed and encouraged. Although chiefs continued to utilize their power for personal benefit and councils were at first uninterested in the responsibility of government, these institutions were increasingly subjected to official prodding and growing public attention. Their gradual exercise of a full advisory role helped change government from an alien imposition to an approachable native function working to solve local problems. Newly created native courts performed similar integrative functions in the legal sphere.

In Eritrea, competing notions of belonging to an Ethiopian and an Eritrean nation arose simultaneously in different parts of the society as a reaction to the Anglo-Italian control. In 1946, with the preparation of the Italian peace treaty, political parties were allowed for the first time; by the following year, pro-Ethiopians had organized into an Eritrean-Ethiopian Union Party, and pro-Eritreans had formed a small Liberal People's Party and a larger Muslim League. Through tribal "polls" in 1948, a United Nations commission determined that the three parties were supported by 45 per cent, 5 per cent, and 40 per cent of the population, respectively; nationalist sentiment favoring union with Ethiopia predominated in the Christian Abyssinian plateau region of Eritrea, and the

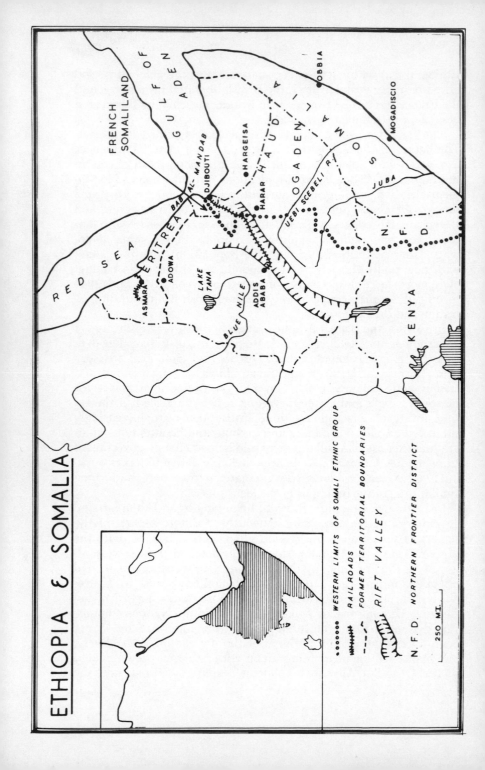

ETHIOPIA & SOMALIA

FRENCH SOMALILAND

GULF OF ADEN

OBBIA

MOGADISCIO

HARGEISA

HARAR

HAUD

OGADEN

SOMALIA

UEBI SCEBELI R.

JUBA

N. F. D.

DJIBOUTI

AL-MANDAB

BAB

ERITREA

RED SEA

ASMARA

ADOWA

LAKE TANA

BLUE NILE

ADDIS ABABA

KENYA

••••••• WESTERN LIMITS OF SOMALI ETHNIC GROUP
ᜒᜒᜒᜒᜒ RAILROADS
—··—··— FORMER TERRITORIAL BOUNDARIES
ᶺᶺᶺᶺᶺ RIFT VALLEY
N. F. D. NORTHERN FRONTIER DISTRICT

250 MI.

Muslim League represented the majority of the population in the rest of Eritrea. Delays and uncertainties in the United Nations, accompanied by violence and factionalism within the Eritrean parties, postponed any compromise between ideas of union and independence until December, 1950, when the United Nations General Assembly voted to "constitute an autonomous [Eritrean] unit federated with Ethiopia under the sovereignty of the Ethiopian crown." Elections to a new Eritrean Assembly were held in March, 1952, and the federation was consummated on September 15, 1952.[2]

The dominant partner within the federation, Ethiopia, had also evolved since the end of the war, although it had done so with less speed because of the strong and cautious leadership of the Emperor. The 1931 constitution was altered in 1943 to provide for indirect election of the lower house of parliament, formerly an appointive body. Senators, provincial governors, ministers, and "crown councilors" all continued to be appointed by the Emperor, and the appointees tended to come from a limited aristocracy that surrounded Haile Selassie. Anonymity was a major characteristic of these advisers of the Emperor, and, in fact, powerlessness went with facelessness, for the Emperor was the government.

One other group reflected Ethiopia's existence in a changing world—the educated minority, including military men with foreign contacts and experience. The Emperor encouraged education in his pronouncements, although school enrollment at all levels was quite limited, no higher education existed at all, and—after an initial expansion right after liberation—the education budget remained stationary between 1947 and 1952.

At the same time, traditional groups remained in positions of power, untroubled by modern ideas. Aristocratic landowners peopled the Assembly and the Senate. The Ethiopian Orthodox Church, which owned a third of the land, was also a powerful force of traditionalism. Government was thus personal, concentrated, and venerable; there was no room in it for the small, young forces that reflected what desire for change there was in the society. It was the Emperor alone who granted a revised constitution in November, 1955—a new step, even if not a new era, in Ethiopian political evolution.[3]

The Rule of the Emperor

The King of Kings, Conquering Lion of Judah, Power of the Holy Trinity, is the supreme ruler of Ethiopia. He claims to be 225th in a legendary line of Conquering Lions that descends from Menelik I, son of King Solomon and the Queen of Sheba; in 1963, he celebrated his seventy-first birthday, his thirty-third year of reign, and, including the regency, his forty-seventh year of rule. His position is founded both in the ancient belief in the divine right of kings and in a theoretical social contract between the Ethiopian people and his dynasty, as stated in the 1931 constitution.

Haile Selassie is head of state and chief executive, legislator, and adjudicator; he is also a meticulous administrator who insists on being personally involved and personally credited in any state action. He makes all governmental appointments, defines powers and duties, declares war and national emergencies, directs foreign relations, convenes and postpones (for thirty days) sessions of parliament, dissolves and replaces parliament, initiates and promulgates legislation, and maintains justice through the courts. Since he insists on personally supervising the details of implementation, these constitutional prerogatives give the Emperor a hand in the entire process of government.* Appointments are shuffled among a circle of officials in order to keep power from being concentrated outside the Throne. All diplomatic correspondence is supervised, and sometimes written, by the Emperor, and the year's program is given in the Emperor's Throne Speech at the opening of parliament in November. Initiative from the ministers passes through the Throne on the way to parliament, and adjudication follows the Emperor's will more than any legal precedent. Haile Selassie delegates little authority, and, in fact, is distrustful of those about him. The result is the concentration of barely limited power in the hands of a single, extremely industrious individual. Whatever may be the Emperor's capacity for work, the system produces more ideas than accomplishments. Projects, committees, cornerstones, and communiqués litter the Ethiopian capital, unfinished.

* Legislation, published in Amharic and English in the *Negarit Gazeta,* includes orders and decrees, promulgated by the Emperor alone; proclamations, passed by parliament; and legal and general notices, issued by a minister under authority of a proclamation.

Haile Selassie is conscious of the underdeveloped position of his country, in the midst of a continent to which colonialism brought an externally imposed take-off stage toward development. He believes in his own destiny, as the one chosen to bring Ethiopia along the road to modernity begun by Menelik II. He is perhaps not aware of the degree of his own country's underdevelopment, however; a 1961 UNESCO report, which stated that Ethiopia had a lower literacy rate than most African countries, reportedly shocked and grieved the Emperor. His deep awareness of the long cultural and historical background of his country makes him think of Ethiopia as a "model for development for other African countries."

The Emperor's ideas themselves seem to have undergone an evolution with the changing world. When the first constitution was proclaimed in 1931, its purpose was to establish a coherent governmental structure and to define the rights and duties of the parties to the contract—the Emperor and the people. It also promised evolution itself, despite provisions for a "perpetual and immutable" system of government, for it looked to measures "for increasing the well-being of Our people and aiding their progress on the road to happiness and the civilization by independent and cultured nations." As early as his coronation, the Emperor said, "I want my people to learn the idea of representation, so that they may one day rise and take part in the government of their country." The second constitution, proclaimed in 1955, turned to the creation of basic patterns of interaction between the Emperor and the people. Newly elected parliamentarians were "now charged with direct and personal responsibility, not only to Us, but also to those who have put their confidence in you and in your abilities by electing you to parliament."

The Emperor believes in progress through gradualism. Although the slowness implied in this approach—and expressed in the twenty-four-year gap between the first and second constitutional steps—has been criticized, the very fact of ordered change is most important. In Ethiopia, change has been brought about by the Emperor alone, for there is still no other force strong enough to pressure the government to change. The danger in the gradualist approach is that at some point it will generate forces for more rapid change, forces that may not be as responsive to the needs of order or the population's unreadiness for speed. Thus, bringing about change while holding it in check is one of the Emperor's dilemmas.

"Democracy evolves by stages, gradually," the Emperor has said. "Democracy as the share of the people's voice in the conduct of their own affairs is not foreign to Ethiopia. It is only that Ethiopia's traditional democratic concepts and convictions have now taken on new expression and fresh forms." There is no intimation in the Emperor's plans and speeches as to what the next step might be. At the pace of his past actions, it would appear that a long time would pass before a new step appeared. "Before you," Haile Selassie told his parliamentarians, "lies the arduous task of educating and enlightening your constituents and fellow countrymen, and of leading them along the path of material and spiritual progress."

Recent changes in the Emperor's thinking seem to have brought new ideas to bear on this element of pace. Although little concrete evidence is available, there are signs that several events have accelerated his notions of gradualism. One such event was the latest in a series of unsuccessful palace coups, which broke out in December, 1960, benefiting from unaccustomed publicity since it took place during the Emperor's absence on a state visit to Brazil. Another was the sudden international pressure exerted on Ethiopia by voluble leaders of newly independent African states. Haile Selassie has calmly stated that the coup would "not at all" change his plans for Ethiopian evolution. But immediately thereafter, he brought new, young blood into government councils, revived long-announced plans for administrative modernization, and began thinking of constitutional amendments. Concrete results are still meager, but, for the first time, the Emperor seems to be aware of the need for greater speed.

Unfortunately, the Emperor's inner circle support not even gradualism, but *status quo* and reaction. The church hierarchy and the landed aristocracy, who sit in parliament and in the ministerial posts, are bound to their own group interests and to the Throne by stronger ties than those which put them in contact with the people. The meager forces of change have no access to governmental machinery, except through the Emperor's conscience.

The group closest to the center of power is the royal family. Death has removed from Haile Selassie some of his closest kin in recent years, and a revolt in 1951 within the imperial family made it imperative to send others to quiet exile in distant provincial posts. Empress Menen died in February, 1962; she had not been active in politics, but was interested in education and in church and social work. Two princes died in 1933 and 1962, and Princess Tsahai died in 1942. The Emperor's favorite son and heir-apparent, Masfen Makonnen, Duke of Harar, was killed in an automobile crash in May, 1957. Since then, the succession has fallen to Crown Prince Asfa Wosen, whose infant son, Abeto Yakob, is next in line. Although he is the eldest son, Prince Wosen was first passed over for succession, and even though he is heir-apparent, his relations with his father have been cool. In the coup of 1960, he was pushed into power by the insurrectionists, and he acquiesced in order to preserve the dynasty.* The Emperor is said to consider him weak, and has given him no responsibilities. The Emperor's oldest child is Princess Tenagne Worq, whose second husband, Andargashaw Masai, was imperial representative in Eritrea from 1952 to 1959. His successor, General Abeye Abebe, widower of the late Princess Tsahai, and now also Interior Minister, rose in royal favor during the 1960 coup, when he remained loyal to the Emperor, kept him posted on events, and immediately moved his military forces against the insurrectionists.

The ministers of the realm are imperial advisers and department heads, rather than true cabinet members. The Council of Ministers constitutes a meeting rather than a collegial body. The most thorough shuffling of ministerial posts since 1942 came at the end of 1960, when the Emperor had to replace nineteen ministers and high officials killed in the final days of the revolt.† Old faces returned to new positions, but young faces were seen in junior positions in important ministries and even in a few ministerial posts. The Emperor retained the Education Ministry for himself.

The Prime Minister (Aklilu Abte Wold, Foreign Minister from 1942 to 1958) coordinates the work of other ministers and supervises the execution of legislation. Ministers may initiate legislation through the Emperor and are individually responsible to him; they can be impeached by him or by parliament, and must answer questions before parliament. However, despite the increased role of parliament in dealing with ministers and the increased number of young men in government, the government is only an impotent

---

* Once earlier, Prince Wosen had refused an offer of the throne—from Mussolini.

† In addition to the military leadership, some ministers and other government officials were also involved in the coup. The Emperor suspected Communist influence behind the coup, and one of the top leaders was reputed to be "sympathetic to Communism."

advisory adjunct to the Emperor. Furthermore, the mixture of young and old in ministerial leadership has often turned out to be a source of friction rather than strength, and was the cause of considerable delay in constituting a new government in 1960–61.

Ministers also function in a larger, older institution—the Crown Council—where they sit with the Archbishop, President of the Senate, and other dignitaries chosen by the Emperor. This body, too, is hardly a true council, but rather a collection of individual advisers, often individually consulted.

The latest constitutional innovation is the partially elected parliament, whose formal prerogatives are greater than its political independence. Parliament was displayed as an exhibit of progress when it was chosen in September–October, 1957. But it has scarcely lived up to its charge of bringing about political integration and education, and its second elections, due in 1961, did not take place. The upper house of parliament is still appointed; its fifty-three members come from the nobility, some of whom have long held government positions, and it has the same functions in the legislative process as the lower house.

In the elections of 1957, 210 deputies were chosen from 491 landowning candidates in 95 election districts; 23 deputies and 3 senators came from Eritrea. There were 3,015,260 registered adult voters, out of a potential electorate officially estimated at 6 million and a population variously estimated at from 8 to 21 million. Each candidate ran as an individual, since political parties are not allowed. The vote was direct and secret, for the first time. Both houses of parliament pass legislation by majority vote, and ten members of either chamber may initiate legislation, although bills that do not have the approval of the Emperor have little chance of success. Conflicting bills are discussed by both houses meeting as a joint committee of the whole. The Emperor must approve all legislation, and, when parliament is not in session, he can enact temporary legislation himself, subject to eventual ratification by the chambers. In fact, the Emperor's political control over parliament is unquestioned.

Although parliamentary sessions are now public, their impact on the population is virtually nil. It is greater on other governmental groups. The ministers are subject to parliament's scrutiny, and their budgets and audits must pass before the chambers. If opposition groups and parties existed, this check might be even more effective in keeping out corruption and improving ministerial performance; but the parliamentarians come from the same governing group as the ministers, and this fraternal interrelation tends to limit dynamism between and within the two groups. Furthermore, the new parliament is a fixed body lasting for a certain time, while the former appointive assembly was shuffled at more frequent intervals by the Emperor; the new deputies, therefore, tend to become an even more conservative status-quo group, responsible to a public that knows neither what they do nor what they should do.

Since the 1960 coup, the Emperor has resuscitated a number of other moribund bodies from among his plans, and has set them back to work accelerating governmental modernization. These commissions deal with reforms in civil service, land tenure, justice, education, fiscal administration and (since August, 1961) constitutional revision. Sporadic reports from them concerning complicated problems that tie them down indicate that the commissions are indeed functioning, but their greatest value seems to be an assuaging one, their existence indicating the Emperor's interest in reform—this interest to be announced with ceremony from time to time.

In Eritrea, there has been more advanced parliamentary democracy. Although election has been by a mixed direct and indirect system, the sixty-nine members of the Eritrean Assembly belonged to political parties and governed their "unit's" internal matters. The elections of March, 1952, gave thirty-two seats to the Eritreo-Ethiopian Unionists, eighteen to the Democratic Bloc (formerly one group of the Eritrean separatists), and fifteen to the opposition Muslim League of the Western Province; remaining seats were scattered among minor parties and one independent. The chief executive of Eritrea (Asfaha Wolde Mikael) was elected by the Assembly. However, in November, 1962, the Eritrean Assembly solved the problems of federalism by simply abolishing the ten-year experiment; Eritrea now has the same constitutional status as a province.

Local government in the other twelve Ethiopian provinces is carried out by appointed governors, some of whom have been princes. The governor has administrative, executive, legislative, and judicial power concentrated in his hands, and he also has military forces at his disposal; he has lost his former autonomy, however, and is only an important relay point in a centralized chain of command. He is regularly available to his people for direct consultation, but there are no popular councils. Appointed advisers and assistants form a consultative provincial body in the nature of an executive council.

The Problems of a Backward People

From the slumdwellers of the capital to the landless serfs of the aristocratic estates, the Ethiopian mass presents a discouraging picture. It is backward, and there is little done—and little that can be done—to hasten its evolution. It is passive to government and generally finds nothing wrong with the traditional concentration of power to which it is subject. Participation in elections has been quite low, and the alternatives presented in each district have generally been indistinguishable. Since all other government institutions are appointive, there are not even local representative councils such as those that rule many traditional societies at the lowest level. The people are in no condition to govern themselves; but they cannot change this situation until they are allowed to educate themselves through contact with evolving institutions. Unfortunately, no one has seen a way—or made one—out of this dilemma.

Ethiopian society is less split by the great horizontal gap than other countries in the developing world; there is practically no modern proletariat or upper class. But the country is splintered by many vertical gaps. It has more than fifty languages, only three of them written and most of them mutually incomprehensible; more than 95 per cent of the population are illiterate. Attempts to spread Amharic, the official language, by government use and through mission schools have so far resulted in diminished communication, instead of diminished provincialism. There are half a dozen newspapers in Addis Ababa and Eritrea, all government-controlled, and their circulation is among the lowest in Africa. Public broadcasts of news and music are heard in the streets of Addis Ababa at two in the afternoon, but the government radio station is only a limited means of arousing public awareness of the outside world.* Fewer than 10 per cent of the school-age children are in public schools, although a larger percentage attend traditional Christian and Muslim classes.

Fifteen per cent of the Eritreans lives in cities, but only 3 per cent of Ethiopia's population is urban. Some 20,000 people are industrially employed. Commercial activity is dominated by for-

---

* The Soviet Union also beams one hour of broadcasting in Amharic each day.

eigners; however, land is owned only by Ethiopians. The majority of the members of the capital city's chamber of commerce are Greeks and Indians, and scarcely more than a tenth are Ethiopians. The same is true of professional services; there are six Ethiopian doctors, and most medical needs are handled by foreign physicians.

Most important in the splintering of society are the racial groups, whose history and distribution reflect the geography of the country. Ethiopia is surrounded by desert; its central plateaus, where the climate is good and agricultural conditions are favorable, are separated from each other by chasms, gorges, and the Rift Valley. Roads built by the Italians had fallen apart by 1951, when a reconstruction program was finally begun; but even today, traffic is meager on many roads, and many areas have never seen a car or a road. The Harar (including Ogaden), populated by Somalis, the northern and coastal portions of Eritrea, and the central and southern lands of the Galla people are all inhabited by Muslims; these lands became part of the empire only during the past century. Unrest and sporadic violence among the inhabitants of Eritrea in 1962 led to the abolition of the special federal status for that area. Along the western and southern borders are Nilotic peoples, mainly pagan and split into diverse tribal and language groups. Thus, the ruling Christian Amharas, who live in the pla tenus, make up only 35 per cent of the population. In the face of Pan-Arab and Islamic propaganda from without, the Amharas tend to feel themselves besieged in their mountain fastnesses, and the problem of national unity is great.

Outside of Eritrea, there are no political parties.* The Emperor believes that parties are not useful, and the recent history of neighboring Sudan has not convinced him that he is wrong. The experience of Eritrea, with its Muslim-Christian political division reflected in its parties, suggests that parties would only reinforce the ethnic splits in Ethiopia proper. Although labor unions are not recognized, there has been some organization and a few strikes among railroad workers and dockers; an unofficial Union of Free Workers has few members.

There are noticeable sectors of discontent, but they are not well enough organized even to be called groups. The small commercial and administrative middle class has frequently been cited as the

* The Patriot Movement, a wartime resistance group that aided Haile Selassie's return, is reported to have been officially revived.

"place to look" for new pressures, but it is still small enough to be quiescent.* A growing awareness that some sort of change will become necessary has been reported by Westerners who have Ethiopian contacts in the capital. But no one suggests what these changes might be in the current context. Opposition, as exemplified by the 1960 coup, comes from some educated and underpaid military groups, such as officers in the Palace Guard. But this is no popular movement, and, significantly, it is not republican.

There exist two minor modern-type groupings that may be used to shape young ideas and increase early contacts with the outside world. The Boy Scout movement has fewer than 5,000 members, but it offers civic training. The Ethiopian YMCA, under the control of the Interior Ministry, has reached more than a million people through its programs (an exercise in adult education). These groups may increase understanding of public life among a narrow audience, but they can scarcely be hoped to generate change by themselves.

The greatest mass organization in the country is the church. It is also the only institution that is above the Emperor, and the only influence that has held the country together at times in the past when political unity has collapsed. Since 1948, the Ethiopian Orthodox Church has been organizationally independent of the Coptic Church of Egypt, its former parent body. Its supremacy, its organization, its wealth and social power, its history, and its national character all make the church a bulwark of conservatism among the Amharas. From the Abuna (Archbishop) down to the family confessors (priests), the church hierarchy is estimated to include at least a tenth of the Amhara male population. Their roots are in the past, and many are illiterate. Their care of Ethiopia's spiritual life is faithful and attentive, and even the external walls of a church arouse respect from the population. The church itself has instituted several reforms of its rules in recent times, and the fact that it commands respect may help to keep even accelerated change orderly. But it is not very interested in fostering evolution and modernization.

---

* However, the depth of antipathy to the Emperor among student and intellectual groups is striking, and has not been well enough appreciated in most Western reports. It results in blindness to the Emperor's good qualities, disrespect of his person, and an expectation of revolt at, or even before, the Emperor's death.

Law and Policies in the Capital of Africa

Ethiopia has bounded into the constitutional stage of legal evolution. Since the constitutions have been used to introduce change rather than reflect it, they are prescriptions for, rather than descriptions of, a political system. Many details of the constitution have already fallen by the wayside, but the broad lines remain, more often as a *loi cadre* to be implemented, rather than an extant normative code. There is no judicial review.

The 1955 constitution,[4] like its 1931 predecessor, confirmed the predominance of the Menelik I dynasty descended through Sahle Selassie, grandfather of Menelik II and great grandfather of Haile Selassie by another line. The new document established firm rules of legitimate male succession, to avoid the internecine strife that traditionally followed the death of an emperor. The 131 articles of this constitution enumerate the powers of the Emperor, the ministers and chambers, judicial and financial procedures, and the rights and duties of the people. It is this last-named section that is particularly advanced. An impressive list of civil rights, going as far as and sometimes even beyond the provisions of the American Bill of Rights—for example, "The family is under special protection of the law"—takes up twenty-four articles. There seems to be no legal or social discrimination against Ethiopia's minorities. There are two major limitations on civil rights; many of the guarantees are to be exercised "according to the law," and the right to form associations is limited to "occupations."

The 1955 constitution contained for the first time a provision for amendment, which is to take place by joint resolution of parliament proclaimed by the Emperor. The first amendments are supposedly still in preparation.

Judicial exercise is far behind the constitution. Judicial precedents are still not codified, and they have little force. Judges rule according to wisdom and the Emperor's wishes. The ancient privilege of every citizen to throw himself down in front of the Emperor and request hearing for his petition has been discouraged, now that the Emperor travels about in a green Rolls-Royce, and petitions are usually taken to one of the courts in the judicial hierarchy. The highest court of appeals is the Supreme Imperial Court, with provincial, regional, and lower courts below it, corresponding to the administrative divisions of the country. *Qadi* courts have also been established in the Muslim areas to judge personal matters. A Security Court and its Court of Appeals judge treason and espionage cases. The surviving top leaders of the 1960 coup, both civilian and military, were tried before a military tribunal. The Emperor exercised great leniency toward most of the followers of the revolt, but at least one leader was condemned to death and strung up publicly for educative purposes.

The security forces of Ethiopia include a 25,000-man army and an 8,500-man Palace Guard, plus large police forces.* The armed forces are under the personal control of the Emperor and are for the most part loyal to him. The 1960 coup arose within the Palace Guard and carried as many as 5,000 of its members with it, but in many cases they seem to have simply been blindly following their leaders. Among the modern, educated officers of the army, opposition is said to continue, held in check by fear of the Emperor; the friction between young and old that is found in the administration is also present in the officer corps. However, little suggests that this opposition is much more than the "palace-guard revolt" that for centuries has rendered monarchy a hazardous profession the world over. The forces of modern opposition are still not strong enough to take over power, let alone rule.

To those who rule, domestic problems are of major concern, even if not of major activity. Probably the most important of these is the question of land reform. Haile Selassie has tried to abolish the serf (*gabbar*) system, although he has also tried to do it without hurting the aristocracy. Through taxes, financial laws, and legal measures, the Emperor has liberated the serfs from their feudal ties to the lord's land and has facilitated their own acquisition of land. But in fact, taxes are ignored as often as not, land ownership is still highly concentrated, and the *gabbar* system remains in many areas.

Yet the country is not agriculturally poor; less than half the estimated arable land is used, but there is no chronic undernourishment, and cattle and grain are available for export. At the present time, coffee is the major export crop. The beginnings of industrialization are concentrated in food processing and mining;[5] the mineral potential of Ethiopia—including oil—is great, but almost completely undeveloped. Of all the countries on the Nile, Ethiopia is the only one that has not tapped the development po-

* After the coup, in January, 1962, the Emperor set about creating a "territorial force" of 1,000 men in each province.

tential of that great river system. The Blue Nile rises in Laka Tana in Ethiopia and loses 5,500 feet in altitude before it leaves the country. Ethiopia is currently host to a large international complex of technical assistants, from Americans to Russians, who advise its economic and social development. But administrative and technical skills among the Ethiopians themselves are sorely lacking, and training possibilities are limited. The latest step—one of imagination and far-reaching potential—is the establishment of a "monument" to Haile Selassie in the form of Ethiopia's first university. Its name and head are Haile Selassie, but its active presidency is held by an American, its language is English, and its faculty is international; students will practice-teach in Ethiopian schools as part of their training. British and American military teams have trained the Ethiopian Army.

One of the healthy signs of the Ethiopian scene is the moderate language that characterizes its foreign policy. Because of its history, anticolonialism is not a popular catch-all for unpleasant problems. The festering border problem with Somalia troubles interior relations in Ogaden, as well as exterior relations, but there is no attempt to channel public dissatisfaction into concern for foreign problems. Probably the most sensible—but most unrealistic—suggestion concerning the nationalist rivalry on the Horn of Africa has been for a regional confederation, involving not a united Somalia but a combination of Somali territories with Ethiopia. Quite naturally, Ethiopia has subscribed to this approach, and the chances of mutual well-being would be enhanced by the association of the two regions. But Somali nationalism makes the solution unthinkable.

Ethiopia is the only country in northern Africa that recognizes Israel. For this reason, and also because of the Somali affair, its relations with the Arab world have been tense. Consequently, Ethiopia has been mending its fences with the other African countries, trying to correct the impression that it is a backward, non-African, Western-dominated nation. Haile Selassie attended the Belgrade Conference of Nonaligned Nations in September, 1961, and sent his representatives to the Accra Conference of Independent African States in 1958; Addis Ababa was the site of the second such conference in 1960. The Emperor has visited Presidents Nkrumah of Ghana, Nasser of Egypt, and Tubman of Liberia, and has received Presidents Touré of Guinea, Othman of Somalia, and Nyerere of Tanganyika, Kenyatta and Mboya of

Kenya, and Kaunda of Northern Rhodesia. All but two* of the thirty-two heads of independent African states were guests of the Emperor at the Addis Ababa summit conference of May, 1963. Not only was the oldest independent African capital chosen as the site of the conference, but the Ethiopian delegation also played an active role in the formulation of the meeting's most concrete accomplishment, the charter that set up the African Unity Organization. Previously, Ethiopia had been a member of the Monrovia group of African states, and was host to the East, Central, and South African Unity Conference (PAFMECSA) in February, 1962. Addis Ababa is also the seat of the United Nations Economic Commission for Africa. Selassie is a staunch believer in the United Nations, despite (or perhaps because of) his experience with the League of Nations in 1935. Ethiopia contributed 3,000 troops to the Congo operations, and also fought in Korea.

Ethiopia's position frequently evokes comparisons, and especially those that recall the evolution of the English monarchy. The similarities are few indeed. Perhaps the most important difference is the absence of powerful figures or forces around the Emperor exerting pressure toward progress. Haile Selassie is pulling the cart of modernization alone, and he is moving as fast as he can. But the world about him is moving faster. At the present time, the passengers in the cart find it natural to be pulled and are undisturbed by the ride. Someday, the cart will hit a bump, and a few people will wake up or fall out. It is possible that they may then offer to help pull. But human nature being what it is, it is likely that even if they do, there will be disagreements over the speed, the direction, and the order of the pullers. At this point, Ethiopian events may begin to resemble the evolution of the French monarchy. It is ironic that, this time, it will probably not be the ruler's fault.

* Togo's Grunitzky and Morocco's Hassan II.

IX

SOMALIA

Somalia, which became a "unitary, democratic, parliamentary" state on July 1, 1960, is one of Africa's few nation-states, although tribalism and irredentism still trouble its young national unity. Somalia is made up of former British and Italian Somaliland. The southern portion, along the Indian Ocean, became an Italian protectorate and colony between 1889 and 1894, during the "Great African Hunt," and was proclaimed a crown colony in 1910. The northern portion, along the Gulf of Aden, became a British protectorate in 1884, although the first British agreement of protection over a Somali chief was signed with the Sultan of Tanjura in 1840. In 1935, Italian Somaliland was used as a springboard for the Fascist invasion of Ethiopia, and the Somali region of Ethiopia (Ogaden) was united with Somaliland under Italian colonial rule. The area was overrun by the British in 1941, and during the war, the British Army united British and Italian Somaliland and Ogaden, with a British Military Administration governing the conquered Italian portion.

After the war, in 1946, British Foreign Minister Ernest Bevin proposed to maintain this unity and complete it by adding the Kenyan Northern Frontier District and French Somaliland to the three united territories; in this way, all the Somali peoples would be brought under one rule. Italy renounced all right and title to its colony in the Italian peace treaty of the following year, but a United Nations resolution in November, 1949, recommended that the Italian area be placed under international trusteeship for a limited period of ten years, with Italy as the administering authority. The possibility of Somali unity was thus postponed. In 1954,

Britain reaffirmed its treaty of 1897 with Ethiopia and returned to
Ethiopian sovereignty the northern border area of Ogaden (the
Haud), which Britain had governed since 1941; Ethiopia agreed
to allow Somali nomads free passage to their traditional pastures
on either side of the border. Somalia, still only an ethnic expression,
was thus again broken up into separate regions for the decade of
the 1950's.

The period of unity under British rule, however, was the incubation period for modern Somali national consciousness. In the original British area, population was less dense, less urban, and more
backward than to the south, and it changed little in the postwar
decade. But in the former Italian region, the British encouraged
primary and secondary education in the towns and introduced
consultative organs of local government. Britain refused to protect
Italian monopolies and thus encouraged local trade. The removal
of Fascist restrictions on social and political clubs led to the possibility of associations among Somalis. The first and most important
of these was the Somali Youth League (SYL), founded (as a club)
in May, 1943, around ideas of national unity, education, national
consciousness, and constitutionalism; it drew its membership from
tribal agricultural and nomadic groups, as well as from urban
areas.[1] By 1946, there were three political associations in the
southern area; by 1949, nine. The notion, written into the Italian
peace treaty, that Italian colonies should be disposed of according
to "the wishes and welfare of the inhabitants" led to the formation
of a U.N. Investigating Commission in 1948 and a burst of activity
among the political groups to broaden their popular base, develop
their programs, and outdo their rivals as representatives of the
population.

Smarting under a bad reputation as colonial rulers, the Italians
attacked their new charge with a vengeance in 1950. They increased education, trained civil servants, prepared democratic consultation, and in general rapidly won the trust of the population by
sincerely attempting to make the most of the decade as preparation for independence. By the first municipal elections of 1954,
there were twenty-one parties. By the first general elections for a
legislative assembly, in January, 1956, there were fifteen, although
many of these were local tribal groups, encouraged by a process of
vote by acclamation in the countryside. The first government exercising full powers was formed in May, 1956, by the SYL (Ab-
dullahi Issa), which had won forty-three of the sixty seats.

In the 1958 municipal elections, the number of parties fell to six, still closely associated with tribal allegiances, even though the voting was confined to urban areas. The SYL was again the largest party, winning 415 of the 663 seats, and was the only party with a national constituency. Opposition came from the Somali Independent Constitution Party (HDMS), founded in 1947 and winner of 175 seats in 1958; it favored Somali federalism and better relations with Ethiopia. A radical group (Hajj Mohammed Hussein), with pro-Egyptian leanings and an anti-Italian message, was expelled from the SYL in June, 1958; as the Greater Somali League (GSL), it won 36 seats. Other groups—the Liberal Somali Youth Party with 27 seats, the Benadir Youth Union with 6 seats, and the Somali Youth Front with 3 seats—all relied on narrow tribal support. In March, 1959, new general elections were held, and the SYL swept 83 of the 90 seats and again formed the government.* On its insistence, the U.N. General Assembly agreed to advance the date of independence to July 1, 1960.

In British Somaliland, the Somali National League (SNL) was founded in 1935, but participation in government was later in coming about. An Advisory Council of traditional elders, appointed in 1946, had no governing power. The British decision to return the Haud to Ethiopia in 1954 led to the creation of a National United Front (NUF) that year. The first Legislative Council, in 1957, was dominated by the NUF and its moderate Christian leader, Michael Mariano, one of the few educated Somalis outside the civil service. However, by 1958, nationalists impatient with the moderates' lack of success broke away from the NUF and revived the SNL; elections for twelve Council seats in March, 1959, were won by the NUF by default, since the other parties boycotted. It was not until later that year that Britain was spurred by progress in the trusteeship territory and pressure from the SNL to adopt a "crash program" of constitutional development and preparation for self-government. The elections that followed, in February, 1960, resulted in the upset victory of the more impatient SNL (Mohammed Hajji Ibrahim Egal), which won twenty seats and formed the first government. The United Somali Party won twelve seats, and Mariano the remaining one. The new legislature immediately requested independence and union with the trusteeship territory, and Britain, although rushed and surprised, agreed. Independence was attained on June 26, 1960, and, after four days of sovereignty,

---

* The HDMS won five seats, which it still held after independence.

former British Somaliland merged with the former Italian area, as it attained its own independence, to form a united Somalia.

Somalia was born a poor country; half of each territory's budget was made up by British and Italian subsidies. The mass of its population is still untouched by education, despite British and Italian efforts, although a small urban elite has benefited from modern schooling, at least to the secondary level. Its national language—Somali—is unwritten, and there is bitter nationalist disagreement over what alphabet to use to write it. Arabic is used to some extent in the cities, but many observers have tended to exaggerate the extent to which the culture is Arabized. Italian and English are also official languages, reflecting the dual colonial heritage. The civil service is Somalized and highly political. The countryside, inhabited by nomads (three-quarters of Somalia's population) and sedentary farmers (one-tenth), is primitive and is organized on the basis of a social kinship unit (*rer*), strongly impregnated with ideas of collective responsibility and autonomy. Although there is a gap, in terms of experiences and expectations, between the ruling groups in the cities and the rural majority of the population, there is a high degree of intermingling between urban and rural society, and no class consciousness.

A Government of Tribes and Parties

As soon as the republic was declared, the united National Assembly met to elect a President.[2] It chose Aden Abdullah Othman, president of the Italian area's parliament, in a compromise designed to bypass rivalries between Issa's SYL followers in the Italian region and Egal's SNL in the British area. A year later, after the constitution was voted, Othman was reconfirmed as head of state by only a narrow margin. SYL leader Abdirashid Ali Shermarke was the compromise candidate for Premier, and he and his fourteen-member cabinet, made up of ten SYL and four SNL leaders, were approved by the Assembly at the end of August, 1960. The government rose to sixteen members, and within a year it resigned because of an Assembly resolution limiting the number of cabinet posts to twelve for reasons of economy. It was reconstituted at the end of August, 1961, with a reduced membership and no new personalities. Issa is Foreign Minister, and Egal was Minister of Education until November, 1962, when the cabinet underwent a major reshuffling. The cabinet also administers a small (6,000) and not too effective civil service.

The cabinet runs the state, influenced by the Assembly, the

parties, and the tribes. An electoral law that permits civil servants to run for office and then return to government service after election or defeat allows the political elite to make the best of two worlds. Since national elections will not be held again until 1964, this is probably less important than the tribal composition of the government; adopting a custom developed under the trusteeship, the cabinet is chosen to reflect accurately the tribal composition of the country. It is therefore geographically representative of Somalia, but family and tribal nepotism is also prevalent. Since the parties and the government are a reflection of the tribal society, they have not been able to take strong measures necessary to make sedentation possible, let alone to encourage it, and the impoverished nomadic society keeps the central government poor enough to perpetuate this condition.

The National Assembly was formed the same way as the new nation—by the union of already existing institutions of the former British and Italian areas. The ninety-member Legislative Assembly, elected in March, 1959, in Somalia, was merged with the thirty-three–member body elected in Somaliland in February, 1960. In the Italian trusteeship territory, election was carried out by a complicated variant of the list system, which effectively inserted the parties in between the voters and their representatives, and which ensured broad representation of the entire geographical area. The territory voted as a single electoral college, but the seats were apportioned on the basis of population to thirty election districts; each party was required to present a nationwide list of candidates, who were elected in each district according to the number of votes the district gave the party's national list. Electoral methods introduced by the British were also adapted to the local scene. The result throughout the country is that the Assembly provides broad representation for the Somali people—under the control of the parties.

Legislation is the charge of the Assembly, but on the initiative of the government. The representatives are particularly conscious of the economic problems of the country and, since the days of the trusteeship, have attempted to implement the irreconcilable goals of economy in government and national development. Since the tribal nature of politics is still dominant, divisive problems of only local interest are brought to the fore. In this sense, the assemblymen are good representatives of the people, but are not always responsive to the needs of national unity.

In local government, an attempt to provide representation has strengthened the tribal structure and effectively blocked direct popular participation. The eight regions are headed by an appointed governor and are subdivided into thirty districts, governed by an appointed district commissioner and an elected district council. These councils have been made up of tribal chiefs and notables and local party representatives. In fact, they are tribal councils, modernized in name only, fulfilling traditional functions such as the interpretation of customary law and the settlement of grazing and watering disputes. The nomadic nature of the society defeats any territorial notion of a "district"; projects such as roads and schools seem distant to the tribes' rudimentary subsistence interests, and the election by which the councilors are chosen is no more than the acclamatory process entrenched in tradition. The forty-eight municipalities are for the most part only villages, but they are practically autonomous units, governed by elected councils and an elected mayor.

Parties in a Pastoral Democracy

The social gap in Somalia is not so wide as it is elsewhere, even though urbanization and education have begun to have an effect on a slowly modernizing minority. The gap, however, is widened by a division of generations; the elders are left behind, and feelings of national consciousness and integration are held above all by a youthful minority. It is significant that then Premier Issa, who was thirty-eight at the time of the founding of the republic, lacked seven years to make him eligible for the presidency. The Five-Year Plan for educational development, begun in 1952, attained only slightly more than three-quarters of its goal of 19,600 adults in basic education, and only 60 per cent of those enrolled had a regular attendance record. Attempts to reach the older generation were, therefore, lacking in cooperation among the very group to be helped, even though the goals themselves were modest. Educational efforts have not succeeded in bringing the elite to a very high level of learning, even though academic skills per se may not be among the basic necessities of a new nation; there were barely 200 graduates of higher educational institutions by 1962, and the very basic need for trained professional men still remains unfilled. Not even half the entire population has come in contact with any type of modern education; illiteracy is variously estimated at 90 to 98 per cent.[3]

The result is that dominant social patterns of long standing still shape political thinking and participation among most of the nation. As long as the *rer* remains the principal social unit, public participation in government will still be channeled through tribal leaders—themselves unsuited and unprepared for modern political life—and notions of tribal loyalty and collective responsibility will outweigh modern ideas of national consciousness and individual participation. So long as more than three-quarters of the population have no permanent homes and only one-tenth of the 8 million arable acres are under cultivation, tribal strife and survival will remain the predominant problems of public attention. As long as the entire population—with the exception of a few city dwellers—belong to one of the four Islamic sects (Qadiriya, Salihiya, Ahmediya, Rifaiya), traditional social ways will continue to be enforced by the web of religious custom.

One means of bridging these gaps should be the political party. Many specifically tribal parties have disappeared because of the electoral law and also because of a law prohibiting the use of tribal names in political organizations. As one result, national parties have become confederations of tribal groups. Before the formation of the republic, the goal of independence served as political glue to hold these groups together. Now the continued presence of tribal interests is frankly recognized. Furthermore, the parties are more effective instruments of political organization in urban than in rural areas; they are thus the result, not the cause, of social integration in Somalia.

SYL predominance in the government does not imply a tutelary, single-party system imposed on the people. It is a true reflection of many social and geographic interests, translated in vague terms of national (Somali) and religious (Muslim) terminology. The party coalition, therefore, is extremely vulnerable to radicalism in these same terms, and the GSL irredentist (pan-Somali) propaganda has more influence on the government than an opposition party might be expected to have, particularly in the testy matter of relations with Ethiopia. On the other hand, the SYL coalition itself is fragile; although the party swept the polls in 1959, it took months to form a government. Splits in the nationalist movement, which other young nations have known—leading to the formation of a multiparty system or to a reaction of autocratic single-party dominance—are a real possibility in Somalia.

Pressures toward the multiparty possibility, and signs of reaction to this within the SYL have appeared since independence. In

January, 1962, Interior Minister Abdirazak Hajji Hussein warned a party group against fly-by-night parties whose leaders, "when speaking in the name of their parties, should know they speak for the common interest of the nation and not for their own interests. . . . We must strengthen our democratic laws. . . . We will not be people who spoil democracy." On the other hand, the GSL expounds a strong Islamic and irredentist message that often leads to pro-Cairo and pro-Peking slogans and activities. The party split on the issue of radicalism in November, 1960, with President Hajj Mohammed Hussein and the more moderate Vice-President Banafunzi reading each other out of the GSL. Such activities indicate a search for an effective opposition message in the absence of a real program. They do little to encourage responsible public participation in government affairs.

Although many tribal parties have died, tribal interests still are the key to the basic understanding of the remaining parties. Ethnically, Somalia is divided into two clans—the pastoral nomadic Samaale and the agricultural Sab—and their component tribal groups. After independence, the Liberal Somali Youth Party merged with the SYL to form a bloc of 85 seats in the 123-man Assembly. The resulting party represents two main Samaale groups: the Hawiya north of Mogadiscio (the capital) and the Darod, who live both along the Kenya frontier and at the country's elbow 600 miles farther north. The party has also made inroads into the Rahanwein group of the Sab. The two Samaale groups alone make up over half of the country's population and provide a broad base of political support; the size and leadership of the SYL have gone far to soften the tribal nature of politics. Since the SYL had little strength in the north, it has joined the SNL to form the coalition government. The SNL has absorbed the United Somali Party since independence; thus it is almost the exclusive representative of the Dir group of the Samaale, who people most of the former British area.

The GSL appeals, above all, to the Darod group among the Samaale; it tries to undercut the SYL in this group, capitalizing first on Darod dissatisfaction with a distribution of government posts under the SYL, and then using the Darod location along the Kenyan and Ethiopian borders as a springboard for irredentist appeals. Difficulties in forming a government in 1959, and earlier, stemmed from the traditional Darod-Hawiya rivalry. The Somali Independent Constitution Party is based on the Sab people living

between the Juba and Uebi Shebeli rivers; the two Sab groups—
Rahanwein and Dighil—are traditional rivals of the Samaale. In
late 1961, a party with a religious appeal—Ittihad al-Ulama—was
added to the north. Although it would be simplistic to say that the
SYL-SNL government is Samaale (minus some Darod) and the
opposition is Darod and Sab, these tribal groups and their rivalries
do play an important role in determining political stability.* Mass
participation in political life through the medium of the parties
thus still tends to follow, rather than overflow, tribal channels.

Since the urban population is small, labor is a tiny segment of
the nation, and labor organization has made correspondingly small
inroads. Unions were begun in 1949; and the Union of Somali
Workers associated with the ICFTU in 1958; some 10,000 laborers
now are organized in the Somali Confederation of Labor. There is
little union activity in the northern zone.

Other projects that serve to integrate developing peoples are
lacking in Somalia. Illiteracy keeps the press small; there is one
daily, in Mogadiscio, printing articles in Italian and Arabic. Eight
towns have telephones. There are no railways; roads are fully
adequate only for primitive transportation, and they provide no
communication at all between the former British and Italian areas.
Radio broadcasting stations operate in Mogadiscio and Hargeisa
to a limited audience; in fact, Somalia is better served by radio
from the U.A.R., by the Voice of America and the BBC, even by
Red China's broadcasts, and by other Middle Eastern national
radios. The single 4-kilowatt transmitter in Mogadiscio is being
increased to 50 kilowatts with Russian help. Three basic education
projects in the Juba farming area have attained only partial success; one failed, but the other two have been able to spread some
basic literacy and new ideas of farming techniques and crafts, despite poor attendance by the wandering tribes and impatience by
authorities. Even viewed realistically, in terms of the long uphill
climb necessary to integrate a poor primitive nomadic society,
their impact has been slight.

The infrequency of mass participation in Somali government
through the ballot box has often been made up for by open and
enthusiastic overparticipation. In the latest municipal elections in
the former Italian territory (1958), 85 per cent of eligible voters

* A Communist Party came into existence for four months during 1956 and
then collapsed. Communist contacts from Russia, China, and Italy appear to
concentrate their attentions on the GSL.

participated, including women for the first time. The campaign was enthusiastic and orderly. But in the elections of 1959, riots broke out, and the opposition charged the government with electoral frauds. The innovation this time was the opening of franchise to all citizens over eighteen, the removal of literacy qualifications, and the installation of a uniform voting system to replace the traditional rural method, which had hitherto allowed the tribe to choose their chief as their "elector" to cast their collective vote for them. The establishment of a national constituency was designed to combat tribalism, but at the same time it prevents close contact between voters and candidate and allows the tribes to come in by the party back door. The latest vote—the first in the newly united nation—occurred on June 20, 1961, when 1,948,348 persons (out of a still uncounted population estimated at a little more than 2 million) overwhelmingly approved the new constitution. It is openly admitted that many people voted many times, as they had in pre-independence elections, and the vote was the subject of a legal complaint by the GSL, SNL, and USP. It should be noted, however, that the vote was low in the former British area (scarcely more than 100,000 out of a population estimated at 700,000) and that there was a slight majority against the constitution in that area, for fear of domination by the south. The referendum was calm, but incidents of disorder have not disappeared since independence. Opposition parties protested the constitutional framework in riots on Independence Day in Mogadiscio in 1960; riots interrupted the President and the Premier as they tried to address the capital in August, 1961; tribal demonstrations in October, 1962, for and against the Interior Minister, resulted in thirty-three deaths; and four died in a clash with police over prices in Hargeisa in May, 1963.

Poverty and Irredentism in an Islamic Republic

Somalia is an Islamic republic in almost everything but name. The constitution was first approved by the National Assembly of the trusteeship territory alone before independence and was promulgated by the newly elected President on the day of independence, to be ratified a year later by popular vote. All legislation must comply with the general principles of Islam, and the *shariaa* is to be the main source of law; laws are also to conform, as much as possible, to the Universal Declaration of Human Rights. Islam is the state religion, and the President must be a Muslim.

The constitution was originally inspired by a unique document—the U.N.-drafted Trusteeship Agreement for the Territory of Somaliland under Italian Administration—to which was appended a Declaration of Constitutional Principles, a prototype constitution. Guarantees for modern civil liberties and social rights, the promotion of democratic self-government, and a pattern of republican institutions based largely on the government of modern Italy have all been carried over from the original ideas of the U.N. document and incorporated by the Italian-Somali drafting team into the new constitution. Thus the constitution is above all a declaration of intent, and it will take time before modern notions of performance, public ideas of responsibility and participation, and real practices of government grow into the patterns laid out in the document.

Formal assistance in this direction is provided by the judicial system, whose highest body, the Court of Justice, is empowered to decide the constitutionality of legislation. A modern hierarchical court system, partially hampered by the lack of trained judges, extends to the lower levels. Yet in the rural areas, customary law is still the deciding pattern of values. *Qadis* have a reduced civil jurisdiction and no criminal competence, but a large segment of the population falls within their purview.

Civil liberties find firm guarantees in the Somali constitution, in accordance with the Universal Declaration of Human Rights. In fact, this is one portion of the document that also reflects traditional values. Freedom of speech, open debate before arriving at decisions, rudimentary vote and elections by public majority, and equality, fraternity, and even nobility among Somalis are all characteristics of Somali tribal society. On the other hand, the institution of tribal vendetta, the payment of compensation in livestock for physical injury to humans, and collective responsibility for individual acts and injuries are ideas alien to modern civil rights and responsibilities, and will take time to eradicate.

Minority rights have less foundation in traditional Somali attitudes. Out-groups, castes, and menial occupations all form a part of traditional ethnic stratification. Yet the position of non-Somali groups has been comfortable; a concentrated Asian minority (40,-000), which practices commerce in the coastal towns, and a small European population (5,000) have not been elements of unrest or persecution. In 1956, ten seats in the trusteeship territory's legislature were reserved for the Asian, Indian, and Italian minorities, but in the 1958 municipal elections and thereafter, separate minority voting was discontinued. Despite political grievances, there appears to be no open discrimination against Sab, Darod, or Dir peoples.

Among the security forces, the urban police has grown up as one of the country's best disciplined units of any kind. It regards itself as servant of the law, not of the government, and has been called "an agent of modernization" as well as a guardian of order. District police (*Ilalos*) also exist and are under the control of the district commissioners. The British-, Italian-, and Egyptian-equipped army is small (5,000) and of little value either in keeping order or in defending the long and disputed land frontier. Its only significant political activity has been an abortive coup carried out by five of its junior officers in the northern (ex-British) regional capital of Hargeisa in January, 1962, and quickly brought under control by other members of the same units. Somalia has increased its close military cooperation with Egypt since independence, but the army is by no means a political elite, and is scarcely capable of either a military coup or a sustained frontier war.

Somalia's domestic and foreign policies are all tied together into one rather discouraging whole. The country is not independently viable in the modern economic world and has little prospect of becoming so.[4] It has a low level of economic activity and little promise for rapid development of its uncertain resources. As it is, important economic sectors such as the textile industry have been priced out of the domestic market by cheaper foreign competition, and banana farming is kept alive only by subsidized trade to Italy. Somalia is thus at the mercy of foreign assistance. Aid programs keep the economy running, and help prime the pump for future expansion; technical-assistance programs, perhaps even more important, attempt to bring modernization to the backward regions. Aid has been given by the United States, Italy, England, Germany, Egypt, Czechoslovakia, and Russia, as well as the Common Market and the United Nations. The outlook is further complicated by the recent recurrence of floods in the southern part of the country and a lack of water in much of the rest. In 1959 and again in 1961, a third of the country went under water, a quarter of the population faced winter starvation, and fifteen nations plus the United Nations joined in food and rescue operations.

Radicalism has made inroads through several doors into Somalia. Egyptian influence, not universally welcome, has increased through Egyptian support of GSL irredentism. Domestic pressure has risen to the point where the SYL government has felt itself forced to preach the "Greater Somalia" message. In early 1960, the SYL government looked to unification of the Somali people "by peaceful and legal means"; a year later, a minister in Cairo declared that "the Somalis are prepared to make sacrifices, no matter how dear, to preserve their independence and achieve their cherished unity." In between these two pronouncements came a bitter eight-month war in Ogaden, between Ethiopian military units and Somali nomads over Ethiopian attempts to close the border and withdraw grazing rights conferred by the 1954 treaty with Britain. To the southwest, across the migrants' traditional grazing lands, the border is set by a 1908 agreement that Ethiopia and Somalia (and Italy before it) interpret differently. The land occupied by some 500,000 Somalis in Ethiopia is a sharp issue of contention between the two countries. To the south, some 100,000 Somalis in Kenya are in a similar situation. In late 1961, the Somali National Assembly called for "support [for] the request of the people of the Northern Frontier Province [of Kenya] to be united with the Somali Republic before the Independence of Kenya," and in March, 1963, Somalia broke diplomatic relations with Britain over the impending independence of all of Kenya. Kenyan leaders are unsympathetic to the Somali position, and since the beginning of 1963, there have been outbreaks of violence comparable to those on the Ethiopian frontier. The border was set by a "three-year trial agreement" between Italy and Britain in 1924. There are also 28,000 Somalis in French Somaliland, where half the population lives in the port of Djibouti. Officially, Somalia has shown interest in the Pan-African Freedom Movement for East, Central, and South Africa (PAFMECSA)—a regional unity plan now centered on Kenya, Tanganyika, Uganda, Zanzibar, and Nyasaland, and, since February, 1962, including also Somalia, Ethiopia, and the nationalist movements of Southern Africa.

Rising irredentism is also a key to other aspects of foreign policy. The United States has given military aid to Ethiopia, while the U.S.S.R. has allowed its large economic-credits program to Ethiopia to lapse, and both the U.S.S.R. and Communist China have shown increasing interest in and attention to Somalia. As a result, the new government has recognized Peking and has moved from a pro-Western position to positive neutrality, although it remains a member of the moderate Monrovia group; it was represented at the Belgrade Conference in the fall of 1961.

Underdevelopment is Somalia's greatest problem, but irredentism is its biggest political issue. Yet, union of all Somali peoples brings no guarantee of a solution to deeper economic and social problems. In fact, it ignores them. A Greater Somalia would be a union of weakness and poverty, with not even any prospect of additional natural resources to bring a promise of hope. It solves no problems, except the problem of irredentist pressure, and exacerbates relations with all of Somalia's neighbors.[5]

Somalia is only on the verge of development—in a social and political, as well as an economic, sense—and, in fact, is only making its entry into the take-off phase in all these fields. A subsistence economy works against both economic development and the effective integration of the population into national life. While the legal system has already attained the level of constitutionalism, the political system is still tied to the uncertainty of the nationalist movement, itself torn between modern leaders and tribal support. The future of this political evolution is cloudy, and already shows signs of disruptive diversionism in foreign policy. Yet, in paying attention to the union of Somalis, the government is responsive to the one genuine aspiration of the Somali people.

X

UNITY AND STRATEGY

The states of northern Africa are interested in each other as neighbors with similar experiences. The East and the West are interested in these states as emerging nations and as part actors, part bystanders in the Cold War. The international relations of northern Africa are dominated by two factors: tremendous local pressures for regional unity and the area's strategic importance in the Cold War.

There are general patterns of similarity among the nations of northern Africa that affect their international relations. Toward the end of the nineteenth century, almost all the countries underwent a period of xenophobia—the last strong motivating force in traditional government before the advent of colonialism. Emir Abdulqader and succeeding resistants in Algeria, Colonel Ahmed Arabi in Egypt, the Mahdi in Sudan, Menelik II in Ethiopia, Moulay Hassan I and particularly his three weak sons in Morocco, the Sanussi under Idris in Libya, and Mohammed Abdullah Hassan al-Mahdi (the Mad Mullah) in Somalia led xenophobic movements in their respective countries in the period between 1832 and 1920; most were active in the 1880's. Only Menelik II was successful in preventing colonial implantation. Although their energy was directed primarily against Christian Europeans—and to some extent against the old Turkish colonialism—in a few cases, such as Sudan or Ethiopia, it was also aimed against neighboring countries.

Thereafter came a period of colonialism, which appeared to impose vast regional unities on northern Africa. To the west, the French governed all of North Africa (with a few Spanish exceptions); to the east, the British ruled the Nile Valley and Somaliland. In between, Italian Libya and Italian East Africa consolidated two large regions. Colonial unity was even more striking at the end of World War II, when there were only two blocs: French North Africa, including the Fezzan, and British-administered Africa, from Kenya to the Canal and from Soqotra to Sirte. This unity was illusory. Colonial rule consolidated national, rather than regional, units and controlled dependencies under many different forms—zone of influence, protectorate, colony, military administration, overseas territory, condominium.

Modern nationalism rose during the war and strove to end colonial rule. Since the nationalist movements grew out of incipient national consciousness, they also broke these general regions into separate states on their way to becoming nations. Although the people of northern Africa for the most part consider themselves Arabs, they slowly grew to regard themselves, above all, as nationals of their countries. There was similarity in the anticolonial policies of the nationalist movements, and often mutual support, but any unity of the area was to be achieved after independence on the basis of cooperation among national governments.

Since independence, the foreign policies of the new states have also shown similarities in their advocacy of neutralism. But there are rivalries and differences, from the pro-Western neutralism of Tunisia and Libya to the positive nonalignment of Algeria and Egypt. However, just as with democracy in domestic affairs, regional unity, which has never really existed in modern times, has become one of the major goals of northern African foreign policies.

There are other, basically nonpolitical factors of unity in northern Africa. One is the region's Arab nature. Africa north of the Sahara is made up of an ancient mixture of peoples, mostly of Hamatic and Semitic origins. Within these general categories, Berbers, Egyptians, Tuareg, Nilotes, Amharas, Danakils, Gallas, Somalis, and myriad other ethnic groups inhabit the region. However, to almost all, the Arabic language and Arab culture give a basic unity. The only real exception is the Amharic culture of Ethiopia, with its own script and history. The cultural meaning of "Arab" is the only one that makes sense; the term has no true validity as an ethnic description. Because of this cultural unity—again with the exception of Ethiopia—it is possible to speak of Arab nationalism in connection with the entire area. By this is meant the fact that the countries of northern Africa are susceptible to appeals made in the name of Arab slogans and will supposedly help each other and share each other's woes in the name of Arab brotherhood. The ideology of Arab nationalism has helped to reinforce the myth of regional unity.

A similar ideology that affects this part of the Arab world is one based on African unity. While in neither case does the prevalence of slogans guarantee that Arab or African unity will, in fact, become a reality, it does mean that there is a powerful symbol under which foreign policies and attitudes can be made appealing. The power of such slogans is great, and leaders who adopt and champion them can end up being their prisoners. There is thus both myth and reality in the pan-ideologies of Arab Africa.

Another factor of unity is Islam. In all except two of the countries, more than 95 per cent of the population are Muslim; in Ethiopia the proportion is about a third, and in Sudan it is over two-thirds. Islam is the state religion in Morocco, Tunisia, Libya, Egypt, and Somalia; in all these countries and in Algeria and Sudan, there have been important movements pressing for an Islamic state. *Tariqas* have played an important role in the emergence of some of the states—for example, the Khatmiya and Ansar in Sudan, the Sanussi in Libya, and the four sects of Somalia. In many areas, Islam has been associated with traditional forces, and in some, such as Morocco, Algeria, and Egypt, the fight against foreign domination has been spoken of as a *jihad* (holy war), although never officially. However, within the walls of the Qarawiyin in Fez, the Zeituna in Tunis, and al-Azhar in Cairo—all of them great Islamic centers of learning more than a thousand years old—modernization, renaissance, and re-examination of the doctrines of Islam have manifested themselves as religious attempts to cope with Westernism and secularism.

Finally, there is a factor of similarity in the geographical location of the northern African countries. With the partial exception of Ethiopia and Sudan, the countries of northern Africa have their centers of population along the Mediterranean shores, to the west along the Atlantic, and to the east along the Red Sea. From Morocco to Egypt, there is a similar, if not common, Mediterranean civilization, based on cultural, geographic, climatic, agricultural, and historical affinities. All the countries have their backs against the Sahara (or, in the Horn of Africa, against another wasteland of the same Arabic name); those areas of population which are not located along the coast are found on watercourses or highlands in the interior. Africa north of the Sahara is thus squeezed between the desert and the sea.

Although this characteristic provides an element of similarity, it also provides the setting for disunity. The countries are stretched out along the top of the continent, side by side, not grouped together. No three states touch each other in an inhabited region, and to pass from one capital to another involves travel across large distances. Great regions of many states are almost totally uninhabited—the elbow of Somalia, northern Sudan, most of Egypt and Libya, parts of the Algerian Sahara. Furthermore, the sea has not provided the contact and unity that the term "Mediterranean civilization" implies. The North African Arabs were not seafaring folk (Barbary-pirate leaders were Turks). Neither the Egyptian nor the Somali coast has any natural harbors, and most of the large ports of today were built (or built up) by the colonial powers, who did depend on the sea. In fact, to the northern Africans, sand was a better highway than water; the major cities of Marrakesh, Fez, Tlemcen, Qairwan, Cairo, Khartoum, Harar, and Addis Ababa were all founded in the interior, and the legendary caravan routes were the real ties that held the region together. All these factors have had an influence on the history and thinking of northern Africa, and contributed to the xenophobia of the past century. Today, although the commercial contacts and maritime development of all Africa north of the Sahara have grown in importance and far outstripped the slow-paced contacts across the desert, the location of the states side by side poses difficulties for the implementation of slogans of unity.

Regional Unity in Northern Africa

The unity and cooperation of the new states of Africa fell apart in the Congo crisis, during the same year that much of Africa attained its independence. The unity of the Arab world showed itself to be illusory in the Palestine War even before most of Arab Africa had joined the ranks of independent nations. Yet, within the area of Africa north of the Sahara, there are still hopes and attempts to attain regional unity, and it is around these that much of the region's foreign policy is centered.

The Arab Maghreb movement[1] looks to a united North Africa. As soon as Tunisia and Morocco attained independence, in mid-1956, a meeting was held between representatives of the two countries in Paris, where a "united North African policy" was pledged. In June of the following year, Bourguiba's proposal for a federal North African union linked with France was turned down by Paris in the heat of the Algerian war. The year 1958 marked the birth and near death of a united Maghreb. In early March, Mohammed V and Bourguiba formally espoused the idea of a Maghreb federation. At the end of the following month, representatives of the Istiqlal, Neo-Destour, and FLN met in Tangier and created a Permanent Secretariat of Maghreb Muttahid. Resolutions recognized the FLN as representative of the Algerian people and suggested the creation of a "provisional government," which was formed within the year; Moroccan aspirations with regard to Mauritania were endorsed, and a consultative assembly was proposed, to be composed of ten members each from the Moroccan and Tunisian national assemblies and from the National Council of the Algerian Revolution. The Secretariat met again in Tunis in June and August, and in Rabat in October. Then it suspended its animation.

Plans for regional unity owed their collapse to both internal and international politics. At the end of 1958, the UNFP government, which replaced the Istiqlal, searching for more fertile fields of foreign policy, turned to Black Africa and the Arab Middle East. The Permanent Secretariat was too much Istiqlal-tainted to be supported by the new government. Relations between Tunisia and Algeria in 1960 were teetering between strain and amity over policy toward the Algerian negotiations, the Tunisian acceptance of the French oil pipeline out of Algeria, and the presence of Algerian troops in Tunisia; Tunisia and Morocco withdrew ambassadors from each other's capital in early 1961 over the question of Mauritania. Above all, the leaders of all three countries gave victory in Algeria higher priority than unity in North Africa, and their silent rivalries came out into the open as an Algerian and Saharan settlement came into view.

However, in September, 1960, Bourguiba again recalled the work of the Secretariat and asked for its strengthening to aid the FLN, making another proposal of "organic political union" between Algeria and Tunisia in order to internationalize the conflict. At the funeral of Mohammed V in March, 1961, Hassan II met with Bourguiba and Abbas to unite North African policy concerning the Algerian negotiations. Concrete proposals for a sound economic basis of Maghreb unity also came from UNFP and FLN representatives, who suggested the possibility of a jointly planned North African economy based on an exchange between Moroccan agricultural production and Algerian mineral deposits. In January, 1962, Morocco and the Algerian Provisional Government signed an agreement setting up a seven-man interministerial council for a United Arab Maghreb. The council has never met since then; the two forces most actively committed to Pan-Maghrebism—the Tunisian Government and the Moroccan Opposition—were left out. A year later, in February, 1963, the Foreign Ministers of all three countries met in Rabat for the first time since Mohammed V's funeral. Beyond the single fact of their meeting, they accomplished little toward overcoming the differences that separated Morocco from Algeria and Tunisia, and Tunisia from Algeria.

Since Algerian independence, the Arab Maghreb has thus returned to the level of slogans, as national problems and nationalized sentiments come to the fore in the three states. Problems of sovereignty over the Sahara and Mauritania, rivalries between the leaders of (and within) the three countries, the position of the Moroccan monarchy in a republican Maghreb, and individual nationalisms brought about by separate independence struggles—all are ingredients that have kept unity plans for the Maghreb from jelling. But the biggest difference of all lies on the level of ideology, in domestic as well as foreign policy. To revolutionary Algeria, an Arab monarchy (such as Morocco's) and an evolutionary bourgeois government (such as Tunisia's) represent only arrested change in an ex-colonial society. To Morocco and Tunisia, a neighbor the size of Algeria with a tendency to export its internal revolution is a manifest cause for concern. For the moment, these differences are more important to the countries of the Maghreb than the geographical imperative of unity.

At the other pole of the African Arab world, Cairo has attempted to extend its influence throughout the African continent.[2] As far back as 1954, in his *Philosophy of the Revolution,* Nasser wrote about the "African Continent Circle," saying, "Surely the people of Africa will continue to look at us—we who are the guardians of the continent's northern gate, we who constitute the connecting link between the continent and the outer world." Whatever may have been Nasser's ideas at that time—before the independence of Sudan and the rebuff from Libya in 1956—it is not likely that present-day Egyptian foreign policy seeks to take over neighboring African states. Rather, Egypt is following a more sophisticated approach in interstate politics—attempting to build up a firm basis of cooperation and support in Africa, and particularly in northern Africa. The contrast between regional unity in the Maghreb and Egyptian influence in northeastern Africa is great. Not only does it involve a difference between institutional and policy unity; relations in northeastern Africa are also different because they are polarized around a single country and because they are in part an adjunct of Egypt's relations with the Arab world.

Egypt's policy makes skillful use of many instruments. In recent years Nasser has shown that he considers Egypt "the connecting link" with the outer world, not in geographic terms, but in terms of modernization. The most important and least tangible instrument of Egyptian policy is its pretense at being a model for African development. Arab socialism is advertised as an indigenous product, not a foreign import; as such, it is argued, it is applicable to the other countries of northern Africa and, paradoxically, is itself exportable. Egypt has already paved the way for one aspect of development by showing that underdeveloped nations can obtain military and economic aid from the Soviet bloc and still retain their independence—*and* their Western aid. If Egypt can show significant growth under its tutelary political system and its Arab socialist economy, not only will it have gained in national power, but it will also have perfected a valuable patent for a bootstrap for its neighbors.

Religion is also used as an instrument of national policy. Egypt has added a religious attaché to many of its embassies in Muslim Africa, has used al-Azhar University for training foreign students in Islamic learning, has established the Voice of Islam as a far-reaching radio program, and has sent Egyptian *imams* (akin to clergy) to help fill the needs of the growing African Muslim community. The Islamic Congress, established in 1954, is the principal organization through which religious exchanges are channeled. The effects of these efforts are difficult to evaluate; needless to say, all that is Muslim is not pro-Egyptian, but the Egyptian religious programs—particularly in a socially conscious religion such as Islam—are also made to carry an Egyptian message.

Another arm of Egyptian policy is education. Egypt has sent teachers to northern African countries from Morocco to Somalia. Their effectiveness has not always been helpful to the Egyptian cause; many returned to Egypt from Morocco after the first year

(1957), because their propaganda was stronger than their academic qualifications and their impatience with Moroccan slowness in paying them was greater than that of French teachers. But some went back to Morocco after 1959, and Egyptians now teach in large numbers in Libya and Somalia and in lesser numbers in Sudan and Algeria. Cairo University has established cultural centers in Rabat and Khartoum. The very fact that Cairo can spare teachers reinforces Egypt's position as a leader of African development, and the message the teachers bring strengthens it even further.

At some point, communication slips from education into propaganda, another instrument of Egyptian national policy. The Voice of the Arabs, the Voice of Free Africa, and the Voice of Islam are all heard throughout northern Africa. Egyptian propaganda is extreme, emotional, and couched in the picturesque language of Arabic insults. It is wholly at the service of Egyptian foreign policy. In place of a detailed analysis, one significant characteristic should be noted: Targets are hit and the chosen are championed not only in terms of anticolonialism and of Arab, African, or new nations' solidarity, but also in terms of internal policies—that is, conformity to the principles of Arab socialism.

The Arab League is also used as an organizational instrument of Egyptian policy whenever possible. At the League, Morocco, Algeria, Tunisia, Libya, and Sudan sit with the U.A.R. and the Arab Middle East; before independence, Algeria took part in the meetings as an observer. As its membership has increased, the League has adopted the problems of its new members; the Mauritanian and Algerian questions have come to occupy a place on the agenda alongside those of Oman and Palestine.

But Egyptian domination of the Arab League has not been without contest since the foundation of the organization. Between October, 1958 (two weeks after it joined), and February, 1961, Tunisia was absent from League sessions in protest against Egyptian support for Salah ben Yussef; when the League met in the Maghreb, at Casablanca, for the first time, King Mohammed V announced that "the Egyptian period of the League is over; the Maghrebian period has begun."* Yet the general effectiveness of Egyptian leadership—Egyptian Abdulkhalek Hassouna was re-

* Egypt's threat in September, 1962, to withdraw from the League reflected these and other challenges to its leadership, but Egypt suspended its resignation almost as soon as it was offered.

elected in 1962 as Secretary General—has strengthened the propaganda position of Egypt, even if it has not brought many concrete accomplishments out of the League. Egypt reinforces its leadership of Arab nationalism through its role as a haven for political exiles, including not only Ben Yussef but also other refugees in the past from Morocco, Algeria, Tunisia, Libya, Sudan, Eritrea, and Somalia, of which only some of the more important—Allal al-Fassi, Ferhat Abbas, Ahmed Ben Bella, Habib Bourguiba, Hajj Mohammed Hussein, King Idris—have returned home. An African Association, established in 1955, has coordinated assistance to African exiles and nationalist movements.

Finally, Egypt uses military aid to further its foreign policy. It has given arms to Libya and Somalia, claimed to have sent arms to Tunisia in 1957 and promised volunteers to Bizerte in 1961, and was the most important source of military support to the FLN in the two years before the independence of Tunisia. Egypt has also been charged with giving military support to opposition movements in Tunisia and Libya.

The states of northern Africa are members of all three "circles"—Arab, Muslim, and African—identified by Nasser as "the theater of our activity in which we should move as much as we can." In this area, the goal of Egyptian foreign policy for the moment is one of leadership and influence rather than federation or takeover. Yet Nasser's neighbors are universally wary of the Egyptians. There is frequently a feeling that predominant Egyptian influence means the loss of independence, if not the loss of sovereignty. The U.A.R.'s two neighbors both give testimony to this feeling. Sudan made it plain after 1956 that Egyptian support for nationalism was a useful weapon against the British, but little more. King Idris, in 1956, made it equally clear that Egyptian interference was considered subversive, not fraternal; and Libya, when looking to regional cooperation, has considered itself part of the Maghreb—partly for the purpose of counterbalancing Egyptian influence. Of all the countries in northern Africa, Algeria and Somalia are the ones that have shown the greatest acceptance of Egyptian influence. Somalia and Egypt are linked by antipathy to Ethiopia—Somalia because of its territorial dispute, and Egypt because of Ethiopia's recognition of and cooperation with Israel. Somalia, with its weak national power and its strong national pretensions, needs allies; Egypt seeks followers. Yet even Somalia is not so closely tied to Egypt that it can be classed as a mere follower; like the other states of northern Africa, it is still jealous enough of its new independence to guard it closely. The case of Algeria is slightly different and is open to even broader possibilities of cooperation with Egypt. The revolutionary or Arab socialist nature of the two regimes gives the two states common outlooks on many problems. Ben Bella and Boumedienne are the leaders of the FLN's Arabist wing, as opposed to Krim's or Khider's Maghrebism. Nasser has included Algeria, along with Egypt, Iraq, Syria, and Yemen, as one of the five liberated Arab countries, and during the exchange of visits between Nasser and Ben Bella in May, 1963, the Algerian premier declared his future hope of seeing Algeria in a broad U.A.R. Short of that day, Algeria and Egypt remain close allies.

Regional unity has made little headway in northern Africa. National rivalries and the Algerian war have kept Pan-Maghrebism from solidifying; national consciousness and national ideologies have kept Nilotic unity, or even foreign-policy cooperation with Egypt, from crystallizing in northeastern Africa. Even in the Horn of Africa, the pattern of relations is conflict rather than cooperation. As the nations discover the differing interests arising out of independent existence, the lure of political unity based on an accident of geographic contiguity becomes overshadowed by difficulties. Competing economies, conflicting ideologies, incompatible political systems, and emerging national interests rise in importance and may even become predominant in the future. In this situation, states have tried to seek "contiguity" on the bases of similar ideologies and of the national interest.

Northern African states were members of two such interest groups—the Casablanca and the Monrovia "blocs."[3] Loose and temporary though these groups may be, they are examples of attempts to create associations on the basis of some political similarities, and not merely because of residence in the same corner of the world. The Casablanca meeting, held in Morocco's largest city in January, 1961, established the framework for cooperation between Morocco, Algeria, and the U.A.R., and Guinea, Ghana, and Mali. A Political Committee for policy coordination, an Economic Committee for the establishment of a customs union, a Joint African High Command for military cooperation, and a Cultural Committee were created; further meetings of all committees have been held at regular intervals, for nearly two years, with few concrete results. The labor movements of this group, along with lesser unions from other African states, met to form the All-African Trade Union Federation in Casablanca in May, 1961, although since then the organization has shown no substance.* The interests of the participating states are diverse: recognition of Nasser's position in Africa, "progressive" support for Hassan II's beleaguered monarchy and for its Mauritanian aspirations, solidarity behind Algerian independence, sympathy for the Pan-African aspirations of the Union of African States (Guinea, Ghana, and Mali), and solidarity against the frequent isolation of these radical states in opposition to the moderate African majority.

The Monrovia meeting in the Liberian capital in May, 1961, brought together Libya, Somalia, Ethiopia, Nigeria, Sierra Leone, thirteen states of former French Black Africa, and the host country. Tunisia attended as an observer. The basis for cooperation was much looser than that of the Casablanca group, reflecting the size and diversity of membership; the resolutions passed were less extreme, reflecting the more moderate policies of the participants. Economic cooperation was anticipated and was examined further in subsequent meetings. The Monrovia states' labor-union international is the African Trade Union Congress (ATUC), founded in Dakar in January, 1962, also quiescent.

The lines between these two groups have been only approximate. Tunisia, with an essentially moderate policy, is still influenced by its need for good relations with Algeria. The Libyan policy of indecision reflects its position between Tunisia and Egypt. Egypt seeks to befriend Somalia, while Ethiopia and Somalia—both of the Monrovia group—have an irredentist claim between them, as do Algeria and Morocco of the Casablanca group. Sudan has kept aloof from both groups, following a policy of neutrality within the neutralist world. Even to the member states, these first attempts at finding ideological rather than geographical allies has not been completely satisfying. The Casablanca group, especially, felt the strains of its own internal contradictions and the pull of the larger Monrovia group on some of its members; it became impossible to hold a meeting of the members after late 1962. However, since its first meeting at Monrovia, the larger group had been attempting to bring the two groups together in the name of the unity of the entire geographic region. An unsuc-

* It has, however, increased pressure for a Pan-African confederation, resulting in the suspension of UMT membership and the termination of UGTA membership in the ICFTU in 1963.

cessful attempt to attract the smaller group was made at Lagos in January, 1962, but by its July, 1962, meeting in Cairo, the Casablanca group was ready for a meeting with Monrovia. The African summit meeting that resulted was the result of careful and lengthy preparation and was held in Addis Ababa on May 23, 1963. The major achievements of the conference include a promise of concerted aid to the nationalist movements of the remaining colonial territories, mainly in southern Africa, and the preparation of an African Unity Organization, which when finally completed and ratified, is to coordinate policy and cooperation among member states. The elusiveness of unity has made it an absorbing preoccupation for northern African foreign policies. But the lack of an agreed definition of "unity," the strength of narrow nationalism, and the absence of an external challenge that poses the overriding need even for cooperation on the continental level have previously kept the eight states divided. There is no assurance that the African Unity Organization will prove any more significant or satisfying than were its two successors; nor is there any reason to believe that the search for smaller, ideologically or geographically compact alliances will disappear, whatever may be the future of the Addis Ababa organization.

Elements of Strategy in Northern Africa

There is basic agreement within northern Africa on a policy favoring Cold War neutralism and the liberation of the African continent from colonialism. Two conflicts are inherent in the northern African position. On the one hand, neutralism is a policy of noninvolvement with either side in the Cold War, and anticolonialism involves a specific rejection of policies of some of the Western states. On the other hand, a number of the northern African states have Western military installations on their soil. Thus, the question of the strategic importance of this part of the African continent is posed.

Strategic value has usually been thought of in geographic terms. Northern Africa's position between Black Africa and Eurasia has given it importance ever since preclassical times. The four focal points of northern Africa are Tangier, Tunis, Suez, and French Somaliland. The symbolic value of these points, where Africa meets the World Island, is perhaps great, but it has faded as far as Cold War strategy is concerned. Historically, all four points have been links in invasion routes in a northerly and a southerly direction. Both Arabs and Spaniards crossed the Strait of Gibraltar; Romans, Vandals, Normans, Arabs, and the World War II Allies and Axis traveled between Tunisia and Sicily; the Pharaohs, the Children of Israel, the Arabs, the British, the Egyptians, and the Israelis have marched back and forth across Sinai; the Arabs and the British have reached hands across the Bab al-Mandab. In a military situation, these routes may again have importance; in peacetime, cultural influences are still felt across these narrow bodies of water. But current military and political strategy has largely bypassed these four hooks by which Africa hangs on to Eurasia.

In the other direction, an invisible line connects these four waterways. Known popularly as the "British lifeline," it has also been the strategic trade route of France and Italy and the crucial lane of commerce for oil supplies from the Middle East to Europe. Essentially (except where it passes through Egypt), this line lies outside Africa; it is Mediterranean, not African. In wartime, it can be cut by forces stationed on either side of the three straits or the Canal, although, during World War II, military traffic to Malta was never completely cut off. The importance of the Suez Canal, nationalized in 1956 and lying wholly within Egyptian territory, is obvious, but the importance of the lifeline itself has been diminished by the airplane and the supertanker—despite the smaller capacity of the former and the higher costs of the latter.

The term "strategic importance" has also been commonly construed as referring to military bases. Morocco, Algeria, Tunisia, Libya, Ethiopia, and French Somaliland all contain British, French, or American installations. Five air bases and a naval air station in Morocco are to be evacuated by the end of 1963, although there is some hope of maintaining some of these facilities in operational readiness by using them as training camps for the Moroccan air arm, according to a Morocco-American agreement of 1963. French bases and training installations in Morocco were evacuated by May, 1962. Mers al-Kebir, the major French naval establishment near Oran, is to be leased by France for fifteen years; a number of military and air installations throughout Algeria are also left to French use for five years. All French bases in Tunisia were evacuated in 1958, with the exception of the large naval and air complex at Bizerte, which is to be evacuated in 1963. The American base agreement with Libya, concerning Wheelus Field, runs until 1970, and the major British installation, Idris

Field, is covered by a similar agreement. Britain also has at its disposal other training areas, although it has already returned some of these to Libya, and French outposts in the Fezzan were evacuated in 1956, with the understanding that they could be used by France under certain specified circumstances. A major American communications facility is located in Asmara, in Eritrea. France maintains sovereignty over French Somaliland, with its large port and airfield at Djibouti. In the long run, these bases are of far less importance than they were in past wars. The development of missile forces and the presence of the Mediterranean Fleet may soon make them totally dispensable as both a peacetime deterrent and a wartime defense. Their value for limited warfare and internal stability is slim, since the propaganda effect of intervention in internal affairs would be highly counterproductive.

"Strategic importance" is also usually associated with raw materials. Algerian and Libyan oil production is indeed great. Italy, France, Switzerland, and Germany are all building costly pipeline and refining installations to handle the oil flowing from North Africa. But the value of Saharan oil is even greater to the two producing countries than it is to Europe. North Africa depends on the continuance of this flow to earn the hard currency necessary to its own development, and it intends to use some of the oil for its own industrial expansion. At the same time, there is a glut of oil on the world market, produced not only by Russian dumping but also by overproduction throughout the world. There is not yet a plethora of capital in North Africa. The element of mutual dependence, even heavier on the African than the European side, does not diminish the strategic importance of Saharan oil. But it does put it in a different light.

Beyond these usual understandings of the elements of strategic importance are some newer considerations. Neutralism in northern Africa is encouraged by the fact that it gives its practitioners a way of obtaining aid from both sides. Therefore (from the Western nations' viewpoint), an element to be taken into account in this region is the degree of penetration by the "other side." In no country is there a legal Communist party, and in no country is local Communist activity of any importance. Yet, in a number of countries—particularly those of the Casablanca group—there is frequently a spirit of admiration and sympathy among the governing elite for Communist methods and policies.

Reasons for this attitude are complex. Much of it is the result of an identity felt by northern African nations with the aims they perceive in Communist propaganda and policies directed against colonialism. Sympathy is also aroused by the Soviet use of the word "socialism"; the African states, in their search for an indigenous system, have not adopted the political economy of class warfare, but they have learned to use some Marxist concepts, and they have adopted some Leninist ideas of party organization. There is also a natural tendency to break away from relations dominated by the former colonial power, particularly as the former colonies seek economic diversification. Yet, with one notable exception, northern African trade still remains closely tied to Europe and, especially, to the former colonial power. The exception is the U.A.R., for the U.S.S.R. is its largest customer, and Egypt's trade constitutes about two-thirds of all of Africa's trade with the entire Communist bloc.

A major reason for relations with the Communist bloc—and at the same time a good index of Communist penetration, revealing both its breadth and its shallowness—is aid. The bloc has given aid to all northern African countries except Libya. Morocco received somewhat less than $5 million in military aid only in 1960–61, although it purchased arms from the Communist bloc in 1962 and possibly before. Algeria received an undetermined amount, estimated at between $10 million and $20 million, before independence, including some assistance from China. Tunisia was granted $28 million in Russian credits in 1961, during the Bizerte crisis, and has received $18 million from the satellites since 1960. Since 1955, the U.A.R. has been given over $500 million by Russia (including $325 million for the Aswan Dam), over $100 million by the satellites, and a $5 million grant from China in 1956; in addition, bloc countries have granted the U.A.R. at least $500 million in military aid. In 1961, Sudan was given $22 million in Russian economic assistance. Ethiopia, long an area of Russian interest, was granted a $114 million credit from the bloc in 1958–59, over $100 million of which came from the U.S.S.R., and over 90 per cent of which was not allocated until 1963, since Ethiopia reserves the right to decide how to spend it. Somalia was given $62 million in credits by the bloc during 1961 and an additional $20 million by Peking in 1963. Despite this attention from the Soviet bloc, no country of northern Africa is in danger of takeover, or even of broadly following Communist doctrine. Africa tends to regard Communist aid and support as as much its right, in the context of Cold War competition, as Western aid, and considers nonintervention a rigid corollary of both. The need for Western attention to northern Africa as a strategic area is thus increased, since the West can know that these countries are not "lost." By the same token, they can never be completely "won."

Despite these reasons for consideration of northern Africa as a strategic area, there is another factor, overshadowing all, that is a unique resource of many of the countries of the area. This is their dynamic leadership. Especially Bourguiba, Ben Bella, Nasser, Haile Selassie and the several leaders of Morocco have been prominent exponents of neutralism, and all aspire to a recognized position of leadership on a continental—not just a national—level. Nasser has probably been the most active, although not necessarily the most constructive. He attended the Bandung Conference in 1955, met as one of the neutralist "Big Three" with Nehru and Tito in Brioni in 1956, and was one of the organizers of the Belgrade Conference of 1961. Morocco has been host to the founding conferences of the Casablanca group and of the AATUF. Morocco and Tunisia also proposed their good offices in the Algerian war on several occasions, notably in 1956 and 1957, and Morocco acted as conciliator between Egypt and Tunisia in 1960 and 1961. Tunisia has been active in the establishment of the ATUC, and was an effective catalyst in the Franco-Algerian negotiations of 1960–62. Ethiopia was the site of a number of Pan-African conferences, including the 1963 summit meeting, and is the seat of several African organizations. Morocco, Tunisia and Egypt aided the Algerian rebels in their war for independence, and all four have given assistance to newer African states south of the Sahara. Examples include Tunisian cultural aid to Cameroun and Niger, Moroccan cultural aid to Senegal and Mali, and Egyptian cultural aid to northern Nigeria, Algerian training for Angolan rebels, Morocco's position as host to the Conference of Nationalist Organizations of the Portuguese Colonies (CONCP) since 1961, and Egyptian aid and interference in Congolese affairs. All of these states have seized upon their membership in the United Nations as an opportunity to gain a world-wide audience and international support for their slogans and policies. Morocco and Egypt have held seats in the Security Council, and a Tunisian (Mongi Slim) has been President of the General Assembly.

The strategic importance of northern Africa thus can be seen in a new light. Like regional unity or unities, it is less geographic than ideological; it depends less on the size, shape, and physical make-up of the countries than on their human ingredients. By the same token, the danger for these countries and the world in which they live is not that of Communist takeover; the preconditions of a Communist society—party, class struggle, important proletariat —are not yet present, and the instruments of takeover are not yet available. The danger is instability and unrest. The dominant factor, which determines what foreign policy and national power will be, is the internal political and governmental system. In northern Africa, domestic politics is of paramount importance. Foreign policy is its adjunct, often directly determined by domestic political maneuvering; Morocco, Algeria, Sudan, and Somalia are cases in point. Of more danger is the fact that foreign policy is often an alternative to internal policy, a diversion from domestic dissatisfaction; Morocco, Tunisia, Egypt, Ethiopia, and Somalia are examples.

Ultimately, these considerations are the deciding factors in the international role of northern Africa, its unity, and its strategy. As neutralist nations with dynamic leadership, but also as emerging nations with promise and problems of development, northern African states face a dilemma. Will their policies reflect a neutralism of positive contribution, or a neutralism of dissatisfaction? The answer depends, above all, on the ability of present leaderships to prepare their mass followings for responsible aspirations and participation in government, and to shape their own promises and performance to fit the needs and capabilities of their nations.

NOTES

Chapter I: Democracy and Independence

1. Edward Shils, *Political Development in the New States* (The Hague: Mouton & Co., 1962). The "gap" is a concept developed by Shils in this excellent essay.

2. *Ibid.*; Gabriel Almond and James Coleman, *The Politics of the Developing Areas* (Princeton, N.J.: Princeton University Press, 1960), p. 53.

3. Max Millikan and Donald Blackmer, *The Emerging Nations* (Boston: Little, Brown and Co., 1961), p. 99.

4. *Ibid.*, p. 74.

5. P. S. N. Prasad *et al.*, *The Economic Development of Libya* (International Bank for Reconstruction and Development; Baltimore, Md.: Johns Hopkins Press, 1960), p. 85.

6. Lucian Pye, "The Non-Western Political Process," in James Rosenau (ed.), *International Politics and Foreign Policy* (Glencoe, Ill.: The Free Press, 1961), p. 293.

Chapter II: Morocco

1. For good treatments of aspects of pre-independence Morocco, see Robert Rezette, *Les Partis politiques marocains* (Paris: Librairie Armand Colin, 1955); Henri Terasse, *Histoire du Maroc* (Casablanca: Atlantides, 1949–50); Jacques Bonjean, *L'Unité de l'empire chérifien* (Paris: Librairie Générale de Droit et de Jurisprudence, 1955); Mohammed Lahbabi, *Le Gouvernement marocain à l'aube du XXe siècle* (Rabat: Editions Techniques Nord-Africaines, 1958).

2. For broader studies of independent Morocco, see Nevill Barbour (ed.), *A Survey of North West Africa* (London and New York: Oxford University Press, 1959); Douglas Ashford, *Political Change in Morocco* (Princeton, N.J.: Princeton University Press, 1961); I. William Zartman, *Problems of New Power* (New York: Atherton Press, 1963); Jean and Simonne Lacouture, *Le Maroc à l'épreuve* (Paris: Editions du Seuil, 1960); Roger Le Tourneau, *L'Evolution politique de l'Afrique du nord musulmane* (Paris: Librairie Armand Colin, 1962).

3. Jean Lacouture, "Morocco: Monarchy and Revolution," *Africa South in Exile*, VI, No. 1 (Autumn, 1961), 90.

4. *The New York Times*, January 9, 1962. Particularly bad strikes cleared many opposition supporters out of the Communications, Education, and For-

eign Ministries in late 1961, as the government kept its promise to fire those who went ahead with the strikes.

Chapter III: Algeria

1. On the evolution of national consciousness, see André Nouschi, *La Naissance du nationalisme algérien, 1914–1954* (Paris: Les Editions de Minuit, 1962). For a biography of Abbas, see Jean Lacouture, *Cinq Hommes et la France* (Paris: Editions du Seuil, 1961).

2. Enlightening parallels can be found in Crane Brinton, *The Anatomy of Revolution* (New York: Prentice-Hall, 1952).

3. For a semiofficial analysis of the institutions and legal position of the nationalist movement, see Mohammed Bedjaoui, *Law and the Algerian Revolution* (Brussels: International Association of Democratic Lawyers, 1961); also Jacques Duchemin, *Histoire du FLN* (Paris: Editions de la Table Ronde, 1962).

4. For a full account of this crisis, see Jean Lacouture, "Les Etapes de la crise du FLN," *Le Monde*, July 11, 1962.

5. Khider, Political Bureau announcement, in *Le Monde*, August 12, 1962.

6. Ben Bella, in *Unità*, August 13, 1962. The following quotations are from this and other interviews, and from the CNRA Tripoli program. There is also frequent use of such language as "a democratic and modern state, cleared of all police dictatorship, assuring all its citizens individual liberty, freedom of expression, and social justice" (Political Bureau declaration, July 24, 1962), but, whatever the degree of sincerity behind them, the words should be read in their revolutionary context. A most important work in the Algerian search for a doctrine is Franz Fanon, *Les Damnés de la terre* (Paris: François Maspéro, Editeur, 1962).

7. Figure refers to industrial licenses granted. For recent reviews of the Constantine Plan, see "Caisse d'équipement et de développement de l'Algérie," *Plan 1962* (Paris: August, 1962); and *The Constantine Plan for Algeria* (New York: French Embassy, Information Office, May, 1961).

8. Nevill Barbour (ed.), *A Survey of North West Africa* (London and New York: Oxford University Press, 1959), p. 249; the chapter on Algeria is the book's weakest. For a good (and not outdated) review of social and economic, as well as political, Algeria, see Germaine Tillion, *L'Afrique bascule vers l'avenir* (Paris: Les Editions de Minuit, 1960); François Perroux (ed.), *L'Algérie de demain* (Paris: Presses Universitaires de France, 1962); and Pierre Bourdieu, *The Algerians* (Boston: Beacon Press, 1962).

9. For an excellent analysis of this shift in the world Communist perspective, see Bernard S. Morris, "Recent Shifts in Communist Strategy: India and Southeast Asia," in John H. Kautsky (ed.), *Political Change in Underdeveloped Countries* (New York: John Wiley & Sons, 1962).

10. For a clear-sighted view of the problem, see Georges Lavau, "Le visage politique de l'Algérie de demain," in Perroux, *op. cit.* For a legal analysis, see Roger Pinto, "Le Statut des européens," *Le Monde*, April 18 and 19, 1962; "Les Accords d'Evian après un an d'application," *Le Monde*, March 19, 1963, and René-William Thorp, "Le Sort des biens français en Algérie," *Le Monde*, May 31, 1963.

11. Bedjaoui, *op. cit.*, p. 50.

Chapter IV: *Tunisia*

1. For a general study of modern Tunisia, see Nevill Barbour (ed.), *A Survey of North West Africa* (London and New York: Oxford University Press, 1959); and Roger Le Tourneau, *L'Evolution politique de l'Afrique du nord musulmane* (Paris: Librairie Armand Colin, 1962). A thorough bibliography is given in Paul Romeril, "Tunisian Nationalism: A Bibliographical Article," *Middle East Journal*, XIV, No. 2 (Spring, 1960), 206–15.

2. Gabriel Ardant, *La Tunisie d'aujourd'hui et de demain* (Paris: Editeur Calmann-Lévy, 1961), p. 35. Ardant infers that the Tunisian middle and upper classes together number about a fifth of the population, a high percentage for a developing nation (p. 79).

3. For an appealing account of Bourguiba's views and an excellent biography, see Jean Lacouture, *Cinq Hommes et la France* (Paris: Editions du Seuil, 1961). The following quotes are taken from Bourguiba's speeches, particularly those of October 2, 1958, and February 6 and 8, 1961.

4. The real importance of the party in Tunisia makes it necessary to treat it along with governmental institutions, instead of separately in the following section. The best up-to-date analysis of the reorganized party is found in Clement H. Moore, "The Neo-Destour Party: A Structure for Democracy?," *World Politics*, XIV, No. 3 (April, 1962), 461–83. The interrelation of party, government, and people is seen most clearly in the position of Tayeb Mehiri, who, as Interior Secretary and also Assistant Secretary-General of the party, controls administration, local appointments, and party organization.

5. Moore, *op. cit.*, p. 472.

6. See *Women of Tunisia* (Tunisian Secretariat of State for Information, 1961).

Chapter V: *Libya*

1. For longer studies of independent Libya, see Majid Khadduri, *Modern Libya* (Baltimore, Md.: Johns Hopkins Press, 1963); Nevill Barbour (ed.), *A Survey of North West Africa* (London and New York: Oxford University Press, 1959); Henry Villard, *Libya, The New Arab Kingdom of North Africa* (Ithaca, N.Y.: Cornell University Press, 1956); William H. Lewis and Robert Gordon, "Libya After Two Years of Independence," *Middle East Journal*, VIII, No. 1 (Winter, 1954), 41–53; "Libya: Seven Years of Independence," *World Today*, XV, No. 11 (February, 1959), 59–68.

2. Figures on population status taken from Prasad, *op. cit.*, pp. 25, 28; verified in Robert Capot-Rey, "Etat actuel du nomadisme au Sahara," *Les Problèmes de la zone aride* (Paris: UNESCO, 1962), p. 33. They differ slightly from those given in *The Worldmark Encyclopedia of the Nations* (New York: Harper & Brothers, 1960), p. 600; and even more so from Barbour, *op. cit.*, p. 346.

3. Lewis and Gordon, *op. cit.*, pp. 44–45; Villard, *op. cit.*, p. 54.

4. A wise discussion of this point, scattered among much other solid socioeconomic information and reflections on Libya, is found in P. S. N. Prasad *et al.*, *The Economic Development of Libya* (International Bank of Reconstruction and Development, Baltimore, Md.: Johns Hopkins Press, 1960), p. 86.

5. For a thorough study of constitution-making, see Ismail Raghib Khadidi, *Constitutional Development in Libya* (Beirut: Khayat's, 1956).

Chapter VI: United Arab Republic (Egypt)

1. Good treatments of prerevolutionary and postrevolutionary Egypt are found in Tom Little, *Egypt* (New York: Frederick A. Praeger, 1958); Maurice Harari, *Government and Politics in the Middle East* (Englewood Cliffs, N.J.: Prentice-Hall, 1962); *Egypt* (New Haven, Conn.: Human Relations Area Files Press, 1957); Jean and Simonne Lacouture, *Egypt in Transition* (New York: Criterion Books, 1958); Nadav Safran, *Egypt in Search of Political Community* (Boston: Harvard University Press, 1962); H. B. Sharabi, *Government and Politics in the Middle East in the Twentieth Century* (Princeton, N.J.: D. Van Nostrand Co., 1962); Mohammed Nagib, *Egypt's Destiny* (Garden City, N.Y.: Doubleday & Company, 1955); Anwar as-Sadat, *Revolt on the Nile* (London: Allan Wingate Publishers, 1957).

2. On the role of the military in the revolution, see P. J. Vatikiotis, *The Egyptian Army in Politics* (Bloomington, Ind.: Indiana University Press, 1961); Morroe Berger, *Military Elite and Social Change* (Research Monograph No. 6, Center for International Studies, Princeton University, 1960); Manfred Halpern, "Middle Eastern Armies and the New Middle Class," in John Johnson (ed.), *The Role of the Military in Underdeveloped Countries* (Princeton, N.J.: Princeton University Press, 1962), pp. 277–317.

3. On revolutionary Egypt, in addition to the books already cited, see Keith Wheelock, *Nasser's New Egypt* (New York: Frederick A. Praeger, 1960); and Marcel Colombe, "Où va l'Egypte?" *Orient*, V, No. 4 (Winter, 1961), 57–66.

4. Despite his rough but insightful *Egypt's Liberation: Philosophy of the Revolution* (Washington: Public Affairs Press, 1955).

5. See Jean Vigneau, "The Ideology of the Egyptian Revolution," in Walter Z. Laqueur (ed.), *The Middle East in Transition* (New York: Frederick A Praeger, 1956), pp. 129–44; Mohammed Hassanein Heikal, in *al-Ahram*, November 7, 1961; Leonard Binder, "Nasserism: The Protest Movement in the Middle East" (paper delivered to the American Political Science Association convention, 1961); also Nasser, *op. cit.* I am grateful to Dr. Binder for sending me his excellent paper. Quotes in the rest of this section come either from Nasser's speeches or from Heikal.

6. See IEDES Study Group, "La Société urbaine égyptienne," *Tiers Monde*, II, No. 2 (April–June, 1961), 183–210.

7. Daniel Lerner, *The Passing of Traditional Society* (Glencoe, Ill.: The Free Press, 1958), p. 218.

8. *Ibid.*, pp. 214–63.

9. See the excellent treatment in Doreen Warriner, *Land Reform and Development in the Middle East* (2d ed.; London and New York: Oxford University Press, 1962).

10. The Planning Commission set the goal for twenty years, but Nasser had the period reduced by half. For an earlier review, see Kurt Grunwald and Joachim Ronall, *Industrialization in the Middle East* (New York: Council for Middle Eastern Affairs Press, 1960), pp. 182–204.

11. See P. J. Vatikiotis, "Foreign Policy of Egypt," in Roy Macridis (ed.),

Foreign Policy in World Politics (2d ed.; Englewood Cliffs, N.J.: Prentice-Hall, 1962), pp. 335–61.

Chapter VII: Sudan

1. The best single-volume study of Sudan from the Mahdist state to modern times is P. M. Holt, *A Modern History of the Sudan* (New York: Grove Press, 1961). On the Mahdist state, see Holt, *The Mahdist State in the Sudan* (New York and London: Oxford University Press, 1958).

2. George H. T. Kimble, *Tropical Africa* (New York: The Twentieth Century Fund, 1961), II, 296.

3. Studies of post-independence Sudan are found in *Africa Report*, Vol. IV, No. 1 (January, 1959), special issue on Sudan; and P. M. Holt, "Sudanese Nationalism and Self-Determination," in Walter Z. Laqueur (ed.), *The Middle East in Transition* (New York: Frederick A. Praeger, 1956), pp. 166–87.

4. Shorter treatments of Sudan after the coup are found in Peter Kilner, "A Year of Army Rule in the Sudan," *World Today*, XV, No. 11 (November, 1959), 430–41; André Ribaud, "Où en est le Soudan?" *Orient*, III, No. 4 (Winter, 1959), 37–45; Kilner, "Seven Generals," *Africa South in Exile*, V, No. 3 (Spring, 1961), 93–99; and Kilner, "Military Government in Sudan: The Past Three Years," *World Today*, XVII, No. 6 (June, 1962), 259–65. See also Manfred Halpern, "Middle Eastern Armies and the New Middle Class," in John Johnson (ed.), *The Role of the Military in Underdeveloped Countries* (Princeton, N.J.: Princeton University Press, 1962), pp. 277–316; and James Coleman and Belmont Brice, "The Role of the Military in Sub-Saharan Africa," in Johnson, *op. cit.*, pp. 359–406.

5. Five seats reserved for graduates of higher education who voted by mail. See T. E. Smith, *Elections in Developing Countries* (New York: St Martin's Press, 1960), pp. 107–8.

6. On the Gezira, see W. A. Hance, *African Economic Development* (New York: Harper & Brothers, 1958); A. Gaitskell, *Gezira* (London: Faber and Faber, 1959); and John Phillips, *Agriculture and Ecology in Africa* (London: Faber and Faber, 1959; New York: Frederick A. Praeger, 1960).

Chapter VIII: Ethiopia

1. For thorough accounts of this reign, see Margery Perham, *The Government of Ethiopia* (London: Faber and Faber, 1947); David A. Talbot, *Haile Selassie I: Silver Jubilee* (The Hague: Van Stockum and Zoon [1960]); and W. E. H. Howard, *Public Administration in Ethiopia* (Groningen: Wolters, 1956), which is a particularly excellent study, in terms of both methodology and content.

2. For a good study of the pre-independence period, see G. K. N. Trevaskis, *Eritrea, A Colony in Transition: 1914–1952* (New York and London: Oxford University Press, 1960).

3. For two good analyses of recent political change, see Simon D. Messing, "Changing Ethiopia," *Middle East Journal*, IX, No. 4 (Autumn, 1955), 413–32; and William Lewis, "The Ethiopian Empire: Progress and Problems," *Middle East Journal*, X, No. 3 (Summer, 1956), 257–69. The first article utilizes a skillful analytical framework. See also Leo Silberman, "Ethiopia,

Power of Moderation," *Middle East Journal,* XIV, No. 2 (Spring, 1960), 141–56.

4. See William Lewis, "Ethiopia's Revised Constitution," *Middle East Journal,* X, No. 2 (Spring, 1956), 194–200.

5. See Kurt Grunwald and Joachim Ronall, *Industrialization in the Middle East* (New York: Council for Middle Eastern Affairs Press, 1960), pp. 205–11.

Chapter IX: Somalia

1. See Sylvia Pankhurst, *Ex-Italian Somalia* (London: C. A. Watts & Co., 1951), pp. 175–85, 222–60; the book is biased, but it contains much information.

2. For studies of pre- and post-independence Somalia, see Alphonso A. Castagno, "The Republic of Somalia," *Africa Report,* V, No. 7 (July, 1960) 2ff.; Anthony Reyner, "Somalia: The Problems of Independence," *Middle East Journal,* XIV, No. 3 (Summer, 1960), 247–55; Castagno, "Somalia," *International Conciliation,* No. 522 (March, 1959); I. M. Lewis, "The New East African Republic of Somalia," *World Today,* XVI, No. 7 (July, 1960), 287–96; and Lewis, *A Pastoral Democracy* (New York and London: Oxford University Press, 1961). The special Somali issue of *Présence africaine* (No. 38, Fall, 1961) has much interesting information but is riddled with errors.

3. For a broader review of education, see George H. T. Kimble, *Tropical Africa* (New York: The Twentieth Century Fund, 1961), II, 130–32; and Helen Kitchen (ed.), *The Educated African: A Country-by-Country Survey of Educational Development in Africa* (compiled by Ruth Sloan Associates) (New York: Frederick A. Praeger, 1962).

4. See Mark Karp, *The Economics of Trusteeship in Somalia* (New York: New York University Press, 1961).

5. See Leo Silberman, "Change and Conflict in the Horn of Africa," *Foreign Affairs,* XXXVII, No. 4 (July, 1959), 649–59 (especially 655).

Chapter X: Unity and Strategy

1. For a further discussion of the Arab Maghreb, see William Sands, "Prospects for a United Maghrib," in Tibor Kerekes (ed.), *The Arab Middle East and Muslim Africa* (New York: Frederick A. Praeger, 1961); Roger Le Tourneau, *Evolution politique de l'Afrique du nord musulmane* (Paris: Librairie Armand Colin, 1962); and I. William Zartman, "The Sahara—Bridge or Barrier?," *International Conciliation,* No. 541 (January, 1963).

2. For a further discussion of Egyptian African foreign policy, see P. J. Vatikiotis, "Foreign Policy of Egypt," in Roy Macridis (ed.), *Foreign Policy in World Politics* (2d ed.; Englewood Cliffs, N.J.: Prentice-Hall, 1962); Jacques Baulin, *The Arab Role in Africa* (Baltimore, Md.: Penguin Books, Inc., 1962).

3. For a full discussion of these groups, see Colin Legum, *Pan-Africanism* (New York: Frederick A. Praeger, 1962); also Zartman, *op. cit.* For a thorough analysis of the role of the Congo crisis in the policy of the two groups, see Robert C. Good, "The Congo Crisis: A Study of Postcolonial Politics," in Laurence W. Martin (ed.), *Neutralism and Nonalignment* (New York: Frederick A. Praeger, 1962).

INDEX